Resettling the Range

The Nature | History | Society series is devoted to the publication of high-quality scholarship in environmental history and allied fields. Its broad compass is signalled by its title: nature because it takes the natural world seriously; history because it aims to foster work that has temporal depth; and society because its essential concern is with the interface between nature and society, broadly conceived. The series is avowedly interdisciplinary and is open to the work of anthropologists, ecologists, historians, geographers, literary scholars, political scientists, sociologists, and others whose interests resonate with its mandate. It offers a timely outlet for lively, innovative, and well-written work on the interaction of people and nature through time in North America.

General Editor: Graeme Wynn, University of British Columbia

A list of titles in the series appears at the end of the book.

NATURE|HISTORY|SOCIETY

Resettling the Range

Animals, Ecologies, and Human Communities in British Columbia

JOHN THISTLE

FOREWORD BY GRAEME WYNN

UBC Press • Vancouver • Toronto

23 22 21 20 19 18 17 16 15   5 4 3 2 1

Printed in Canada on FSC-certified ancient-forest-free paper
(100% post-consumer recycled) that is processed chlorine- and acid-free.

Library and Archives Canada Cataloguing in Publication

Thistle, John, 1971–, author
Resettling the range : animals, ecologies, and human communities in British Columbia / John Thistle.

(Nature, history, society)
Includes bibliographical references and index.
Issued in print and electronic formats.
ISBN 978-0-7748-2837-6 (bound). – ISBN 978-0-7748-2838-3 (pbk.)
ISBN 978-0-7748-2839-0 (pdf). – ISBN 978-0-7748-2840-6 (epub)

1. Range ecology – British Columbia – History. 2. Grassland ecology – British Columbia – History. 3. Wild horses – Ecology – British Columbia – History. 4. Grasshoppers – Ecology – British Columbia – History. 5. Human ecology – British Columbia – History. 6. British Columbia – Environmental conditions. I. Title. II. Series: Nature, history, society

SF85.4.C3T55 2015   577.409711   C2014-906098-X
                                                           C2014-906099-8

Canada

UBC Press gratefully acknowledges the financial support for our publishing program of the Government of Canada (through the Canada Book Fund), the Canada Council for the Arts, and the British Columbia Arts Council.

This book has been published with the help of a grant from the Canadian Federation for the Humanities and Social Sciences, through the Awards to Scholarly Publications Program, using funds provided by the Social Sciences and Humanities Research Council of Canada, and with the help of the University of British Columbia through the K.D. Srivastava Fund.

Printed and bound in Canada by Friesens
Set in Garamond by Apex CoVantage, LLC
Copy editor: Judy Phillips
Proofreader: Francis Chow
Indexer: Patricia Buchanan
Cartographer: Eric Leinberger

UBC Press
The University of British Columbia
2029 West Mall
Vancouver, BC V6T 1Z2
www.ubcpress.ca

To Raquel

Contents

List of Illustrations / ix

Foreword: Mapping the Ecology of Place / xi
Graeme Wynn

Acknowledgments / xxii

1   Introduction / 3

PART 1: WILD HORSES

2   Wrestling with Wild Horses / 13

3   The Biogeography of Dispossession / 32

4   Eradicating Wild Horses / 59

PART 2: GRASSHOPPERS

5   Grappling with Grasshoppers / 85

6   Resisting Range Monopoly / 108

7   New Enemies, Enduring Difficulties / 130

8   Conclusion / 158

Appendices
1 Accounting for Extermination / 163
2 Grazing Fees, Nicola Valley, ca. 1920 / 164

Notes / 167

Selected Bibliography / 193

Index / 208

Illustrations

1.1 Study area map / 5

2.1 Typical open cover of bunchgrass / 18

3.1 Gang Ranch and reserves map / 49

3.2 Ranches and Indian reserves, Nicola Valley / 51

4.1 Overgrazed range and horses, St. Mary's Reserve / 75

6.1 Gang Ranch, winter hay / 118

6.2 Gang Ranch / 118

6.3 Gang Ranch / 119

7.1 Badly depleted range, Riske Creek area / 134

7.2 Overgrazing at Riske Creek, with ruler for scale / 135

7.3 Overgrazing at Riske Creek, with hat for scale / 135

7.4 Exclosure on Nicola Range / 136

7.5 Riske Creek exclosure, 1931 / 137

7.6 Reseeded and protected stand of Kentucky bluegrass / 138

7.7 Crested wheatgrass on reseeded and protected area / 138

7.8 Depleted lower grasslands on Tranquille Range / 139

7.9 Four-year-old sagebrush seedlings on depleted range / 139

7.10 Cheatgrass/downy bromegrass in foreground on overgrazed area / 140

7.11 Deadfall from bark beetles / 146

Mapping the Ecology of Place

Graeme Wynn

G rasslands are not easy to know. Massively transformed in the short span of ten to fifteen decades, North American grasslands challenge ecologists, who have had little time to understand their "original ecology and function."[1] Contemplated from afar, "they are almost featureless, a horizontal, double-stitched seam between earth and sky. Moving up close is equally challenging. By the time the infinitely narrow, windblown stems and leaves come into focus, all larger perspective is lost."[2] So mused Don Gayton – a student of western Canadian landscapes whose collection of lyrical essays exploring the transformation of the prairies, titled *The Wheatgrass Mechanism,* won him a reputation as a writer with "the eye of a scientist and the soul of a poet" – as he contemplated *Spirit in the Grass,* a coffee-table book on the Cariboo-Chilcotin region of British Columbia.[3]

The photographer's challenges are real. Every "shot" encapsulates a series of decisions: which lens to use; where to direct it; when, in what light, to press the trigger. Every image is composed and framed, as a close-up, a long shot, a view of the middle distance. But are grasslands more difficult to encapsulate than other landscapes? Rugged snow-capped mountain peaks, the impressively broad and soaring trunks of old-growth rainforest, rugged shorelines – the classic images associated with western Canada's parks and protected areas, and beloved of tourists and camera buffs – are not typical of these areas.[4] But does the photographer out on the range really face a stark choice between uninteresting depictions of a horizontal world and myopic close-ups of ground-hugging vegetation? Although Gayton suggests as much, he praises photographer Chris Harris for images that focus on the "broader landscape," a sort of middle ground that is certainly not without its charms. Harris "feasts," observes Gayton in one telling phrase, "on the contrasts of the velvet-textured grasslands as they press against the jagged bareness of the cliffs"; in another similarly evocative sentence, Gayton marks the scale and grandeur of an image by noting the presence of two hikers, tiny figures "in the tawny, contoured grassland expanse of Churn Flats ... like two insignificant ticks on the broad, muscular back of some huge animal at rest."[5]

Yet, Harris's pages include close-up studies of birds and butterflies, and stems of bunchgrass backlit by the burning orb of the sun dominate his book's arresting cover. Effective photographic essays – and the most reverberant coffee-table books – usually encompass a range of scales. They are grounded in detail: they depend upon their materiality, upon their capacity to make things recognizable, imaginable, real. But they cannot stay there alone. To be effective they must move beyond the myopic close-up and attend to wider horizons, both actual and figurative. Sweeping vistas and wide perspectives are essential complements to tightly focused imagery. They allow viewers to "place" or find larger meaning in the specifics.

But there is more to it than this. Exhibitions and picture books juxtapose particular representations – and the selection of these images, and the order in which they are presented, shape the story they tell. Yet, the moral (so to speak) of that story is not quite the same for all who come to (or go from) it. As Gayton's focus on representations of the "broader landscape" in *Spirit in the Grass* suggests, curators and photographers may make decisions about the inclusion and placement of particular images according to the message they seek to convey, but viewers make their own interpretations of what they see.

All skillful storytellers know that much the same is true of the webs they weave in words. The historian, the novelist, the student of this or that "human science," the raconteur – all these people need to make choices and shape their material. Like Gayton's cameraman in the grasslands, they need to frame a point of view that lies somewhere between the dull banality of generalization – that uninteresting line between earth and sky – and the overwhelming, indecipherable welter of specificity symbolized by the stalks and shoots of dryland vegetation. The challenge, expressed in terms made famous by English philosopher Isaiah Berlin, is to stand between the hedgehog (oblivious to all but the big idea it holds dear) and the fox (driven to distraction by an insatiable curiosity about all things).[6] Yet, wherever this ground is found, and however compelling the resulting narrative, the account it offers remains malleable, subject to interpretive whim, vulnerable to misreading, and open to question for what it emphasizes and ignores.

These are the challenges and perils of discourse, and they are well worth bearing in mind when considering John Thistle's achievement in *Resettling the Range*. This is a book about the grasslands of British Columbia. Its story is important. But it is also partial. Grappling, as historical geographers have done for years, with the challenge of tracing change through time and across space, Thistle offers neither a thorough chronology of grassland settlement nor a complete treatment of the almost two million acres of grassland in British Columbia.[7] Although his book is concerned (as he notes) "with the different ways that ranches and cattle interacted with natural and economic processes, and each other, to remake, and in some cases degrade, the grassland environment," it is neither an economic nor an ecological history (p. 7). Nor is it a social study, or a work akin to Michèle Dominy's exploration of "the mutuality of spatiality and cultural identity" in New Zealand's high country, intended in part to address the atopia or neglect of place in social scientific research.[8]

Resettling the Range is a work of regional environmental history, and as such it reveals something of the ways in which "human communities and their environments change and become tangled together through time" (p. 7). But it is also less, and more, than this. Less because its main focus is on how people understood and responded to wild horses and swarming grasshoppers in the grasslands, and more because the spotlight it turns on these unlikely topics reveals each of them to be a synecdoche – a part that represents a rather more complex whole. So Thistle's stories of horses, grasshoppers, people, and cattle on parts of British Columbia's rangeland encourage readers to "fill in gaps," and to consider the larger implications of human-environment interactions. To put this somewhat differently, the twinned accounts unfolded in these pages invite readers to think again, and anew, about the processes of dispossession that newcomers inflicted, in different ways, upon indigenous peoples across the American hemisphere and beyond. They also offer new understanding of the course of development in North America's interior grasslands, make a fresh and distinctive contribution to the history of British Columbia, and limn new ways of thinking about questions of importance to environmental historians, historical geographers, and historians of science.

The strikingly beautiful Cariboo-Chilcotin region photographed by Chris Harris has been described as "one of the great ecological jewels of Western North America."[9] Encompassing some 550,000 acres, it accounts for almost a third of the Interior grassland of British Columbia.

Far from being homogenous, it includes about 310,000 acres of river terraces, benches, and slopes along the Fraser River and its tributaries between Big Bar and Williams Lake, as well as extensive undulating plateau areas to east and west – described by one of their early chroniclers as a series of "gentle swells and swales in a mantle of drift."[10] In sum, almost 80 percent of the grasslands in this region occur within twelve miles of the Fraser and Chilcotin Rivers and their tributaries. These grasslands occupy an important place in Thistle's account of rangeland resettlement. But they are neither the whole of that ecosystem nor the sole focus of this book. Rolling to hilly grasslands, with fewer swamp meadows than occur further north, are also extensive in the valley bottoms of the Thompson and Hat Creek Valleys and, as in the Cariboo-Chilcotin, they interlace with ponderosa pine and Douglas fir forests at higher elevations. There are another 250,000 acres or so of grassland/dry forest south of the Thompson River in the Nicola Valley, and Thistle draws upon developments in both these areas in telling his story. Beyond this, but less central to Thistle's account, grasslands occupy approximately 250,000 acres of land in the valleys of the Okanagan, Similkameen, and Kettle Rivers and, further west, extend over about half this area in the East Kootenay Trench.[11]

Developed through millennia in the absence of large herds of grazing animals, all of these grasslands are differentiated most markedly from those of the prairies east of the Rocky Mountains by the presence of a fragile microbiotic or "cryptogrammic" surface crust that profoundly affects their capacity to sustain herds of introduced cattle and other species, and that therefore imparts a particular inflection to their ecological histories. Part of a once considerably more extensive realm of grasslands and savannahs that encompassed much of the semiarid intermountain west from the Palouse country of eastern Washington, northeastern Oregon, and northwestern Idaho through the Interior valleys of southern British Columbia, this ecosystem now occupies less than 1 percent of British Columbia, and its current extent has been reduced (in various ways) by approximately a third in the last fifty years. Elsewhere, as in the Great Columbia Plain south of the forty-ninth parallel, large parts of the bunchgrass range were turned to cultivation in the nineteenth and early twentieth centuries, and extensive areas were lost to the plough.[12]

Writing of ranching on the interior range of British Columbia in the 1950s, geographer Thomas Weir – one of the first, and for a long time one of very few, scholars from beyond the rangeland sciences to focus attention on this region – identified three kinds of grazing practice that had evolved since the 1860s.[13] By his account, these practices were shaped by "physical controls," among which the "natural vegetation" was the most important. Drawing upon the work of ecologist Edwin Tisdale, Weir identified three grassland zones shaped by the impact of altitude (and, indirectly, the influence of precipitation – which increased from less than 6 inches per annum in the lowest, driest areas to exceed 25 inches above 3,300 feet) – on grass and tree growth.[14] The first zone, between 1,100 and 2,300 feet, was characterized by bunchgrasses and sagebrush; between 2,300 and 2,800 feet, forbs were interspersed with bunchgrasses; and between 2,800 and 3,300 feet, a heavier growth of forbs as well as bluegrass and other sod-forming species largely replaced the bunchgrasses. Fairly open stands of aspen and aspen fir above the grasslands provided good range too, but above 4,000 feet, thickening stands of lodgepole pine and spruce reduced grazing opportunities. Overall, stocking ratios estimated by Weir were lowest in the dry, low-lying – and by 1950 often degraded – areas, where as many as 40 acres were required to maintain each steer; in the best of situations, other parts of the region were capable of sustaining stock at four times this density. But these limits were in some sense notional, as cattle were moved from one environmental zone to another to take advantage of changing seasons and available grazing.

The superimposition on such a diverse landscape of tenure arrangements that allowed the preemption of 160 (later 320) acres and gave access to extensive tracts of rangeland through leases and permits led, said Weir, to markedly different patterns of ranching in lowland, upland, and transitional zones. The largest ranches, with hundreds of thousands of acres and up to ten thousand cattle, were based in the southern lowlands, where they were able to use the vast expanses of bunchgrass found on valley slopes and terraces for spring and fall grazing. Typically, they moved cattle onto the timber-covered Crown ranges in early summer and continued upslope as the season progressed, sometimes grazing areas 2,000 vertical feet above their home paddocks. These operations had to put up winter feed, but this was generally required for only a few weeks, and in favourable winters the most favoured operations might not have to feed at all. The smallest, and perhaps least profitable, ranches were in the northwestern uplands, where stock might have to be fed for three to five winter months before being turned onto limited areas of home range and then moved to graze small upland meadows sequentially during the summer and early fall. Typically found at intermediate elevations, in the north-central part of the grasslands, transitional ranching units used the limited bunchgrass of shallow valley sidehills for spring grazing their herds of several hundred to one thousand cattle, before moving them through 500 to 1,000 vertical feet to forage in the timbered uplands during summer and to rustle in upland meadows in the fall. They too depended upon winter feed, but less markedly than did the upland ranches.

To read Thistle and Weir together is to recognize how scholarship changes, and to be reminded of the ways in which shifting societal and disciplinary concerns produce radically different accounts of phenomena. Geographers writing about the same region, and about the major economic activity that shaped its landscapes, Thistle and Weir actually have a lot in common. Beyond their shared interest in ranching and the Interior grasslands, they draw upon many of the same sources (Tisdale's work is important to both, for example), have things to say about the same operations (such as the Douglas Lake Cattle Company), and ultimately tell us a good deal about the development of the inland range of British Columbia. But writing sixty years apart, they tell very different stories about this place. Weir's pioneering work reflected the descriptive regional approach of a discipline still tinged with an environmental determinism in its concern to characterize types of economic activity (ranch units) and its ready attribution of land-use patterns to physical factors. The grassland was a tabula rasa upon which the ranchers effectively wrote the destiny dictated by nature. Land tenure regulations and market circumstances had some small influence on the pattern of human activity, but imprinted in response to the challenging and limited opportunities afforded by the physical environment, this pattern seemed entirely natural and secure.

Thistle's grasslands are, by contrast, places of ongoing contestation and change, unstable in all sorts of ways. Whereas Weir took the idea of "native grassland" as a convenient enduring given, Thistle interrogates it and recognizes that Interior grassland ecosystems existed in almost constant flux, sustained by light fires every decade or so, and subject on their upland, forested margins to more severe conflagrations every century or two. For Weir, overgrazing – putting too many animals on the range – was one cause of low carrying capacity; for Thistle, overgrazing is not just a matter of stocking densities but a contingent outcome of weather conditions, prices for stock, the rhythms of transhumance (or the timing of stock movements), the presence of sheep, and so on. Rather than offering a view, as Weir did, of a landscape produced by "impersonal, even autonomous underlying forces," Thistle aspires to know "how people and groups understood change, both social and ecological, and how they responded when those changes came to seem undesirable" (p. 7). Here, both people and "nature" are actors, and the former often face the need to make choices without a complete understanding of circumstances or full knowledge of the consequences of their actions.

Weir paid no heed to indigenous people, whereas Thistle marks their presence in the grasslands in his title (by describing the development of the ranching economy as a "resettling") and makes the dispossession and marginalization of the region's original human inhabitants a centrepiece of his book. For Weir, the extension of ranching into the Interior plateau was an unproblematic part of the great and continuing story of Canadian economic development. For Thistle, the Victoria *Colonist*'s perhaps somewhat incredulous observation, in 1930, that "the Indians assert that the country and the ranges belong to them," is literally and figuratively a starting point for analysis. As elsewhere in the province, Indian Reserves were created in the grasslands as European settlement advanced, but no formal treaties ceded indigenous territory to newcomers. Today, the Grasslands Conservation Council tells us that slightly less than 10 percent of BC grasslands lie in Indian Reserves – although the proportional significance of these reserves varies considerably, as they account for barely 3 percent of the Cariboo-Chilcotin and almost a quarter of the Okanagan basin.[15] But, Thistle shows, even these stark figures reflect contested histories: colonists, indigenous people, and officials held different views of how much land Native people needed, and how much they should be allowed. A few, such as the Oblate priest C.J. Grandidier and Indian Reserve Commissioner Gilbert Malcolm Sproat, noted the injustices being perpetrated and the sense of grievance stirring among indigenous people as newcomers allowed their cattle to graze on reserve land and tightened their grip on the range.[16] But their voices, like those of the indigenous people of the region, were soon drowned out by endorsements of economic growth and the benefits of making the grassland "productive" through "rational land use" and "range improvement."

By Thistle's account, tension and conflict also marked relations among ranchers. As the Douglas Lake Cattle Company and a small handful of other operators expanded their already significant holdings late in the nineteenth century, those with smaller ranches and fewer cattle feared the engrossment of both land and water by the larger companies. Size conferred all manner of advantages: it allowed strategic seasonal use of different types of range; it offered economies of scale in the development of improvements such as irrigation ditches; it encouraged labour specialization and the employment of workers with special skills; and it made for more efficient marketing arrangements. "Smallholders," a diverse group of people who did not share these benefits, grew anxious about the growing concentration of resources and lobbied for changes – such as the creation of grazing commons and community pastures – that would help their operations and interest. Some government officials suggested that large corporate enterprises damaged the range, and others denounced the drift toward oligopoly as undemocratic and contrary to the agrarian vision that enshrined yeoman farming as a way of life and underpinned the development of agriculture through British North America and early Canada.[17] When grasshoppers swarmed and the need to do something to counter their decimations seemed urgent, ranchers and government officials argued over who should implement and pay for extermination programs or anticipatory precautions. Buffeted, if not silenced, by circumstances, people sought variously to take advantage of propitious situations, to hold what they had, or to resist or reduce the effects of change driven by forces beyond their immediate control. Recognizing this, we begin to see how the three kinds of ranch units that Weir "naturalized" as the logical consequences of environmental conditions were actually created from a complex conjuncture of economic, entrepreneurial, historical, legal, social, and even perhaps psychological circumstances.

Grasslands may not be easy to know, but *Resettling the Range* develops a nuanced and complicated picture of British Columbia's Interior rangelands and offers a distinct and unusual perspective on British Columbia and the environmental history of settler colonialism. It makes clear that the ranching industry that drove development across the province's broad expanses of bunchgrass and forbs was (and is) a "modern capitalist institution" (p. 161). Its underlying rationale was that very human concern, "improvement." But it also notes the ironies implicit in this narrative of progress. So Thistle demonstrates (among other things) that the newcomers' notions of rationality and improvement spelled dispossession, marginalization, and death for people and creatures. His stories reveal officials and ranchers with little capital opposing range "monopoly" and describing "the fencing of large tracts of public land by private individuals [as] a great evil" while barely pausing to wonder at their own society's metaphorical "fencing in" of other people and animals on reserves, and the exclusion of indigenes and their once sizable herds from the range (p. 23). Nor, Thistle makes clear, did the newcomers' rhetoric of complaint about huge bands of wild horses eating out the grass, or government legislation encouraging their elimination, pay much heed to the fact that many of these animals belonged to local Native people who had earlier been encouraged to become (as surveyor Peter O'Reilly observed of members of the Alkali Lake, or Esk'etemc, band in 1881) "heavily involved in ranching," to the point that they owned "significant numbers of cattle and horses."[18]

Neither the wild horses nor the grasshoppers that are the focus of Thistle's approach to the Interior grasslands offered a simple target for those who wished to eradicate them from this ecosystem: "wild" horses ran free, but some were owned, and it was often difficult to tell these apart from their truly feral cousins; grasshoppers irrupted on no predictable schedule and then almost disappeared, and they also confused the entomologists, who posited phase-changes to explain their seemingly inexplicable behaviour. Thistle's accounts of attempts to grapple with the problems that wild horses and grasshoppers became for many British Columbians draw much detail from local archives, but they also have an eye to wider horizons as they attend, for example, to the potential value of wild horses to the military and the ways in which early-twentieth-century campaigns against pests were shaped by the discourse of warfare. Beyond this, Thistle's work also gives careful consideration to scientific efforts directed, in Canada and elsewhere, to understanding grassland ecology and "locust plagues." Yet, this book is, above all, an account of some important facets of the human history of the Interior grasslands, a work in environmental history that sits firmly in the humanistic tradition.

Much has been written in the last quarter-century about "putting science in its place," and there is a significant double entendre in this phrase. Used forthrightly, it signals the claim that geography (or location) is crucially influential in the development and dissemination of scientific understanding. In short, this is to maintain that inquiry is shaped by the spaces in which it is carried out, that scientific inquiries are affected by provincial cultures and the social milieu, and that scientific practices have influenced the formation of local identities.[19] Used obliquely, the phrase can also connote a certain skepticism about scientific claims to objectivity and universality: science is put in its place as just another story about the world, one no more efficacious or deserving of attention than any other. This second implication fuelled the so-called science wars of the 1990s, and it has not entirely disappeared from scholarly imaginations.[20] Thistle, by contrast, seeks to develop an engaged and rigorous discussion of the relations between science and rangeland resettlement (and vice versa) by following the dictum of historian of science Theodore

Porter: that although science is made by interested human actors subject to various influences, "they cannot make it however they choose" (p. 9). Working along this line, Thistle considers past and present scientific research on the grasslands in context, mindful of the "epistemologies and past worlds of the historical actors" who produced and consumed it, to shed light on the scientific as well as the economic, material, and social relationships that mediated human interactions with the nonhuman world and to offer an environmental history "deeply informed by the technical content of science."[21]

In this way, *Resettling the Range* tills the "very fertile ground" that Don Gayton found at the "mutual border" between the "aged realms of 'science' and 'the humanities.'"[22] Writing in 1990, ecologist Gayton saw this liminal space as "a narrow seam that may someday blossom into a domain itself"; in the quarter-century since, scholars have approached it from many different directions, to encourage its cultivation, to ensure its flowering, and to uncover antecedent interest in its promise. So Canadian literary scholar Laurie Ricou argued, less than a decade after the appearance of *The Wheatgrass Mechanism*, that "students of literature interested in writing about place ... need now to be students of ecology at some level."[23] A few years later, American historian Dan Flores, reacting to the "cultural turn" in humanities scholarship that privileged "the World according to the Word" over more material considerations, felt it necessary to remind his colleagues that "we remain biological even with all our bewildering array of cultural dressings."[24] History, he averred, required a bioregional perspective and a commitment to understanding the "tangible ecologies of place." At much the same time, eco-critics began to celebrate the "intertextual, interdisciplinary, and multi-vocal nature" of an "incipient" form of environmental literature.[25] Drawing from William Least Heat-Moon's *PrairyErth (A Deep Map)*, they quickly termed work of this sort "deep mapping" and associated it with Stegner's *Wolf Willow*, Lopez's *Arctic Dreams*, McPhee's *Annals of the Former World*, and even Thoreau's *Walden* and Leopold's *Sand County*, to sketch a tradition and identify a genre.[26]

According to Susan Naramore Maher, one of the leading commentators on this approach, also known as the literary cartography of place, its significant features include a "multivalent, cross-sectional understanding of history," close attention to the environment, a bioregional sensibility, and "an interest in a specific place, a particular biome, or a unique landscape." *Resettling the Range* is not a deep mapping exercise in the eco-critical sense of that term, but it does share important characteristics with work of that kind. Indeed, it might well be described – as Maher has written of Gayton's *The Wheatgrass Mechanism* and John Janovy Jr.'s *Dunwoody Pond,* both of which she places firmly within the deep mapping genre – as a work that forces us "to decenter the human, to reconsider the primacy of a larger biological reality, and to reexamine the political and cultural precepts that attempt to control natural systems."[27]

In the end, though, the stories at the heart of *Resettling the Range* are stories about people making choices. Thistle's purpose in telling them is to emphasize that history is contingent: "There was nothing inevitable about the decisions early British Columbians made: they might have restored the range rather than simply put poison in it; they might have reclaimed wild horses" instead of annihilating them; they might have envisaged a land-use system weighted toward communal rather than individual property rights; they might have heeded the voices of Native peoples and listened more attentively to those of their own recognizing the inequities of Indian reserves (p. 162).

There are big "ifs" around most of these conditionals. But long immersion in the archives, close observation of what transpired on the landscape, and prolonged reflection on the history that you hold in your hands has left John Thistle convinced that "early British Columbians could have done better, not just by each other, but also by First Nations peoples, and the nonhuman world of nature" (p. 162). He comes to this conclusion with characteristic humility. His purpose is not to condemn those who came before us as benighted fools, but to draw wisdom from the past and foster a thoughtful approach to the future. It was Shakespeare who wrote that "All the world's a stage, / And all the men and women merely players."[28] Plays are structured by their texts, just as powerful streams of tendency shape the thinking of all who act in the world, but Thistle would remind us that both playscripts and zeitgeists are pliable, and that the measure of any performance lies in the choices made by those who deliver it. Like Don Gayton's and John Janovy Jr.'s very different books, this one encourages us to ponder our humanity, and to be more considerate of humans and the rest of nature than the societies to which we belong have been in the past.[29]

Acknowledgments

Writing a book, I now realize, requires a great deal of help, and so it gives me great pleasure to thank the people and institutions that helped see this book through to publication. At the top of the list is my wife, Raquel Larson. Without her love and support over the years, this book would not, probably could not, have been written. My name is on the cover, but this is her achievement too. I would also like to thank my parents, John and Sharon, and my brother, Steve, for their support over the years. My family has supported me in everything I've ever done and for that I am thankful. Likewise I am very grateful to Brad, Tracey, and Abbey Green for all of their support and encouragement over the years.

I would also like to offer my gratitude to Graeme Wynn and Cole Harris. Graeme Wynn is not only an outstanding scholar, he's also an exceedingly generous one, and one of the kindest I have known. I am very grateful to Graeme for encouraging me to write a book about wild horses and grasshoppers, and for all the ways he helped see it through to publication. Cole Harris has been both a mentor and a good friend. I will always be grateful to Cole for introducing me to British Columbia and for encouraging me to think long and hard about its historical geography. Anyone who knows Cole's work will see traces of it in mine, and probably much more visible markings as well, not least of all in the title.

I would also like to offer special thanks to Mark Fiege. Mark is both a brilliant historian and a brilliant writer, and his timely advice to simply read more fiction when I was struggling with the writing of this book helped, I think, to turn a study into somewhat more of a story.

Numerous other people also contributed to the completion of this project. Matthew Evenden, Jim Glassman, Doug Harris, Jay Taylor, and Coll Thrush all provided advice and encouragement at various stages of the research and writing process, as did my good friends Derrick Carew and Tony Mitchell. At UBC I was lucky to be part of a vibrant environmental history community. In one way or another, David Brownstein, Matthew Dyce, Lynn Hilchie, Geoff Mann, Jonathan Peyton, Joanna Reid, Matt Schnurr, Shannon Stunden-Bower, Helen Watkins, and Bob Wilson all contributed to the completion of this book. Stephen Jenkins graciously responded to my emails out of the blue about wild horse ecology and helped me to think more clearly about the complexities involved. I would also like to thank the staff at the BC Archives, the BC Ministry of Forests and Range Library, the Geographic Information Centre in the Department of Geography at UBC, Library and Archives Canada, UBC Archives, and UBC Rare Books and Special Collections for their assistance with this project. I am also grateful to Arn Keeling and John Sandlos, who, along with the Labrador Institute and the Faculty of Arts at Memorial University, supported me through a postdoctoral fellowship in 2010–11. I would also like to thank everyone at the Labrador Institute of Memorial University, especially our director, Keith Chaulk; our assistant director, Martha MacDonald; and Ron Sparkes, for giving me the opportunity to live and work in the north.

I also want to thank everybody at UBC Press, especially Randy Schmidt and Ann Macklem. I can't imagine better guides though the publishing process than Randy and Ann and I want to thank them for all the ways they helped see this book through to publication. I'd also like to thank Judy Phillips and Nicole Hilton for the great work they did copy-editing and reviewing the documentation toward the end of the writing process. Two anonymous peer reviewers commented on two drafts and the result, I think, is a much better book. Any remaining errors in fact or judgment are my own. Finally, I would like to thank Eric Leinberger, who made the maps for this book and who, through a series of basic questions at the beginning of this process encouraged me to think more carefully about the challenges and opportunities of mapping environmental history.

Portions of this book appeared in modified form in the *Journal of Historical Geography* and *BC Studies* and I am grateful to these journals for permission to republish these portions here.

Resettling the Range

I
Introduction

My interest in British Columbia's Interior drylands began with a weekend field trip through the lower Fraser River Canyon with graduate students and faculty members from the University of British Columbia Geography Department. The purpose of the trip was to see the remnants of Aboriginal house pits, as well as some of the landscapes made more recently by colonialism. Starting off from the coastal city of Vancouver on a misty Saturday morning, we slowly made our way to remote Cameron Bar, on the west bank of the Fraser River.

Like all good "archival fieldwork," our route through the canyon revealed traces of an astonishing sequence of human occupation: at Yelakin, the edge of an Aboriginal village otherwise obliterated by the arrival of the Canadian Pacific Railway in the early 1880s; at Boston Bar, a small Aboriginal cemetery elevated several feet above the surrounding surface, sacred space left behind as the rest of the landscape was desecrated (washed away by the powerful jets of hydraulic mining operations) and then essentially abandoned to its current use as an industrial log sorting yard (guarded by two large dogs); somewhere near the mouth of the Stein Valley, a failed settler farmstead, one of many in the province; and, finally, at Cameron Bar, the remains of an orchard and farm buildings, a desiccated pocket of land designated as an Indian reserve, the great linear piles of rock left by Chinese miners, and the impressions left in the land by a pair of long abandoned Aboriginal house pits.[1] The precise history and meaning of these places was often far from obvious, but each had something important to say about the "resettlement" of British Columbia.[2] I remember being deeply impressed by what I saw, and anxious to learn more: about the origins of these features; about the people who made and gave meaning to them; and about how and why they had changed over time.

Equally impressive as we moved through the canyon was the way the land itself changed. At some point, dense coastal rainforests of cedars and Douglas fir gave way to relatively spacious stands of ponderosa pine, and even patches of open grassland. The reason for the change, I later learned, was the north-south trending mountains uplifted millions of years ago, which block the movement of moist maritime air, creating what climatologists call a rain shadow – basically a big dry patch – over much of the interior of the province. Bunchgrass, sagebrush, cactus, and many other plant and animal species adapted to dry conditions are common in this place. So are cattle. The largest herds were along the middle Fraser and Chilcotin Rivers and in the Nicola Valley near Douglas Lake – too far to travel in a single weekend field trip. Just past the settler community of Lytton, however, we saw a few head of cattle in the shady understory of a ponderosa pine forest. We also saw what appeared to be a ranch, or perhaps it was a farm, or a vineyard. Whatever it was, the only green patch in a dry yellow landscape dotted with dark green pine trees was irrigated.

By early Sunday evening, we were back on the coast (if memory serves, it was still misty when we arrived). I knew then that I wanted to write a history of the rain shadow environment we encountered on the weekend. I also knew that I wanted my environmental history to be basically ecological, both in the broad sense of thinking relationally about species (including our own) and the spaces they inhabit, and in the narrow sense of documenting changes in the land. Essentially, and in retrospect too ambitiously, I wanted to do for the drylands of Interior British Columbia what it seemed to me William Cronon had done for New England, or Arthur McEvoy had done for coastal California, or Richard White had done for Island County, Washington.[3] Years later, this book is the result.

The plan to write an ecological history of the ranching economy held promise for several reasons. I knew from reading Cole Harris's work that ranching had been the leading edge of settler colonialism in the drylands and that it remained the dominant land use there during the late nineteenth and early twentieth centuries.[4] I also knew that, unlike other forms of settler agriculture, ranching was spatially extensive. In addition to fenced winter lowlands that ranchers reserved for winter pasture or converted to hay crops, the province's ranching landscape included huge areas of unfenced upland, collectively known as Crown range, that was grazed in common by settler and Native livestock for eight or nine months each year, from about mid-April to mid-December depending on the weather. Ranchers also used forested areas for grazing. Together, forest and range covered pretty much the entire Southern Interior (Figure 1.1). It stood to reason, in other words, that an ecological history of ranching would also be a story about the wider rain shadow environment we encountered en route to Cameron Bar.

An ecological history of ranching also made sense in the context of Canadian historical scholarship. When I started working on this project, the "standard," and only book-length, study of cattle ranching west of the Rocky Mountains was geographer Thomas Weir's *Ranching on the Southern Interior Plateau*.[5] First published in 1955 by the Dominion Geographical Branch, *Ranching on the Southern Interior Plateau* was a work of regional economic

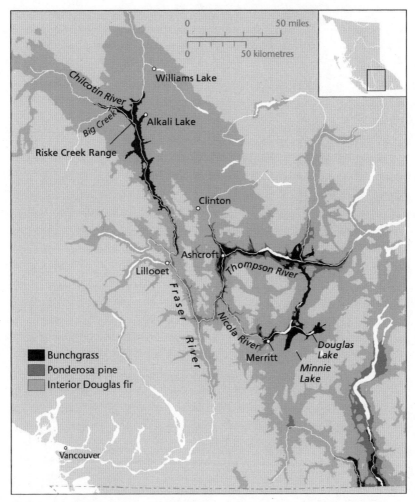

FIGURE 1.1 Study area map. *Eric Leinberger*

geography that sought, in Weir's words, "to show the relative importance of physical controls underlying ranch practices; to describe and analyze such basic patterns as the distribution of cattle, sheep, range types, and ranches; to analyze the historic and economic factors responsible for the form of settlement and finally to analyze the ranch as a functioning unit." This was a narrow analysis in some ways, but Weir also had a wide vision of his subject. His argument was that the "integration of the physical and the cultural, of time and place" had "fashioned a landscape predominantly rural with an elementary economy."[6] At the heart of that landscape were lowland areas that ranchers fenced for winter pasture. The pastoral landscape revolved around these spaces because they could easily be irrigated, and because in most cases upland areas were useless for ranching without them.

I admired Weir's emphasis on ranching as a way of organizing space and environment (and still do). In particular, I appreciated his attention to environmental factors, especially the role of winter range, in shaping the regional economic landscape. Like all books, however, *Ranching on the Southern Interior Plateau* was the product of a particular historical context, and that context had changed considerably in the fifty years since the first edition was published. Perhaps because he was writing in the early 1950s, when colonialism tended to be assumed rather than questioned, it never occurred to Weir that the rural landscape he sought to describe and explain depended on, and ultimately was made possible by, the dispossession of Native people. But it did, and it had been. Unlike in some other parts of Canada, no treaties were ever signed in British Columbia. Instead the colonial state created small Indian reserves. By the time Weir arrived in the late 1940s, indigenous people lived on Indian reserves that were but a tiny fraction of their former ancestral territories. According to Cole Harris, *all* Indian reserves account for a little more than one-third of 1 percent of the provincial land base. But indigenous people never disappeared. Moreover, in addition to being hunters, fishers, gatherers, guides, and wage labourers, indigenous people were stock raisers. Yet, apart from a single passing reference to "Indian" fur traders in the "colonial period," no Aboriginal people featured at all in this book. It was as if they did not exist.

On the other hand, in a sense, there were no white or other ranchers in his book either. Weir provided wonderfully detailed maps depicting the seasonal movements of people and animals through the pastoral landscape. He discussed the role of provincial range policy in promoting or discouraging settlement and good land use (as Weir understood it). He also interviewed numerous ranchers and range managers to learn how ranches worked and to understand what kinds of economic challenges they faced. But he never gave these people voice. Nor did Weir allow readers to hear from the government scientists and administrators who were responsible for range management in the province (although their work informed his analysis). In the final analysis, *Ranching on the Southern Interior Plateau* was less a book about the interactions of people and place than it was a geographical analysis of impersonal, even autonomous, underlying forces – the physical environment, technology (especially the railway), and above all the invisible hand of the market. The overall impression was one of rational economic actors using scarce resources to make a commodity for the market. I had no doubt that technology and market forces were important, or that ranchers and range managers aspired to "rational" land use. But I also suspected that in real time the story of ranching was more complicated. After all, as Weir observed, much of the range was overgrazed. Rational land use may well have been the espoused goal since the gold rush years (1858–65), when range use was both transient and unregulated, but it was by no means always the outcome.

So I began, and *Resettling the Range* is the result. It can still be read as an ecological history of the province's ranching economy in the broad and narrow senses described above, and as a response to some of the absences and shortcomings in Weir's analysis of *Ranching on the Southern Interior Plateau*. It deals with the different ways that ranches and cattle interacted with natural and economic processes, and each other, to remake, and in some cases degrade, the grassland environment. It also examines how individuals and groups understood environmental problems, and when deemed undesirable, how they responded. In these ways, it is a work of regional environmental history that, like others in the field, seeks to show how human communities and their environments change and become tangled together through time.[7] But it does so, I think, from a unique, even unlikely, vantage point.

Rather than focus on ranches and cattle or even range science, the focus of *Resettling the Range* is on wild horses and grasshoppers. Partly this is because, like other environmental historians, I am interested in telling stories that are not confined to humanity alone. As Reviel Netz observes, "We tend to concentrate on humans because we consider humans as actors in history – they have desires, they move about, and thus they shape history. But all living things have desires and move about, and so they shape reality as well; and in another way the same is true of material reality itself." I do not think that nonhuman entities and natural processes shape reality in the same way, or to the same extent, that humans do. Unlike penguins, humans as a group

now have the power to render the planet uninhabitable for all but the most
resilient living things. They (we) also have the power to *choose* to do otherwise. This book is a lot about the choices some early British Columbians
made when faced with complicated environmental problems that were also
complicated social problems. Yet, it is also a book about the historical and
geographical *contexts* in which these problems and their solutions unfolded,
and those contexts, I argue, were as much ecological as they were social. To
borrow again from Netz, in this book "there are no extras, and they are all
actors – humans, animals, and their shared terrain."[8]

Mainly this book is organized the way it is because of the archival records
I consulted. Even though I studied many kinds of documents for this
project, at some point I began to realize that a lot of what I was learning
about the ecological history of ranching, my original project, was coming
not from records related to cattle but from records related to pests, particularly herbivores that competed with cattle for grassland. Animals
targeted for extermination thus opened windows onto ecological history.
Even more surprising was how much I learned about the human communities of the grasslands by looking at these animals. It turned out that
one could learn a lot about the ecological history of a place, and of the
people who lived there, by looking carefully at the animals those people
sought to exterminate.[9] What I learned was that all three – the people,
pests, and ecological history of the place – were connected. Perhaps not
always obviously or directly, but nevertheless connected.

The histories of wild horses and grasshoppers overlap in time, and many
actors appear in both narratives. But rather than adopt a strict chronological
approach, I have found it useful, even necessary, not only to write themat-
ically but also to move between time scales, placing early-twentieth-century
debates about overgrazing and environmental change, for example, alongside earlier ideas as well as more recent understandings that are essentially
evolutionary in nature. The point is not to suggest, ahistorically, that more
or better science would have solved or avoided environmental problems
in the past. People in the past knew what they knew, just as we do now.
The reason for tacking back and forth between time periods in this book
is that the contexts being described defied neat and tidy chronologies. To
tell the stories of grasshoppers and horses, it was necessary at times to step
back from the late nineteenth and early twentieth centuries – sometimes
way back – to a time when there were neither grasshoppers nor horses,
nor even any grass in the grassland. Likewise, it was useful to look ahead
to future understandings of range ecology, especially when such understandings were clearly anticipated in the past.

Science was hardly determinative in establishing British Columbia's early range policies. It barely figured in the story of wild horses, and in the case of grasshoppers its central conclusions were largely ignored. Entomologists in the early 1920s concluded that worsening grasshopper outbreaks in the grassland were directly associated with overgrazing, which among other things had created favourable breeding areas for egg-laying insects. But rather than reform land use in the region – the preferred strategy of early scientists – for a variety of practical, political, and economic reasons, the province opted to put arsenic, and later more harmful synthetic chemicals such as DDT, in the grassland. Entomologists were only too willing to help with poison control, but it was not their preferred strategy, at least not initially. The more durable solution suggested by scientific research in the first half of the twentieth century was range restoration. In fairness, new land-use practices were introduced after 1919, when the province passed its first Grazing Act, but only slowly, and often subsidiary to quicker, and usually less controversial, fixes such as pest extermination. Thus, while the rhetoric of "rational" land use was pervasive in British Columbia, particularly after 1919, the influence of actual scientific research was often secondary, and at times was simply irrelevant, in determining range policy in the province before the early 1960s, the point at which the discussion in this book ends. Science mattered. Just how it mattered is one of the central themes of this story. But economic considerations and political expediency were almost always more important. It was always easier to advocate new land-use practices than it was to implement them.

Nor, in occasionally drawing from past and present science in a work of environmental history, am I insensitive to the epistemological difficulties involved, though I do think these can be overstated.[10] I am not convinced that science is merely one "cultured way of knowing" among others; that it is simply "made up ... like fairy tales and nursery rhymes"; and that by implication it must be irrelevant or meaningless to historians and geographers except as a discourse or set of ideas and practices to be studied.[11] It is a culture; it is a discourse; and it is a set of ideas and practices to be studied.[12] But this is not at all the same as saying it is simply made up, like *Mother Goose* or *Green Eggs and Ham*. As historian of science Theodore Porter puts it: "Interested human actors make science, but they cannot make it however they choose. They are constrained, though not absolutely, by what can be seen in nature and what can be made to happen in the laboratory."[13] With Porter's comments in mind, I use past and present science selectively, and as much as possible contextually, in this study while appreciating the practical and epistemological difficulties in doing so. Science may be cultured and socially constructed (how could it be otherwise?). The fact remains, though, that many of the stories in these pages – and arguably many environmental histories – would have been impossible to write without it.[14]

For the most part, this book avoids explicit engagement with these issues, seeking instead to tell contextualized stories about how people and nonhuman nature have changed together through time. To tell these stories, I have relied heavily on historical materials held in federal and provincial archives. Using old government records, provincial statutes, private correspondence, maps, surveys, newspapers, photographs, scientific studies, and unpublished transcripts from public meetings and royal commissions, I have assembled paired historical narratives about the relations among animals, ecologies, and human communities in a large but little known part of northwestern North America: the drylands of present-day British Columbia. I begin with a "war on wild horses" that also worked to dispossess Aboriginal people and discredit their competing claims to land, and conclude with a campaign against grasshoppers that exposed economic inequities among immigrant cattle ranchers. If this seems unconventional, my argument in this book is that it is also a powerful way of doing environmental history.[15] In the pages that follow, horses and grasshoppers become lenses through which we come to understand that stories about "range improvement" and "rational" land use in British Columbia were also – and for some people and creatures primarily – stories about dispossession and marginalization, and that these were not just social but deeply ecological conditions. Neither narrative has a happy ending, and several disheartening subplots thread through the larger plotline: some people suffer arsenic poisoning; others become embroiled in bitter, even violent disputes; and countless animals are killed. I am convinced that these are important stories to tell because of the unique perspective they provide on the resettlement of British Columbia. I am also convinced that these stories have something important to tell us about the danger in separating "environmental problems" and their solutions from their intertwined social and ecological contexts, because when some British Columbians did this in the past, they not only made matters worse in many cases but also created new problems that nobody anticipated. Even though it only gestures toward recent events on the range, and makes no policy recommendations, this book, I hope, will inform current discussions about how to achieve fairer and more sustainable futures for people and nonhuman nature alike. At least, and more assuredly, it will point to what has been unjust and unsustainable in British Columbia in the relatively recent past.

PART I
Wild Horses

2

Wrestling with Wild Horses

In April 1930, a group of Nlaka'pamux women and men led by Jack Swakum, Felix George Buckskin, and Myers Michel gathered along with their lawyer, a settler named M.L. Grimmett, outside the government office at Spences Bridge, British Columbia. They had come to Spences Bridge to meet with Thomas Mackenzie, the province's grazing commissioner, and to discuss with him the government's decision to shoot "wild horses" next winter as part of its new "range improvement" program. There are no records of exactly what was said at the meeting, but local newspapers in Vancouver and Victoria soon ran headlines that the Indians "resented" and were "sullen" and "aroused" by the decision to shoot these horses – even though it was necessary to "save the range from ruin for pasture" – and reported, perhaps not entirely in the language of yellow journalism, that "reprisals were threatened." According to Grimmett, "The Indians pledged to obey and be guided by the law, but if the shooting of horses is begun, anything may happen." Indeed, according to the *Victoria Colonist*, an "ugly situation" was developing in the drylands. "The Indians assert that the country and the ranges belong to them," the *Colonist* exclaimed. "They claim that they are non-treaty Indians and must live by their own resources, that horses are cash, as they are used in their trading, and that they and no other rangers know what horses are of value and what are not, and what should be shot and in what manner."[1] "One Indian Chief, who interviewed the late Queen Victoria in England years ago, claims that her late majesty told him the land belonged to the Indians," the *Vancouver Sun* added in a passage that undoubtedly raised the ire of its British-Canadian readership, "and protests in strong terms against the government taking any of their rights away."[2]

This was not the first time that First Nations in British Columbia had appealed to the Queen, and thus the power of the British Crown, in asserting Aboriginal rights and title to land; nor would it be the last.[3] The Nlaka'pamux had done so themselves in 1879 in a well-known example in which Aboriginal leaders "invoked the Queen as their ally in their dealings with authorities in settler society that were intended to secure state recognition of a form of indigenous self-rule."[4] Although similar arguments about indigenous self-rule were in the air at Spences Bridge in April of 1930, the context in this case was highly unusual. Reading accounts of this episode for the first time at the BC Archives, I wondered, how on earth did "wild horses," creatures usually considered a range pest to be exterminated, become a means for asserting Aboriginal rights and title to land? The short answer is that not all "wild horses" in early British Columbia were actually wild – or feral, to use the preferred terminology of modern range managers. Although allegedly unbranded in many cases, or bearing what the provincial government referred to as "unregistered" brands (which from the perspective of settler law was no better than being unbranded), many of these animals had Aboriginal owners. The Nlaka'pamux, along with other First Nations, not only claimed these animals but also defended them.

The long answer is more complicated. In retracing the road to Spences Bridge, it helps to step back from the land and wild horse conflicts of the early 1930s and simply ask, what was a wild horse? The question is basic, but the answer is tricky because, like all creatures, wild horses have histories. Today, the phrase "wild horse" usually refers to a feral horse of domestic origins, but in early British Columbia it had wider and more ambiguous meanings. Some wild horses were the progeny of lost or abandoned pack animals brought to British Columbia in the late 1850s and early 1860s during the Fraser River and Cariboo gold rushes; others were likely feral escapees from settler ranches and Indian reserves. All of these animals were feral in the usual sense. More than a few wild horses, however, must have descended from animals that went feral during the disease epidemics of the late eighteenth and nineteenth centuries. Measles and influenza arrived in succession in the Southern Interior in the 1840s, and smallpox arrived in 1862. The evidence for disease-related feralization is sparse, but it had happened elsewhere in early British Columbia. Writing from Kootenai territory (near present-day Invermere), David Thompson noted in 1808 that wild horse herds in that area had "very much multiplied, as every year the mares have a foal. There are several herds of wild horses in places along the mountains, these have all come from tame horses that have been lost, or wandered away from tents where sickness prevailed."[5]

These were not the only "wild horses" in early British Columbia, however, and numerically they may not have been the most important, though admittedly a precise count is impossible. Curiously, many newcomers to the grasslands also used this phrase to identify horses that Aboriginal people owned. In doing so they not only conflated wildness with ownership (a contradiction in terms under settler law) but also conflated animals with race, while at the same time condemning Native people for not knowing how to use land properly. An 1888 report on grazing lands by Indian Reserve Commissioner Peter O'Reilly was typical. The open ranges of the Okanagan Valley and Nicola Valley near Douglas Lake, O'Reilly wrote, were being "greatly eaten out, principally by bands of wild horses belonging to the Indians, which greatly injure the pasturage of the country and from which the tribe derives little or no benefit, and the sooner they are got rid of the better it would be for ... Indians and settlers" alike.[6] Two years later, an Indian Agent writing from Williams Lake likewise reported of the Alkali Lake (Esk'etemc) Indian Reserve that the Native people there had 150 head of cattle, adding that it would be to their "advantage if they would procure more, by selling their numerous wild horses, of which they own 600 – which are of no use to them, and are gradually eating out the grass – and purchase horned cattle with the proceeds."[7] A few years later, a cattle rancher from Clinton asserted that the "worst pest in this part of the country is wild horses ... I believe the descendants of Indian horses," he continued, "and I am told the Indians lay claim to them in an indefinite sort of way."[8] In early British Columbia, wild horses did not just descend from Aboriginal horses, however. In many cases, they *were* Aboriginal horses.

Regardless of their origins, and at times it was probably pretty hard to tell – horses, after all, are social animals and at a distance it would have been difficult or impossible to identify and distinguish between brands or markings, if there were any – ranchers and range officials distrusted, even despised, these animals because (allegedly) they interfered with the production of more valuable settler livestock such as cattle. Complaints about interbreeding and the recruitment of "tame" mares into "wild bands" were common among many ranchers. Rancher John Saul of Clinton argued that wild horses were "continually running off the tame mares so that often well bred mares produce worthless colts."[9] J.D. Prentice, manager of the massive Gang Ranch on the middle Fraser and Chilcotin Rivers, agreed with others when they said that the "wild horse evil" was "a great one, annually destroying feed."[10] But like Saul, he was just as concerned about wild stallions "interfering detrimentally with tame bands." Wild stallions "not only get to the gentle mares and so deteriorate the band, but frequently run them off and it is difficult and sometimes impossible to recover them."[11] Another rancher added that wild stallions "were the worst kind of nuisance, as they run off the tame mares, which in a short time become wild."[12]

As infuriating as these things could be – and judging from archival records, they drove many ranchers mad – they were not the only arguments against these animals. For many ranchers, wild horses were not just profligate interbreeders and polluters of better bloodlines but also pathogenic vectors that transmitted mysterious diseases to domestic stock. According to rancher John McKay, "a very malignant distemper" affected horses in 1889 and apparently "quite a number of animals died." By his account, the disease appeared first among "the Siwash [i.e., Aboriginal] ponies, and from their habit of roving with large bands, it was impossible to keep their more valuable stock free."[13] Victor Engstrom of Coldwater, in the Nicola Valley, also noted a strange "stamper" in Aboriginal horses and thought it "advisable to exterminate such wild or nearly wild Cayuses" (yet another settler name for Aboriginal horses) that were "not attended to in the winter or never used as pack horses or rounded up and corralled at regular intervals."[14] Not all ranchers were as aggressive as Engstrom. A rancher from Dog Creek, for example, also reported a "stamper" in horses in the late 1890s, but unlike his friends and neighbours in nearby valleys, he wanted the provincial government to "ascertain [the disease's] true nature" before embarking on an eradication program. Meanwhile, he reported, "I am treating with sulphur burnt with old boot leather and making the cattle and horses inhale the smoke." Suffice it to say that most ranchers and range officials preferred to treat what they presumed to be the source of the disease rather than simply treat its symptoms.

Disease and interbreeding were not the only, or more important, arguments against these animals. Their role in degrading the range was by far the more serious problem, even though, as we will see, settler cattle were almost certainly more to blame. By the early 1890s, it was becoming clear to many people that the range in some places was both badly trampled and heavily overgrazed. "The pasturage is not so good as in former years," complained an Okanagan Valley rancher in 1894. "The country having been overstocked, the original grass has in many places disappeared."[15] Rancher T.G. Kirkpatrick of Ashcroft agreed: "Before the country was overstocked it was good pasturage land. In the open land bunch-grass dominated."[16] But now things were different. Bunchgrass was less abundant, and weeds and woody shrubs such as sagebrush and antelope brush (both indigenous plant species that ranchers nonetheless sometimes referred to as "pasture weeds") were more common. The areas in and around small creeks and rivers and seasonal watering holes were especially degraded, not just by years of sustained heavy grazing but also by the cumulative effects of trampling as cattle herds approached, or made their way through, the water. Even on upland ranges, where water was usually more plentiful and range capacity was higher, one observer noticed that the grass in some places had been trampled and overgrazed.

Less clear was what to do about these problems. From one perspective, range degradation was a numbers problem. Some observers felt that there were simply too many cattle grazing too little grassland. Others added (not incorrectly) that the timing and duration of grazing was often just as important as the total number of animals involved. Still others added (again not incorrectly) that there was something in the very nature of the bunchgrasses that made them vulnerable to both grazing- and trampling-related range degradation.

In fact, all of these stories contained an element of truth. It is impossible to know how many horses there were in the grassland when the first Europeans arrived in the early nineteenth century. In 1891, nearly three decades after the first Indian reserves were created, the Indian Agent for the Kamloops-Okanagan Agency estimated that the Native people in that area had 12 "graded" stallions, 5,520 "other" horses, and 1,030 cattle. Similarly, the Indian Agent for the Williams Lake Agency reported that Native people in his region had 3,244 horses, 521 cattle, and 1,020 pigs. That puts the total number of Aboriginal horses at around 8,000 or 9,000 at the end of the nineteenth century. After that, things get murky. We do know, however, that the number of cattle in the grassland increased dramatically during the resettlement period: from zero in 1800 to nearly 100,000 at the turn of the century. Moreover, according to current science, it did so in an environment that for evolutionary reasons was perhaps predisposed to grazing and trampling-related range degradation. British Columbia's grasslands are part of a much larger intermountain ecosystem that extends, albeit not unchanged, into the present-day American states of Washington, Oregon, and Idaho. The origins of this environment are complex, but apparently it began to emerge some 6 million years ago when the Cascade and Sierra Nevada Mountains began impeding the inland flow of moist maritime air. The result was a massive rain shadow on the leeward side of those mountains in which only dry forests and grasslands would grow. The rise of the Rocky Mountains millions of years earlier had much the same effect further inland, helping to create the various grassland communities of the Great Plains. But considerable differences in the annual distribution of rainfall encouraged very different plant communities east and west of the Rocky Mountains. In the Great Plains, the prominent grasses were rhizomatous: reproduction occurred underground by way of a dense mat of roots and stems because the growing season extended well into summer. In the Intermountain West, in contrast, moisture came mainly in the form of winter rain and snow, but there was still not enough water at the right time of year to support extensive underground root systems. Several species of bunchgrass dominated instead, at least on south-facing slopes and the dry valley bottoms below them. Unlike their rhizomatous relatives, the bunchgrasses of the Intermountain West grew in tufts, were surrounded by a delicate crust of nitrogen-fixing lichens and mosses, reproduced above ground with seed, and went dormant during the summer drought (Figure 2.1).[17]

Another important feature of these grasslands was that they had evolved in the absence of large herding herbivores. Antelope, deer, elk, bighorn sheep, and evidently several small bison herds in parts of present-day southern Oregon apparently exerted some grazing pressure in these grasslands, as did grasshoppers and numerous other small herbivores at the other end of the ecological spectrum. But unlike the Great Plains, which were grazed and trampled by some 20 to 40 million bison for millenniums (nobody knows for sure how many), grazing pressure west of the Rocky

FIGURE 2.1   Typical open cover of bunchgrass. *Edwin Tisdale Summary Report*

Mountains was relatively low before domestic animals arrived.[18] The result was an evolutionary dichotomy with important implications for North American environmental history. The point is not to suggest that cattle and bison were ecologically interchangeable animals, because they were not. Nor is it to suggest that the Great Plains has not had its share of grazing problems, because clearly it has. Ironically, when the bison were all but eliminated in the late nineteenth century, *under*-grazing became an ecological problem.[19] It is to suggest, however, that the grasslands of British Columbia, like those of the wider Intermountain West, were in some ways relatively susceptible to grazing- and trampling-related range degradation, especially in the spring before individual plants had an opportunity to seed. Of course, none of this was known in detail in the nineteenth century when the first settlers arrived. But one local observer may have anticipated as much in 1898 when he noted that the "Native grasses in most places cannot stand too close cropping or too much trampling."[20]

Overgrazing by cattle was important in many cases, but it was only part of the ecological story because others noticed that the grassland was changing in even more ominous ways. By the late nineteenth century, it was clear to many people that in some areas bunchgrass was giving way not just to weeds (dandelion, Canadian thistle, and even cheatgrass were becoming common in many places by the late 1880s) but also, and in several ways more seriously, to native trees and unpalatable woody shrubs. The cause of tree and shrub encroachment was unclear. Overgrazing by horses and cattle, particularly along the forest-grassland border where pine and fir seedlings were naturally more abundant, probably contributed to the process. Likewise, in the lowlands it seems likely that the removal of bunchgrass by cattle afforded woody shrubs opportunities to expand. But some ranchers also pointed (rightly, it turns out) to changing fire patterns over the past half-century as Aboriginal people were confined to reserves and the province's first fire laws were enforced. Here too it helps to take the long view of environmental history, for the story of fire and grass was essentially evolutionary in nature.

On the basis of burn marks or "fire scars" found in cross-sections of Douglas fir and other long-lived tree species, biogeographers know that fire has been a prominent part of forest and grassland ecology for a very long time.[21] Tree ring records from British Columbia antedate the arrival of Europeans by hundreds of years, but charcoal deposits in ancient soil profiles and the historic dominance of arid and semiarid ecosystems by so-called fire-adapted and fire-resistant plants and trees suggest a much longer tenure.[22] As the BC-based ecologist and nature writer Don Gayton recently remarked, "We are slowly coming to the realization that the drier landscapes of North America – forests, grasslands, shrublands, even deserts – evolved in the presence of periodic fires."[23] Current science tells us that, historically, British Columbia's grasslands and adjacent dry forests probably experienced light fires every 4 to 16 years, with larger, stand-replacing conflagrations in the uplands occurring only every 100 to 250 years.

Given its prevalence in ecological history, it should come as no surprise that the written record relating to Interior British Columbia is full of references to forest and grassland fire. The earliest and in many ways most vivid accounts come from the Interior fur trade in the first half of the nineteenth century. A 26 August 1841 entry by Hudson's Bay Company chief trader John Tod was typical: A "great part of the woods in our neighbourhood [is] on fire and [has] been for a long time past. A thick cloud of Smoke is therefore continually hanging over us, and so oppressive at times as to affect the eyes." The following spring, Tod wrote that the "weather continues excessively warm and dry, and in consequence of the country being on fire in the vicinity, the Smoke very thick." Another fire burned in August 1842. "The neighbouring hills are all on fire," Tod wrote with awe, "which have a splendid appearance during the darkness of night." And almost a year later to the day, on 17 August 1843, Tod reported that the "atmosphere is surcharged with a dense smoke proceeding most likely from fires in the neighbourhood."[24]

A now indecipherable mixture of natural and purposeful Aboriginal burning, such fires probably performed numerous ecological functions. Not the least of these would have been to accelerate periodically the rate at which key nutrients, such as phosphorus and nitrogen, were returned to the soil. This gave plants such as ceanothus and Saskatoon berry a sudden boost and short-term edge in the region's evolving plant ecology. Fire also influenced the distribution of animal, insect, and parasite populations, and because fire altered soil chemistry, it also affected the distribution of soil organisms. At the landscape level, the principal effect of fire was to limit tree and woody shrub regeneration. Especially on lowland flats and rolling hills, frequent fire favoured grass and discouraged the growth of sagebrush and antelope brush. In detail the result was a complicated patchwork of plant types and densities depending on fire history and micro-scale ecological conditions, such as moisture availability, soil surface texture, exposure, and aspect that influenced sagebrush seedling establishment. Generally speaking the result was a landscape dominated at lower elevations by bunchgrass with occasional patches of brush, and presenting a "parklike" aspect at higher elevations where grasses and forbs grew below relatively open stands of ponderosa pine and Douglas fir.[25]

Geologist and naturalist George Dawson, among others in the late nineteenth century, noted the park-like nature of the Interior country. "All the lower and larger valleys are either free from forest or dotted over with irregular groups of open wood or individual trees," observed Dawson in 1895. "With increasing elevation," however, "the nearly treeless slopes are exchanged ... for open woods, consisting of Douglas fir (*Pseudotsuga douglasii*) or yellow pine (*Pinus ponderosa*)."[26] An able ecological interpreter but still a man of his times, Dawson did not know what caused the "sparsely wooded condition of the lower valleys," only that "a limited number of trees with their widely spaced roots practically absorb all the moisture which the soil is capable of yielding, and, so long as they exist, prevent the establishment of any new arboreal growth."[27] Water and soil in this case were important but not determinative. The most important ecological factor was fire. Frequent light fires punctuated by larger burns over long periods kept low elevation forests relatively open and prevented seedlings of pine, fir, and woody shrubs such as sagebrush and antelope brush from colonizing nearby grasslands.

Not surprisingly, when the long pattern of burning that had helped to create and maintain these landscapes was disrupted after 1860 – coinciding with disease-related depopulation in Aboriginal communities and the first wave of European resettlement – the land itself began to change.[28] As one rancher reported as early as 1902 of the area around Lillooet, traditionally the territory of the Stl'atl'imx people, "No fires in this district such as there used to be in earlier times. Then they were purposely caused by the natives, with the object of burning off the grass, which otherwise was not touched from years end to years end." But now things were different because Native people lived on Indian reserves and no longer burned the range. "In consequence," he noted, "cottonwood and other deciduous trees have sprung up in many places where formerly there was nothing of the sort, so continuously was the ground burnt over." To what extent this applied to other areas was unclear, but apparently the decline of Aboriginal burning triggered a new ecological process whereby open grasslands began to be colonized by pioneer tree species. It also anticipated broader ecological changes when the province's first fire prevention laws were enforced in the first half of the twentieth century. As we will see in subsequent chapters, the decline of natural and strategic Aboriginal burning in the second half of the nineteenth century and first half of the twentieth set important changes in train.

Many ranchers rightly pointed out that not all grazing was overgrazing. A stocking rate of ten animals per acre (as recommended by the colonial commissioner of lands and works as early as 1870), for example, might constitute overgrazing in one area but not in another or even in the same area in another year. Moving animals from one range to the next and from lowlands to uplands over the course of the year – a pattern known as transhumance – was intended to address this problem. The precise timing of animal movements varied annually in response to geography and changing ecological conditions, but usually cattle were fed or left to rustle on a ranch's winter ranges from about mid-December to mid-April. Spring grazing might last for a month or more, until late May or early June. During the summer, cattle grazed on upper grasslands or the grassy understory of open ponderosa pine forests, and sometimes this lasted well into the fall, depending on the weather. Usually by late October the cattle were herded onto fall ranges at lower elevations and left there to graze stubble and second growth until winter feeding began again in about the middle of December. On the other hand, weather and markets could conspire to undermine even *good* range practice. Low prices in the fall, when most of the cattle were sold, sometimes led ranchers to hold stock in hopes of obtaining better prices the following year. This was risky business because the ability to carry cattle through the winter depended on whether one had sufficient winter range on hand, and that depended in part on the weather. A long, hard winter followed by a cold, wet spring could be disastrous. With hay supplies running short, some ranchers would have to sell off surplus stock at much reduced prices or turn their animals onto open ranges before the grasses had a chance to develop. This worst-case scenario – low prices in fall followed by a long icy winter and a cold wet spring – rarely materialized in full-blown form. Nor did it affect all ranchers and rangelands equally. But micro-scenarios affected individual ranchers annually throughout the grasslands.[29] Although impossible to estimate, the cumulative effect of these market-environment interactions at the local scale was probably considerable.

The result in some areas was increasingly overgrazed range, which ranchers initially tried to compensate for by regulating the grazing habits of sheep. As early as 1876, the Act to Provide for the Better Protection of Cattle Ranges enabled two-thirds of the settlers in any ranching district to create a common in which "no sheep shall be allowed to pasture ... except while being driven from one district to another."[30] There were probably no more than 15,000 sheep in the grassland in 1876, and only about 35,000 horned cattle. On the other hand, most ranchers considered sheep to be relatively ruinous because they cropped the grasses too close to the ground. By this logic, a few sheep were much worse for range quality than many more cattle. This was followed in 1879 by a more comprehensive piece of legislation known as An Act to Protect Winter Stock Ranges that enabled the election of a "board of overseers" in any polling district with the power "to make by-laws for the regulating of the depasturing of cattle, sheep and swine on land unenclosed by a lawful fence"[31] Two commonages were created in the Nicola Valley in the 1880s, though as we will see in Chapter 6, this had more to do with curbing range monopoly than with protecting the grassland.

Publicly managed commonages called for a collective approach to range problems, but this was not the only strategy. By the early 1890s, a few ranchers were also advocating the opposite approach: enclosure. In British Columbia, as elsewhere in the North American West, settlers were engaged in an extensive, open range system of ranching involving fenced winter ranges that were owned, and unfenced Crown ranges that were not.[32] But some of the province's larger ranchers promoted the enclosure of the common grazing grounds in order to encourage investments and, just as important, to prevent these areas from being degraded. As Clement Cornwall, a prominent and politically connected rancher from Ashcroft, argued in 1894 in the pages of the province's annual report on agriculture, the "government should do all in its power to induce private interests to purchase the hill pastures. Then they will be protected instead of ruined as at present by over-stocking."[33]

It was easy for men of means like Clement Cornwall to advocate the enclosure of the so-called hill commons, but ranchers with little or no capital and thus no ability to purchase large tracts of land opposed it on the grounds that it was inequitable. It never occurred to these ranchers or to the government officials with whom they corresponded in the early 1890s that indigenous people, themselves stock raisers on a large scale when the first settlers arrived, had been unfairly excluded from the grasslands, or that the province's expanding ranching economy ultimately depended on and was made possible by dispossession. And yet ironically, they were deeply opposed to range monopoly. Remarkably, and without any sense of moral inconsistency, one rancher among many in the 1890s considered "the fencing of large tracts of public land by private individuals a great evil."[34]

Partly in response to these arguments, some within the provincial government advocated a modified concept of public land in which an annual grazing fee was used to fund various range improvement projects. By "range improvement" late-nineteenth-century land managers in the West meant more than just improvement in the everyday sense of simply making something better, though they meant that as well. As a general, and in the 1890s largely informal, program of land use, it also included the elimination of so-called scrub bulls (usually older, mixed-breed animals) from the range and their replacement with better quality, and thus more valuable, breeding stock; the construction of more and better fences for controlling cattle movements and interactions and thus to some extent the breeding process and spread of infectious diseases such as mange and blackleg; the fencing of small seasonal ponds that during the spring and summer months turned to cattle-miring "mud-holes" as the winter melt-waters receded; and the reseeding of depleted ranges with cultivated plants, as well as what one official called "closer" herd management, or more frequent moving of cattle from one range to the next in order to avoid "overstocking."[35] It also meant better, and thus more, irrigation. Admittedly, one official observed, the region's water supply was largely a matter of winter rain and snow, neither of which could be controlled. Nevertheless, irrigation was often highly inefficient. Some irrigation ditches, the official suspected, probably lost as much water to seepage and evaporation as they carried to ranchers' hay fields. Better dams and ditches, he reasoned, would not only effectively increase the total water supply but also enable ranchers to cultivate more of what their cattle consumed each year, thereby reducing grazing pressure.

Even range improvement (as defined by provincial officials) proved surprisingly controversial, however. The important issue for many people was time. Reseeding and the rest of it were are all well and good in the long term, but ranchers needed help now. Even those in settler society who advocated a broad approach to range improvement admitted it would take years, perhaps even decades, and ultimately a considerable sum of private and public money to purchase better breeding animals, build all those fences, improve irrigation, harvest more hay, and reseed or otherwise restore depleted rangelands. And, of course, there were always questions about how to pay for range improvements. Enclosure was controversial, but so was paying an annual grazing fee for "public" land. Even closer herd management, which many ranchers supported, was nonetheless somewhat frowned upon because of the additional time and labour costs that more frequent cattle movements necessarily entailed.

Ranchers and range officials sought simpler solutions to the problems they faced, and in the 1890s nothing seemed simpler than eliminating competing claims to grassland. Like many other early British Columbians, rancher John Moore of Big Bar was also convinced that the "public pasture lands" were "overstocked and getting run down in consequence" and that "we must therefore consider the best way of protecting the pastoral lands." Rather than focus on cattle, though, or even grasshoppers (which, as we will see, were also becoming a problem), he made wild horses the villains of his environmental history. By his estimate, there were "5000 wild or nearly wild horses in the 40 or 50 miles between Lillooet and Big Bar."[36] Moore never defined what a "nearly wild" horse was, nor did he say how the horses in question were counted. Nor did he do the math on how many cattle could be fed if these animals were eliminated. He did not have to because ranchers could do it themselves. Using contemporary estimates ranging from 2:1 to as high as 3:1, they could quickly calculate that 5,000 wild horses on the range all year long were equivalent in grazing and trampling terms to 10,000 or 15,000 head of cattle. To put these estimates into perspective, it helps to know that the largest cattle ranch in the grass-land in the 1890s had around 6,000 head of cattle, and that most ranches had fewer than 500 head. By this logic, exterminating *just* the wild horses between Lillooet and Big Bar would save enough rangeland to support two or three relatively large ranches or twenty to thirty average ones. It was precisely the kind of quantitative logic that newcomers concerned with improvement found irresistible.

It never occurred to these ranchers, or to the officials with whom they corresponded, that there might be problems in assuming cattle and horses were interchangeable in exactly this way. Yet, we now know that although they certainly overlapped ecologically – both, after all, were herbivores – wild horses and cattle probably occupied different ecological niches at different times of the year. As Stephen Jenkins and Michael Ashley recently observed in a review and synthesis of the literature on wild horses, "Sympatric ungulates [such as cattle and horses] may have similar diets but forage in different habitats within a common range."[37] Now, in all fairness, there was almost no research on wild horse ecology in North America until after the Second World War, by which time most wild horses in British Columbia had already been eliminated. Even today, after years of experience and study, the question of ecological competition between horses and cattle is fraught with uncertainty. As Jenkins explains, "Ecologists make a distinction between resource partitioning – the extent to which species differ in their use of resources in an ecological community, and competition – the impact of each species on the distribution, abundance, and physical and behavioral characteristics of the other. The best evidence for competition is often experimental, but there are few if any rigorous experimental studies of competition between feral horses and other ungulates."[38] There were clues, however, even in the late nineteenth century when ranchers used simple calculations to condemn these animals, that the problem of competition was complicated. Judging from archival records, the sharpest ecological conflicts between cattle and horses occurred in late winter or early spring, when ranchers ran low on hay and had to turn their animals onto the open range.

Even if horses and cattle were simply assumed to be *equivalent* in the grazing terms (i.e., 1 horse = 1 cow), the argument for exterminating them would have been convincing, especially when applied to the grassland as a whole. Nobody knew exactly how many wild horses there were in the 1890s, but one estimate put the number as high as 25,000. As the total cattle herd in the mid- to late 1890s was only about 80,000 head, ridding the range of wild horses would increase the total amount of forage available to cattle by as much as 30 percent (enough to support perhaps 25,000 head of cattle). Even if there were only half or a quarter as many wild horses (i.e., 12,500 or 6,250 head), the ecological benefits of eliminating these animals would have appeared considerable to ranchers running fewer than 500 head of cattle. As one rancher put it, "As to the wild horse pest it ought to be entirely stamped out."[39]

Certainly British Columbians were gaining plenty of experience stamping out other animal pests. In one seven-year span for which there are records (1909–16), the province paid bounties on 2,871 wolves, 1,951 cougars, 38,804 coyotes, 7,396 owls, and 382 golden eagles (51,314 animals in total).[40] The total for the late nineteenth century is impossible to determine but according to geographer Lillian Ford's study of coyote extermination, in some years the body count in British Columbia was so high that the provincial government had to defer payments until the following fiscal year.[41] A bounty on wild horses was another matter, however, because not all wild horses were actually wild. As rancher J.S. Place of Merritt observed, in a telling passage that appeared in the pages of the province's annual report on agriculture for 1892, "The *Whites* would cause no trouble. We are all of the opinion that they ought to be totally exterminated."[42]

The province's apparent enthusiasm for extermination and J.S. Place's prediction that the "whites would cause no trouble" notwithstanding, a number of settlers in the 1890s balked at a bounty on wild horses because of concerns about killing domestic horses. In reality, many settlers also kept horses on Crown range. They worried that at a distance it would be difficult or impossible to tell a branded animal from an unbranded animal: distance and common grazing, and the socializing tendencies of the horses themselves, obscured – and for all intents and purposes dissolved – the social categories that divided owned and ownerless animals. It was also true that some wild horses had brands, making it difficult or impossible for bounty hunters to differentiate between those animals that were ownerless and thus open to destruction under the law and those that were not. In this blurry context, where the wild and owned were indistinguishable, some ranchers feared that "unscrupulous" horse hunters would simply hang around ranches and Indian reserves in order to shoot tame and thus more easily targeted horses just for the bounty.[43]

Others preferred what they understood to be a subtler approach to wild horse extermination in order to avoid (or at least minimize) a conflict with Native people. One rancher thought the "evil might be mitigated by reasonable and practicable regulations as to wild colts and stallions," but stressed that because "these regulations would chiefly affect the Indian's [sic] horses, they should be plain, brief, and not too harsh."[44] Others agreed that any measures against wild horses would mainly affect Native people, but proposed targeting mares instead of stallions, to limit their reproduction. Still others wished to see a law that targeted wild stallions as well as mares, yet opposed an open season backed by a bounty. These ranchers hoped to avoid the problem of indiscriminate shooting of settler and Native livestock by having specially appointed horse hunters armed not just with rifles but also with brand sheets identifying legally owned livestock do the work instead. For his part, the deputy minister of agriculture, James Anderson, focused on the fact that most wild horses had owners: "As most of these useless Cayuses are ... claimed by Indians, could they not be compelled to keep them on their own reserves?"[45] "It seems too bad," he lamented in the pages of the province's annual report on agriculture for 1895–96, "that the Indians, besides having the *best* of the country as reserves, should be allowed to make use of the public domain in this most wasteful manner."[46]

The cultural background of these comments was formed by colonial assumptions about civilization and savagery that even the most enlightened in early British Columbia shared. As historical geographer Cole Harris has written, "Hardly a white person questioned the distinction between civilization and savagery or the association of the former with Europeans and the latter with native people ... From this it followed that until Europeans arrived, most of the land was waste, or where native people were obviously using it, that their uses were inadequate."[47] Even Gilbert Malcolm Sproat – the Indian reserve commissioner who Harris argues "struggled mightily" to reconcile the needs of Native people (as Sproat understood them) with the requirements of an incoming settler society – had serious misgivings about indigenous land use in the grassland, prophetically noting as early as 1878 that "by and by they [Native people] may be told to limit the number of horses they keep, which, except in intertribal traffic, have small or no market value."[48]

I return to Sproat in the next chapter. For now, it is important to understand that even in 1896, at the height of British colonialism, it was still possible for settlers like James Anderson to see that indigenous people simply did not have the "best of the country as reserves." Reserves were small and rarely contained good grazing land or the water resources necessary to irrigate hay crops. Taken together, as noted already, reserves accounted for less than one-third of 1 percent of the total provincial land base. In the grassland, the largest reserves were still smaller than the largest settler ranches yet had to support numerous Native families and their livestock. Settlers like James Anderson who said that Native people had the best of the country as reserves were not only self-interested, in that they simply wanted the grassland for themselves, but also delusional.

While Anderson discussed Native peoples' grazing needs and land-use practices with the Dominion Department of Indian Affairs, provincial legislators attempted to reduce the wild horse population with legal instruments. An Act for the Extermination of Wild Horses, passed in 1896, made it "lawful for any person licensed by the Government to shoot or otherwise destroy any unbranded stallion over the age of twenty months which may be running at large upon the public lands, provided that such person shall theretofore have unsuccessfully used reasonable endeavours to capture such stallion."[49] The logic was to eliminate reproduction so that wild horses would eventually disappear, but in ranching country this legislation was a disappointment, judged limited in scope and entirely inadequate to the situation. Even James Anderson, whose government had passed the legislation, agreed that the act, "while good and calculated to mitigate the evil in the course of time[,] affords no immediate relief." In his view more "stringent" legislation was needed.[50]

Four years later, however, the wild horse problem remained unsolved. According to one report, "Huge bands of these worthless beasts" still roamed over the "best" ranges of the Interior, "doing incalculable damage to the detriment of the cattle industry." Disease was still a problem, the production of high-quality horses had been "rendered abortive" by interbreeding, tame mares were still being run off by wild stallions, and the range in many places was still being "overgrazed."[51] Two years later, in 1902, one government official lamented that the "vexed question" of wild horses was "as unsettled as ever" and that there had been no reduction whatsoever in the number of these "worse than worthless animals." Predictably, the 1896 legislation targeting wild stallions had failed to limit their numbers. These horses showed "no sign of diminution" and it was "evident" that something "much more drastic in nature" was required.[52]

In the meantime, settlers tried out several less drastic plans. In 1901, the *Vancouver Daily Province* reported that an "organized effort" involving settlers and some Native people was being made to round up wild horses in the Nicola Valley for use in the British Imperial Army during the Boer War. Contrary to settler complaints that British Columbia's wild horses were often small, weak, and disease-prone, one local newspaper reported that these "wiry" and "excellent" horses were in fact "very acceptable" to army purchasing agents. There were some selection criteria, however. The army's advertisement specified that horses "thin in flesh need not be shown." Nor, the newspaper continued, were military officials interested in white and light grey horses. Captured horses should be "brown, black, chestnut, or iron grey."[53] As Lieutenant Colonel H. Thomson of the British Imperial Army explained in an 1895 lecture titled "Our Military Horses," "White and light coloured horses not only lacked stamina and were prone to disease, but also tended to be quite skittish and thus highly likely to buck their riders in battle.[54] Otherwise, the newspaper noted, "settlers and Indians" were free to round up for sale however many wild horses they could. Indeed, according to the paper, those who captured such animals would be well rewarded for their efforts.[55] After touring other parts of western Canada, two British Army purchasing agents arrived at Kamloops as planned. But there is no record of how many wild horses, if any, were rounded up for military use in Africa.

Another plan, described in local newspapers as a "sporting proposition," involved using well-heeled English sport hunters to rid the range of wild horses. Appealing to the "sporting tendencies of Englishmen who had time on their hands," J.B. Hayne, himself an avid sport hunter and Englishman of apparently considerable means, suggested bringing one hundred of his countrymen to British Columbia to round up the province's wild horse population. The plan was to form "a far stretching cordon" around the Okanagan hills and move systematically from section to section in that district. "The line of hunters would be stretched around say, a lake," Hayne explained, "and as they closed in the wild animals would be driven toward the centre and eventually would take refuge in the lake. Then it would be an easy matter to shoot them or dispose of them otherwise."[56] If Hayne's plan to round up wild horses and then slaughter them in a lake seemed laughable to some and unsportsmanlike to others, several provincial politicians supported it nonetheless. Indeed, according to one representative, "It was quite probable that the services of sporting Englishmen might be enlisted for the purpose."[57]

Hayne's proposal to recruit elite British sport hunters had its historical antecedents. In early Greece, as elsewhere in the ancient world, aristocrats had eradicated predators to protect human settlement, crops, and livestock. Protective hunts also occurred in early modern Britain and led locally to the extirpation of wolves and wild boars in the late fifteenth and the early sixteenth centuries. From these early efforts emerged elite-oriented blood sports. Fox hunting, for example, became a popular and much ritualized practice among the English elite in the late eighteenth century. But like all blood sports, the hunt for foxes "involved curious contradictions." Although the fox was "a danger to all domestic poultry and to the eggs and young of pheasants reared for slaughter," explains historian John Mackenzie, eventually the "farmers and gamekeepers who killed them were dubbed 'vulpicides,' people who failed to comply with the elaborate rules of the countryside, the restricted access and ritualised forms of vermin destruction." Moreover, as local fox populations declined, elite hunters took steps to protect and husband them by introducing breeding stock. In so doing, Mackenzie observes, "The logic of 'protective' hunting had been inverted. The ritual of protection against vermin had become so necessary to rural social relations that the vermin had to be preserved and increased. The sporting needs of the hunt had turned the 'vermin' into a protected species."[58]

Nobody in early British Columbia ever contemplated protecting wild horses for hunting purposes, but as with the English fox hunt, Hayne's plan to recruit British horse hunters also had its curious contradictions. One was how it combined the perceived virtues of hunting – that hunting encouraged, among other things, a kind of rugged masculinity – with ordinary practices of pest eradication and range improvement. In this way, Hayne's proposal to hunt wild horses resembled somewhat the protective hunts of ancient Greece, Assyria, and early modern England, the major difference being that it was bunchgrass and not people that the wild horse hunt sought to protect. Indeed, in organization, Hayne's horse hunt strongly resembled the communal hunts of colonial British India that in part also sought to protect people from predators. But again, wild horses threatened only the grass that fed settlers' cattle, not the settlers themselves. The most curious contradiction of all, however, surrounded the actual animals involved. Even though wild horses may have been wild enough to establish a blood sport, they were not exactly wild in the way that lions, rhinos, elephants, and pronghorn antelope are wild. In colonial British Columbia, the usual boundaries between the wild and the tame were being blurred.

Partly in response to this problem, in 1908 the provincial government amended an existing piece of legislation known as the Animals Act, enabling "at least five owners of horses ranging upon the public lands of any district east of the Cascades" to request a licence authorizing any one of those named in the request to "shoot unbranded horses running wild upon the public lands within the portion of the said district mentioned."[59] This fell well short of an open season backed by a bounty, but it did constitute a much more aggressive stance toward wild horses than the aforementioned 1896 act, which targeted only unbranded stallions. Yet, few if any wild horses – and as far as can be ascertained, no Aboriginal horses – were ever killed under the province's amended Animals Act. Details are hard to come by, but according to later reports, some ranchers refrained from taking advantage of the law because of concerns about threats and reprisals from Native people.[60]

Certainly some ranchers resorted to threats and intimidation. One ranch manager wrote ominously about free-ranging horses around Big Creek, on the middle Fraser River: "The Indians will be warned by me once [to keep their horses on the Indian reserve] and if they continue [grazing them in this area] I think a way will be found to stop them."[61] Most settlers, however, opted for less aggressive strategies such as letters and petitions to government suggesting, as others had done before, that Indian horses, like Indian people, should be confined to Indian lands. By this logic, Aboriginal horses and their owners were a federal problem, not a provincial one. Even in the Interior of British Columbia, when it came down to conserving grassland, the old problem of federal-provincial relations could not be escaped. Rather than accommodate Native peoples' grazing needs, settlers simply tried to eliminate them. Meanwhile, in order to force a few Aboriginal horses off the range, some of the larger ranches in the grassland simply started buying them. As the foreman of a large Chilcotin ranch property explained in 1910, the Natives around Big Bar, on the east bank of the Fraser River, "are hard up and need the money and it helps to get them off the range. Besides," he added, "we should make a little on them."[62]

In truth, as we will see in the next chapter, it was not only the Native people at Big Bar who were hard up and in need of cash. Nor, despite what many settlers said, was it possible for Native stock raisers to keep to their reserves all year. Indian reserves not only were small but rarely contained the specific natural resources – winter range and water – needed to raise horses and cattle together on anything more than a modest scale. It is impossible in these pages to detail fully the pattern of ranching and resettlement that was produced in the second half of the nineteenth century. Instead, in the next chapter, I offer a generalized account of ranching and resettlement along the middle Fraser and Chilcotin Rivers and in the Southern Interior spanning the ancestral territories of Tsilhqot'in, Stl'atl'imx, Secwepemc, Okanagan, and Nlaka'pamux First Nations peoples.

3
The Biogeography of Dispossession

This chapter steps back from the wild horse conflicts of the late nineteenth and early twentieth centuries in order to show how deeply rooted these were in the processes of resettlement and dispossession that began decades earlier, when the first ranches and Indian reserves were established. Essentially, it shows what First Nations people understood all too well: that a map of ranches and Indian reserves in the grasslands approximated the distribution of lowlands suitable for wintering cattle or cultivating hay crops. Settler ranches had most of these lowlands, whereas Indian reserves had only a little or none. This was the pattern of ranching and resettlement – the biogeography of dispossession – that prevailed throughout much of the grasslands by the late nineteenth century.

British Columbia may be best known for its wet and dense coastal rainforests, but large parts of the Interior are dry. Average annual precipitation in the drier areas is usually less than thirty centimetres, and overall it is low. Weather and climate vary with local differences in altitude, exposure, and latitude, but in general terms, winters are cold, summers are hot, and the air is dry.[1]

But it was not always that way. Like that of northern North America in general, the environmental history of Interior British Columbia was reset during the last Pleistocene ice age. At its height, about 18,000 years ago, a massive, more or less continuous blanket of ice covered present-day Canada and extended into what is now the northern United States. But eventually the climate warmed. By about 13,000 years ago, the glaciers had begun to retreat, and by about 10,000 years ago, except at elevations where alpine glaciers persisted, the Interior of present-day British Columbia was probably ice-free (although as earth scientists observe, some glacial features probably persisted longer).[2]

Initially, the surface was too unstable and the climate too cold to support plant life, but eventually the land become stable enough, and the climate warm enough, to support pine forests in the uplands and more extensive stands of sagebrush, forbs, and grasses in the valley bottoms. Pollen analyses indicate that grasslands were more extensive in the past than they are today, reaching a maximum area around 8,000 years ago, a sure sign that the climate was much warmer and drier than it is today. It also shows that forests expanded at this time and that the forest-grassland border continued to fluctuate thereafter with fires and short-term changes in climate.[3] Grasslands contracted as the climate cooled and became slightly wetter, reaching roughly their current size and distribution around 4,500 years ago.[4]

Before resettlement, this was Native space. Current archaeological evidence indicates that there were people present in this area as early as 8,250 years ago. Not much is known about the culture and lifeways of these first people, but important clues appear in the archaeological record as we move closer to the present. Numerous artifacts and especially an abundance of projectile spearheads suggest the presence of nomadic deer and elk hunters by about 7000 BP. By 5,000 years ago, indigenous people had begun to harvest salmon and larger winter villages soon followed. Circular house pits, ranging in size from 7.6 to 16.0 metres in diameter, began to appear around 4,500 years ago, and numerous artifacts – spears, nets, hooks, chisels, blades, bracelets, pendants, beads, and a wide variety of artwork – suggest the development of separate, relatively sedentary, and increasingly complex fishing societies over the next 2,000 years.[5] Land-based activities, such as hunting and gathering, remained important, however, and were greatly enhanced by the arrival of the horse. Precisely how and when the horse (*Equus caballus*) arrived is impossible to determine. We know that the horse evolved in North America but became locally extinct there about 11,000 to 13,000 years ago and that the continent remained horseless until the Spanish reintroduced them in the fifteenth and sixteenth centuries.[6] In 1808, David Thompson noted that "wild horses" were "common" and "frequently seen in large groups" near present-day Invermere, and Simon Fraser encountered indigenous people on horseback near what is now Soda Creek.[7] However, earlier accounts were impossible to locate.

Nevertheless it seems clear from ethnographic records and recent oral histories that horses were important in Aboriginal history. Like other

animals, horses were incorporated into an animated universe wherein
people could be animals, animals could be people, and the actions of
nonhuman actors carried social meaning for the human communities
attached to them. Anthropological accounts emphasize the practical utility
of horses in hunting and warfare and the way that horses encouraged
marriages and political alliances or facilitated movement and trade across
an enormous area. They also emphasize how the arrival of a new animal
altered existing social and subsistence relationships. It is impossible to
know how the arrival of horses affected grassland ecology, though it must
have increased grazing and trampling pressure on grasslands that previously
experienced few large herbivores. There is evidence, however, that mounted
hunting parties of Secwepemc and Nlaka'pamux people contributed to
the extirpation of elk in the present-day upper Nicola Valley area by the
late eighteenth or early nineteenth century.[8] The wider effects of this
elimination of elk are also impossible to determine, but recent ecological
theory suggests that removal of a large ungulate probably altered existing
predator-prey relations in the region, opening new forage resources to new
browsers and grazers such as deer and bighorn sheep.[9] There is evidence
too that the horse increased the scale and frequency of warfare, and seemingly the same can be said of trade.[10] Apparently, the horse itself became
an important marker of status and wealth, and its arrival in the so-called
"plateau culture area" – including present-day Interior British Columbia
and the American states of Washington and Oregon – may have helped
to foster "an incipient, social class system of rank" in what were previously
much more egalitarian societies.[11] Many years later ethnographer James
Teit reported, ethnocentrically perhaps, that some indigenous groups
considered horses to be private property, and that some chiefs and families
had very large herds.[12]

Like others of his generation, James Teit had come to the grasslands to
"salvage" a timeless, authentic Aboriginal culture that many newcomers
believed (perhaps self-servingly) was rapidly disappearing.[13] Native cultures
were neither static during the precontact period nor destined to disappear
in the postcontact period.[14] The pace and scale of change in the nineteenth
century, however, was probably unprecedented. In 1811, the continental
fur trade connected the peoples and animals of the grasslands to a world
capitalist system centred on Europe.[15] The fur trade introduced new trade
items and notions of use and exchange value that had no analogue in
Native society but were the very basis of the European society that was
about to claim the grasslands for itself. More disruptive in the short term
were the effects of old-world diseases. Influenza and measles appeared in

succession in the 1840s, reducing the Native population by at least 10 percent.[16] There were no non-native ranchers in the grassland in the 1840s, just transient explorers and fur traders. Yet, the region was being reconfigured from afar by the diplomacy of distant imperial powers. In 1846, the Oregon Treaty between Canada and the United States extended the existing international border along the 49th parallel west to the Pacific. In the process, Native space north of the new border "was reproduced as an absolute space of British sovereignty."[17] Then the miners arrived: the Oregon Treaty notwithstanding, a gold rush up the Fraser Canyon brought 25,000 to 30,000 Americans and others to the grasslands after 1858. Like others before, the rush for gold in British Columbia was marked by violence. Fights between Native people and armed miners moving in "paramilitary" formation were not uncommon, and colonial customs officers reported that miners abducted Native women.[18] The gold rush also brought countless sheep, mules, cattle, and horses to the grasslands. According to one account, some 22,000 head of cattle crossed the international border at Rock Creek between 1858 and 1862. Scattered reports suggest that Native people defended some grazing areas against encroaching American cattle drovers, but in other cases they were overwhelmed – a problem that would persist into the 1860s and 1870s.

The gold rush also brought a smallpox epidemic to the grasslands. Although many Fraser Canyon Native peoples had been vaccinated by Christian missionaries – themselves a powerful force for change in the nineteenth century – an 1862 smallpox epidemic apparently "spread faster and farther" than any previous epidemic.[19] A decade later, George Grant, secretary to a transcontinental survey for the Canadian Pacific Railway, wrote from Fort Kamloops that smallpox had reduced the number of Native people "in this part of the country" to "the merest handful."[20] Anthropologists believe that the 1862 epidemic probably reduced the indigenous population by one-third. Depopulation had serious and lasting consequences for Native societies; it also had important implications for nonhuman nature. In addition to changing the scale and pattern of Aboriginal burning, and thus to some extent the pattern and distribution of forest and grassland plants affected by fire, disease-related depopulation caused some horses to become feral when their Native owners died.

In addition to people and pack animals, the gold rush brought ranching to British Columbia. Unlike fur trade and mining economies, ranching economies implied settlement, and settlers required land. Recognizing as much, but also eager to impose some administrative order on the gold rush and establish settlers in a space that was British by the terms the 1846

Oregon Treaty yet occupied increasingly by American gold miners, in 1858 colonial officials established the mainland colony of British Columbia. Two years later, they passed a land ordinance enabling British subjects "and aliens who shall take the oath of allegiance to Her Majesty, her heirs and successors" to pre-empt 160 acres of land.[21] The reason for the amendment was essentially environmental and reflected the intense ecological effects of the gold rush. As early as 1865, there was evidence that the range in many places was both badly trampled and heavily overgrazed. As one colonial official put it, 160 acres of land was "insufficient" in the grasslands, "where overstocking soon destroys the range."[22] The 1870 amendment also provided for potentially enormous pastoral leases, subject only to a minimum stocking rate set by the commissioner of lands and works within six months of obtaining the lease. The stocking rate for leases varied somewhat according to local conditions, but usually it was one head of cattle for every 10 acres of land. To give just two examples of land acquired this way, the owners of the Cornwall ranch leased 10,000 acres at Ashcroft in 1873, and John Wilson (dubbed the "Cattle King" of early British Columbia because of his large cattle herd and extensive landholdings) leased 10,980 acres in the Thompson Valley. In just one year for which there are records (1873), the government of British Columbia sold 102,500 acres of rangeland.[23]

These early efforts to control common grazing lands with leasing anticipated similar developments elsewhere in the "British West."[24] In 1882, the Dominion government introduced legislation enabling individual ranchers to acquire 100,000 acres on a twenty-one-year lease. However, the origins of this approach were in the antipodes, where similar challenges around the control and colonization of common grazing lands occurred much earlier. Faced with "illegal alienation" of land and an "uncontrolled dispersion of settlement," in the late 1840s and early 1850s, the British government made it possible to acquire fourteen-year pastoral leases in Australia, and similar legislation was soon introduced in New Zealand.[25] The point of these leases was to promote ordered settlement while providing would-be pastoralists with land and the security of title they needed to establish ranches.

Ranches required more than environmentally undifferentiated grassland, however.[26] As cattle required range and shelter in winter, ranches tended to concentrate in areas with very particular ecological and geographical attributes. In the BC context, these were lowland ranges where snowfall was relatively light and occasional thaws from warming mountain winds left the ground bare and thus available for winter grazing. Even though all bunchgrass was considered hard grass because it cured on the ground, making it available for grazing after other forage plants had succumbed to the effects of frost, not all hard grass was winter range. Geographically, winter range was usually coextensive with what range ecologist Edwin Tisdale eventually dubbed "lower grasslands."[27] The best winter lowlands were found along the middle Fraser and lower Chilcotin Rivers, in the Thompson Valley, and in the Nicola Valley from Merritt to Douglas Lake; good winter ranges also existed in the Similkameen Valley near the settler communities of Princeton and Keremeos. But such spaces were not widely distributed beyond these areas. According to one recent estimate, *all* types of grasslands account for less than 1 percent of the provincial land base.[28] Recognizing the importance and perhaps limited extent of winter range, ranchers quickly pre-empted, purchased, and leased as much of this ecosystem as possible, and in some instances, such as the Gang Ranch or Alkali Lake Ranch, this was quite a lot. A relatively small area of land with specific geographic and environmental qualities thus bore the concentrated brunt of settler colonialism.

Yet, the reach of ranching was considerable. A few examples from British Columbia help to make to this point. By the early twentieth century, the Douglas Lake Cattle Company had access to 450,000 acres, perhaps only a quarter of which was alienated. Likewise, the Chilco Ranch, which held exclusive grazing rights between the Taseko River and Big Creek, in the Chilcotin District, controlled some 850,000 acres of open range and forested upland, only a fraction of which was alienated. Only the massive Gang Ranch on the middle Fraser and Chilcotin Rivers controlled more. With nearly 50,000 acres of alienated winter range in 1898, its ranching hinterland (including leases and Crown range) amounted to approximately 1 million acres, effectively making it one of the largest ranch properties in the West.[29] Admittedly, these are extreme examples, but they illustrate a general pattern in which control of lowlands – because uplands were often worthless for ranching without them – enabled a few ranchers with property rights in winter range to control a valley. Collectively, even small cattle ranches controlled much larger areas of land.

Ranching was just one part of the spatial reordering that occurred in the drylands in the mid- to late nineteenth century: it was also during this period that the first Indian reserves were created. In the summer of 1861, William Cox, the gold commissioner and colonial magistrate at Rock Creek (near the American border), was instructed by Governor James Douglas to create Indian reserves in the Okanagan and Kamloops areas. By the end of October, there were reserves at the head and foot of Okanagan

Lake totalling some twenty square miles – "some of the best land" in the area, according to one colonial official – as well as reserves in the Kamloops area totalling some 600 square miles.[30] In 1862, he "marked off by substantial and prominent posts the lands on the Bonaparte River which the Indians wished to be reserved for their use." He also "notified the settlers and travelers" in this area that "their said lands must not be encroached upon."[31] In retrospect, notes Cole Harris, the Cox reserves were among "the most generous ever identified in British Columbia."[32] But when Governor Douglas left office in 1864, colonial officials in the capital city of Victoria raised questions about the legality of these reserves and eventually they were significantly reduced. In 1865, the colonial magistrate and cattle rancher J.C. Haynes reduced Cox's Okanagan Lake reserves to just over five square miles (3,342 acres), and in 1866 Cox's Kamloops reserves were divided into five smaller reserves. The largest reserve was now just three square miles (1,920 acres). In relatively short order – really not much more than a decade – an entirely new system of land use had been imposed, and the intentions of the colonial government had been established. Indian reserves would be small and the remainder would be opened to British-European settlement.[33]

Not surprisingly the sudden influx of settlers and cattle into the grasslands in the 1860s and 1870s, and the massive reordering of space and environment that this influx entailed, nearly caused a war in the grassland. In the summer of 1874, amid reports of Native unrest in the grassland, and rumours that a war was looming, Isaiah Powell, Superintendent of Indian Affairs for British Columbia travelled to the Interior to gather intelligence. Kler.klick.ten (Louis), the chief at Kamloops complained, "Our feeling are hurt because we do not have enough land ... We have many horses as you can see. We have many cattle. I see one white man can take a large quantity of land [referring to the system of pastoral leasing]. Our cattle and horses have been driven away from the open country[,] this is not right. Do you think this is just? We complained about this and I heard soldiers would soon come to live at Kamloops. I do not like this. My people talk about it." Similarly, Sys-sy-as-cut, the chief at Deadman's Creek, complained, "A little while ago we owned all the land, now my people have very little and we are surrounded by the Whites and they are continually driving off our cattle and horses [again referring to the system of pastoral leaseholds] ... I want you to give us land for our horses and cattle to feed on. Some white people claim it all. This is not right." Likewise, the chief at Bonaparte complained, "White men are always now driving away our Cattle and Horses and claiming the whole Country. They do not fence their land to keep it or show which is theirs but claim it all. If our horses go out now as they used to the whites drive them off and say we shall be punished. I do not think this is right." For his part, Powell felt it was his "duty" to report that the Native people had many legitimate grievances and that "among the assigned causes of discontent" was the removal of their horses and cattle from "unfenced lands or those held under pastoral lease." In his report he recommended that the government refrain from issuing pastoral leases until the "land question" had been settled.[34]

Meanwhile Native people made more formal complaints to the colonial government with assistance from C.J. Grandidier, an Oblate priest at Kamloops. An 1875 petition argued that Indian reserves in the grassland were too small to feed Native families and livestock, and that Native people needed more range. "We consider ourselves unfairly treated by not having a large pastureland secured to us to keep our horses and cattle," the petitioners complained. "White men can lease or buy pasture lands but we have not the same privilege."[35] Grandidier agreed that Native people were being "hemmed in on all sides by the settlers who have leased all the pastureland to the very limit of the reservations," adding that "many head [of cattle and horses] die every winter for want of food because they are obliged to winter on the spot where they have fed all the summer and the grass is all gone." Native people needed more and better rangeland, to be sure, but according to Grandidier it was also crucial that these lands should be fenced. "Large cattle raisers," he noted, "may overrun the pastureland next to the Reservation with thousands of head at a time so that in a short time the grass may be all eaten up."[36]

Reflecting more generally on these matters in an 1874 letter to the editor of a BC newspaper, Grandidier recalled a time not too long ago when there were no ranchers in the grassland and Interior Native people had the range there to themselves. "Before the settlement of the Province the natives were in possession of it," he observed. "There was no one to restrain them in that possession. Their horses had wide pasturelands to feed on." But then everything changed. "The whites came in, took land, fenced it, and little by little hemmed the Indians in their small reservations. They leased the pastoral land that they did not buy and drove the cattle of the Indians from their old pastureland." To make matters even worse, "their reservations [were] repeatedly cut off and made smaller for the benefit of the whites and the best and most useful part of them taken away till some tribes are corralled on a small piece of land, as at Canoe Creek or elsewhere, or even have not an inch of ground, as at Williams Lake." According to

Grandidier, "the dictates of justice" had been completely abandoned in British Columbia. Native people had "protested against those spoliations from the beginning," he noted, "but they have not obtained any redress."[37]

By the mid-1870s, as Harris has observed, the situation in the Interior was dire: "an Indian war in progress south of the border; messengers and spies from the American Okanagan circulating in the Okanagan and Thompson Valleys and some young Okanagan warriors joining their relatives in American territory [and] deep dissatisfaction over the land question going back to the Cox reserves and fomented by the land rights acquired by each incoming settler."[38] When the Joint Indian Reserve Commission (JIRC) established by British Columbia and Canada in 1876 to solve the land question arrived at Kamloops in the summer of 1877, one of its members, Gilbert Malcolm Sproat, reported that Native people were meeting at the head of Okanagan Lake and that "the continuance of peace [here] hangs by a thread." "Their dissatisfaction is chronic, they know their power, and do not fear war." The settler population was defenceless. Unlike on the coast, where officials could anchor gunboats in areas of Native unrest, in the Interior they had to rely on mounted soldiers that were usually many days away. Indeed, according to Sproat, "if these Shuswap Tribes – bold, fierce, well-armed Indians who can ride 60 to 70 miles a day – broke out, I do not see what force there is in this country to put them down."[39]

The purpose of JIRC in this fraught colonial context was not to sign treaties with Aboriginal people. No treaties were signed in British Columbia. Rather its job was to allocate Indian reserves. This task proved more difficult than expected, however, because by the early 1870s many of the best lowland ranges and bunchgrass pastures had already been fenced or leased.[40] This was problematic from several perspectives. For one thing, fenced lowlands sometimes blocked access to salmon fisheries. In these cases the commissioners created easements or worked out informal arrangements with ranchers whereby Native people could traverse a grazing lease to reach a fishery. In a letter to a Joseph Guichon, a prominent Nicola Valley rancher, Commissioner Sproat explained that "the Indians have the right of access, but they must not take horses through the white men's lands so as to damage them." Instead, "they are to walk on foot through the lands of the white men and not to go on horseback and not encamp in such lands." Sproat reported that the chiefs resented having to leave their horses behind; they also complained about not being able to camp close to their traditional fishing sites. As one chief explained, it would be "hard on the women and children carrying the fish" if his people had to camp further away, a powerful reminder that while all Aboriginal people were dispossessed, individuals and groups within Aboriginal society experienced the process of resettlement somewhat differently depending on their social position.[41] But apparently the ranchers insisted because in their view leased lowlands constituted a private property right for which the ranchers in the province had paid and that had, therefore, to be protected.

The deeper issue was that Native people needed water for hay crops and lowlands to use as natural winter range. "What really governs the stock farmer's business here is his available winter range," Sproat wrote, "as it is worthless to feed cattle in summer if they have to die for want of food and shelter in winter. Horses," he continued "can live on the higher lands in winter as they paw through the snow to get at the grass, but cattle require sheltered spots with little snow on them."[42] The problem in 1877 was that the best "sheltered spots" in the grassland had already been alienated. This was problematic from another perspective because usually lowland areas were easier to irrigate and ranchers usually had the water rights to do so. The commissioners had no answer to these problems, nor any mandate to disturb settlers who had acquired their land and water rights by legal means, as defined by the colonial government. In a few cases the JIRC challenged the legality of settler pre-emptions, but in most cases they did not because as far as could be ascertained most ranchers in the province had acquired their winter ranges and water rights legally through practices and procedures established and backed by the colonial state.

Property rights in water and winter range were only part of problem that the reserve commissioners faced. The already difficult task of allocating Indian reserves in the grassland was made even more difficult by range degradation. Sproat noted that the "well known bunchgrass formerly grew on the valleys and lower hillsides as well as the mountains generally." But apparently this was no longer the case. In many cases, the range in these areas had been overgrazed, and in some areas woody shrubs were taking over. "When eaten closely," Sproat observed, "this grass does not grow again – sage takes its place." Contrary to reports from some ranchers and government officials, Sproat concluded that the "pastoral wealth" of British Columbia had actually been "considerably overestimated." In his view, there were but three grades of range in the grassland: "No. 1 Grazing Land" was grassland in its "natural character" (in other words, grassland that was either lightly grazed or not grazed at all). "No. 2 Grazing Land" included ranges that were modified by grazing but still useful for ranching, as well as (less helpfully) ranges that were "permanently damaged." And "No. 3 Grazing Land" was "browsing land among the rocks and woods." Sproat estimated that unmodified grassland (No. 1 Grazing Land) probably comprised half the total. The rest was either somewhat modified, permanently damaged, or found mainly in patches among the rocks and woods.[43]

Convinced nonetheless that ranching was the only viable, reserve-based economy available to Native people, but still unsure about how much land was needed to feed cattle and horses, Sproat tried to establish the grazing capacity of the grasslands. He began by interviewing twenty-three settlers – all of them "experienced" ranchers and thus presumably well positioned to pass judgment on how many acres of land were needed to raise horses and cattle. But this turned out to be of little help because the ranchers he interviewed gave very different estimates. The highest estimate was ten times the lowest. According to Sproat, the highest estimate originated "in the condition inserted many years ago by the Government Leases of pasture lands ... that lease holders should not keep more than one animal to every 10 acres." This was a far cry from the lowest estimate of just one acre of land for every animal, but ultimately these interviews did little to clarify the situation, so Sproat started a grazing experiment, testing the problem "practically" by fencing horses and cattle and "measuring the area they cropped in a given time," and "judging the probability of its recovery before the animal within a given area would have to come around to pasture again."[44]

In a society where numbers mattered, good estimates of grazing capacity were perhaps a way to convince settlers that somewhat larger Indian reserves were justified. As Sproat explained, "The Indians want in kind, if not in quantity [because they had far fewer stock overall] what the white settlers require." This was "but common sense," he continued, "as an Indian's ox will eat as much as a white man's ox. His appetite is not affected by the accident of his ownership." Like his interviews with ranchers, however, his grazing experiment with horses yielded uncertain results. "The truth," Sproat conceded, "is that the question is extremely difficult to answer." It could not even "be answered of land in an enclosed, long farmed country like England." On the other hand, he concluded, "We should be surprised if in most parts of the Thompson country, an enclosure of 1,000 acres of good bunch grass land ... would not give out entirely if continuously cropped by 1,000 steers" (i.e., to the lowest estimate offered by ranchers of one acre for each animal). Ultimately, it was determined that Indian reserves would average twenty-four acres of grassland for each animal.[45] This was more than twice the highest estimate offered by ranchers (ten acres for every animal). On the other hand, it was not nearly as much as white settlers with little or no capital were able to obtain through purchase, pre-emption, or lease.[46] Nor was it the best land from an ecological perspective because the best areas in many cases had already been alienated. Nor, according to Sproat, was it exactly what the Native people wanted. "One of the reasons why some of the Chiefs troubled us so much by large demands," Sproat speculated, "was that they themselves, as in times past, before reserves were laid out, might get rentals for grazing." Sproat called this the "baronial argument" and "invariably" the commissioners "rejected it saying let us make yeomen not barons."[47] In retrospect, they would simply help to transform them into part-time wage labourers.[48]

Convinced nonetheless that Native people needed better access to grazing resources, but ultimately unwilling to create larger reserves containing what little winter range was left in the region, and thus leave settlers short of grassland, the Commissioners created a new land-use category: commonage for shared use of settler and Native livestock. If the land was overgrazed by either group, according to Sproat, it would be managed by the Dominion. Otherwise it would remain in the hands of local users. They also suggested – perhaps in an effort to force the issue of common grazing politically – that if either government disallowed these commonages they should become Indian reserves.[49] Thus, by 1879, there were not only numerous small Indian reserves in the grassland, but also two relatively large grazing commonages: approximately 18,000 acres at Douglas Lake and roughly 24,000 acres at Okanagan Lake. In Sproat's opinion, commonages were spaces of compromise and shared responsibility where Native and non-Native stock raisers could graze their animals in winter. Nonetheless a colonizer, he hoped that somewhat larger Indian reserves combined with common grazing would help to foster viable reserve-based ranching economies and, even more important, peaceful coexistence in the grassland.

Yet there were problems with these arrangements from the outset. Initially some ranchers simply disregarded the province's new Indian reserves. In November 1879, with winter fast approaching, Sproat complained to the province that several "Indian winter ranges" had already been overrun by "thousands" of head of settler cattle. He worried that "as winter approaches again ... these intrusions will be repeated and these pastoral reserves will be completely ruined." But nobody responded. Increasingly frustrated by what he took to be provincial indifference on Native land problems, but ultimately unable to do anything about it, Sproat appealed to Indian Affairs officials in Ottawa. "Some of the settlers drive large bands upon the Indian lands and the Indians stand helplessly looking on," he explained. "Their objections are not heeded. If an Indian goes to a local Justice of the Peace, probably the latter has no copy of the Indian Act, knows nothing of the position of the Indians or their lands, and in most cases he himself is a stock owner. Practically there is no redress." In one case, Sproat recounted, "an Indian cripple had a small garden patch by the roadside, his only means of living. A man driving cattle down the road tore his fence down and put his cattle in the garden for the night. The Indian was ruined. There was no redress."[50] Admittedly, these were extreme examples. Nonetheless, they illustrated to Sproat a disturbing pattern of settler indifference to Native land problems in the grassland. Even though these lands were legally designated as Indian reserves, the decisions of the Indian reserve commissioners were in some cases simply being ignored. To make matters worse, the province did nothing about it. Indeed, long after Sproat resigned his post in 1880, Native people continued to complain that ranchers grazed cattle on unfenced Indian reserve lands. But their complaints went unanswered. As one Indian Agent explained in 1885, "At present more cattle belonging to white settlers are being are pastured on the reserves than belong to the native people themselves. The land is overstocked and the indigenous grasses are nearly exterminated."[51]

Meanwhile, ranchers found other ways to tighten their grip on the grasslands. Although, according to Sproat, Native people were content with the commission's common grazing arrangements, many settlers strongly objected to these spaces and eventually the province disallowed the commonages at Douglas and Okanagan Lakes on the grounds that the JIRC had no authority to create this land-use category. Nor, the province insisted, could the lands in question become Indian reserves. As Peter O'Reilly, who became Indian reserve commissioner in 1880 when Sproat resigned, noted in 1889, Nicola Valley Indian reserves were more than "sufficient for the requirements of the Indians without any commonages."[52] Indeed, as Forbes Vernon, who in addition to being O'Reilly's brother-in-law was the province's chief commissioner of lands and works, put it: "To allow these commonages to become Indian reserves would simply mean the destruction of the cattle industry."[53] Vernon should have known: a cattle rancher himself with large landholdings in the Okanagan, he was probably that industry's most prominent and politically connected member. Not surprisingly, the Nlaka'pamux at Douglas Lake strongly protested the government's decision to disallow the commission's commonages. An 1889 petition insisted that contrary to settler opinion the Native people there were in "great need of the piece of land promised to us" and that "if the land called the commonage is taken from us we have no resources for our increased stock and we have no land for growing grain and vegetables for ourselves."[54] But the province demurred. The commonages created by Sproat and the JIRC, Vernon said, "could not be recognized by the province" because the Indians did not need them and because they would impede the development of the grassland. Instead the lands were "thrown open" to purchase and pre-emption and before long the last patches of winter range in the region were added to a few large cattle ranches, including the Douglas Lake Cattle Company.

The great land grab continued, however. The system of pastoral leasing that caused so much trouble in the 1870s was abolished in 1884 when the Canadian Pacific Railway arrived and a greater influx of eastern settlers suddenly seemed imminent. But a provision in the amended Land Act allowed leaseholders to purchase the land in question at a dollar an acre. Some of the largest and most influential landowners in the province at the time were involved in these acquisitions. Thaddeus Harper, an expatriate American rancher who came to British Columbia from California in 1858, added 12,146 acres of excellent bunchgrass range to his already massive landholdings along the middle Fraser River; Lawrence Guichon, an immigrant farmer from France (and relative of Joseph Guichon), added 5,814 acres of range to his Nicola Valley ranch; J.B. Greaves and C.M. Beak, whose ranches would eventually amalgamate (with others) to form one of province's large corporate ranches, added 4,611 acres and 5,963 acres respectively to their landholdings; provincial magistrate J.C. Haynes added 2,908 acres to his Similkameen Valley cattle ranch; and the aforementioned cattle rancher cum commissioner of lands and works, Forbes Vernon, added fully 4,739 acres of land to his already large Okanagan Valley ranch property. The immediate result of the 1884 land amendment was a brief but consequential land rush. In just one year for which there are records, 1884–85, ranchers alienated nearly 110,000 acres, much of it excellent winter range.[55]

Away from the major river valleys in forested uplands, an archipelago of meadows offered a somewhat greater range of grazing possibilities. Yet, the problem of winter pasture persisted. The origins of these meadows, which are widespread in the northern portion of the Interior but comparatively absent to the south, can be difficult to determine. Most were likely natural in origin, having derived from underlying and ancient patterns of relief and drainage associated with the operation of basic earth processes over tremendous amounts of time.[56] It is possible, however, that purposeful Aboriginal burning created, or at least encouraged, the formation of some meadows in the precolonial period. Others were almost certainly the product of abandoned beaver dams, but to the extent that abandonment was related to the fur trade, these too were partly a product of human culture.[57] The evidence for abandoned beaver dam meadows comes from scattered references in ranch diaries, but a historical-ecological relationship between beaver dams and hay meadows can also be deduced from submissions to a Royal Commission on Forestry by Cariboo-Chilcotin ranchers in 1944.[58] One showed that Cariboo ranchers opposed a plan by southern ranchers to replenish depleted beaver populations to alleviate a water shortage problem. Their resistance stemmed from a belief that beaver dams would eventually reflood meadows that the ranchers had come to rely on, making them useless for grazing or for winter hay. As the authors of one report noted, "We submit that in areas such as some parts of the Cariboo where a great deal of hay is grown on natural meadows, and drainage is essential to enable the farmer to cut hay, the operations of the beaver must be carefully controlled."[59] In fact, by the mid-1950s, beavers were a "general problem" throughout the grasslands, flooding meadows used for grazing. The reason for the increase in the number of beavers over the years was unclear because no beavers had actually been reintroduced, but apparently it had to do with declining markets and a concurrent decrease in the price paid for beaver pelts. As one local observer reported in response to these problems, "Registered trapline holders won't bother to trap beaver if the returns are not commensurate."[60]

Given the wide range of local ecological conditions, it should come as no surprise that there were many kinds of meadows. *Swamp meadows* may have been most common. These usually featured a slow-moving stream or perhaps a small pond at the centre derived from spring runoff. Either was an important source of water for plants and animals. The most common plant associations were sedges and horsetail, with forbs and grasses found only around the drier, outer edges. Strategies varied, but in the late nineteenth and early twentieth centuries, swamp meadows were primarily used for fall grazing, with a portion of the forbs and grasses cut and set aside for winter feeding. *Dry meadows* usually occupied former lakebeds and beaver ponds. Sometimes these formed in swale bottoms where water tables were high in the spring but low in the summer and fall. Ranchers prized these areas because they often contained valuable forage plants like spear grass, brome grass, and June grass, as well as foxtail, dandelion, and several kinds of sedge. Dry meadows were used for spring and fall range. They also provided a supplementary, and for some ranchers and Native people a primary, source of winter range.

Willow bottom was the final type of meadow used by ranchers and Native people in the nineteenth and twentieth centuries. Found only on the flood plains of streams and creeks twenty to a hundred feet below the uplands, willow bottoms included significant numbers of the trees that lent their name and a diversity of plants that served as forage. Aspen, dwarf spirea, arctic birch, and wild rose were common, as were several grasses and sedges. Before the first fire prevention laws were passed in the late nineteenth and early twentieth centuries, some settlers, apparently following Native practice, burned willow bottoms to encourage grasses and sedges.[61] Others opted to save a few shrubs for early winter, when snowfall made the grasses difficult to crop. Although ranchers purchased and fenced some of these meadow types, just as often they used them in common with other ranchers. In some instances, users regulated access and even set stocking rates and grazing seasons informally as they established customary use rights.[62]

Native people were increasingly excluded from these meadow commons, and their segregation became a bone of considerable contention. The best-documented and most enduring conflict involved a large swamp meadow located forty-five miles from the mouth of the Chilcotin River. Anaham people had used this area for as long as anyone could remember, but in the late nineteenth century, it was taken over by about half a dozen or so immigrant cattle ranchers. The documentary record of this dispute dates to the late 1880s, when colonial official Peter O'Reilly created Indian reserves in the area, though scattered evidence suggests problems at Anaham even earlier. Arriving on 6 July 1887, O'Reilly laid out a reserve of 8,930 acres, about 1,500 of which he thought could be cultivated "without any expense other than ploughing." "The soil on the low land is for the most part excellent," he wrote, "being deep, and of rich loamy character." Moreover, the "mountain side affords good grazing, and there is timber sufficient for the purpose of fencing, fuel etc."

How O'Reilly, a man with little or no agricultural or natural history background and thus no means to make these claims, could ascertain all this in a day is extremely difficult to fathom. Most likely he did not. According to historical geographer Ken Brealey, between 1881 and 1897, O'Reilly laid out six hundred reserves in approximately a thousand days, suggesting that he rarely spent more than one day allocating any particular reserve.[63] In truth, they were laid out as quickly as possible, usually with very little input from Native people and with no specific knowledge of local conditions or the wider environmental setting. Nevertheless, in O'Reilly's view, the No. 1 Reserve at Anaham was "one of the most valuable reserves" in the province and the Indians there were "satisfied."[64]

The next morning, O'Reilly, the Anaham chief, and perhaps a dozen or so Anaham men rode up to a swamp meadow where, according to O'Reilly, "the Indians had been in the habit of cutting small quantities of hay for winter use." The chief wanted the entire meadow set aside as a reserve, but O'Reilly declined to do this on the grounds that it was "altogether in excess of the requirements of the tribe." Instead he pointed to the reserve allotted to them the day before and set aside a second reserve of 640 acres, or less than one-third of the total meadow that he declared ample to feed their two hundred horses. The rest of the meadow became commonage for immigrant cattle ranchers. Later that morning, O'Reilly left Anaham for Soda Creek, pleased with the work he had done and believing that the Anaham were content with their reserves. But it soon became apparent that the Anaham were not content with their reserves.[65]

According to provincial surveyor James Fletcher, whose job it was to resurvey O'Reilly's reserve allocations and record them on provincial pre-emptors' maps when he arrived at Anaham, "Old Anaham [the local chief] and about 15 of his men came to camp and told me that he understood he was to get all the meadow, and unless it was given to him he would prevent me from surveying it." Part of the problem, from Fletcher's perspective, was that by the time he arrived there were more ranchers in the region, and all of them wanted a part of the swamp meadow for winter range. Moreover, a local missionary reported that settler cattle had already encroached onto the 640-acre No. 2 Reserve, causing "considerable dissatisfaction" among the Anaham people.[66] In this fraught context, Fletcher said he would survey the meadow "as instructed until prevented by force," which he feared might be exercised by the Native people. His anxiety was not simply personal paranoia. He further noted that "if any white settlers are given the balance of the meadow ... [the Indians] will never allow them to cut hay from it, and for that reason none of the settlers around here would take it." This was probably not entirely true, but other comments corroborated his conclusion that the Anaham were determined to keep the swamp meadow for themselves. O'Reilly responded to these claims by reiterating his original conclusion that the balance of the swamp meadow should be reserved as commonage for settler stock. And the ranchers followed suit. Contrary to Fletcher's prediction, the ranchers at Anaham were more than willing to graze their animals on the meadow commons, including (at times) the 640 acres still legally denoted an Indian reserve.[67] In retrospect, these conflicts seem overdetermined, the inevitable consequence of a superficial reserve allocation process, a culturally blinkered resettlement process, and an ecologically constrained landscape.

Two maps help to illustrate the challenges indigenous stock raisers faced by the early twentieth century. The first shows Gang Ranch properties and Indian reserves along the middle Fraser and Chilcotin Rivers (Figure 3.1).

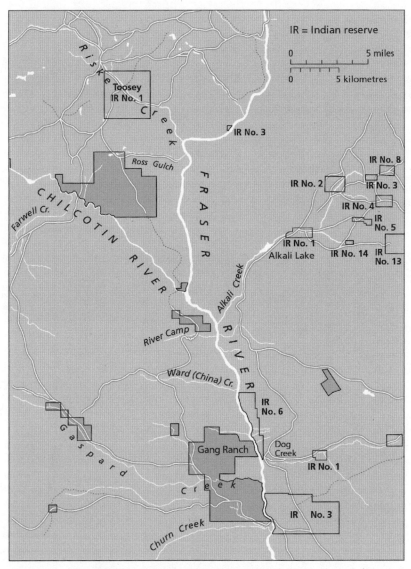

FIGURE 3.1   Gang Ranch and reserves map. *Eric Leinberger*

Like so many ranches in early British Columbia, those along the middle Fraser River were often established before the process of reserve creation had begun. The precise origin of each ranch is difficult to determine, but the Alkali Lake Ranch, said to be the oldest ranch in the province, dates to 1861, and the Gang Ranch, the largest ranch in the province, was largely assembled from 1870 to 1883. Numerous smaller ranches (not shown on the map) were also established along the middle Fraser, especially at the junction of the Fraser and Chilcotin Rivers on the so-called Riske Creek range, at Alexis Creek in the western Chilcotin, and on the east side of the Fraser River at Big Bar, though in some cases these smaller operations became the basis for much larger land holdings. The massive Chilco Ranch, for example, was an amalgamation of ranches and range and water rights acquired between 1890 and 1910. Small Indian reserves were established along the middle Fraser and Chilcotin Rivers in the 1860s and again in the 1880s. As elsewhere in the grasslands, these enclaves were usually located at the margins of large settler and corporate ranch properties.[68]

Figure 3.2, showing Indian reserves and ranch property at Douglas Lake in the Nicola Valley, suggests a similar pattern of resettlement defined the Southern Interior rangelands. Although the No. 1 Reserve there was larger than most and contained some good grazing land, the best winter ranges and open grasslands belonged to the Douglas Lake Cattle Company, the Guichon Ranch, and an unknown number of much smaller ranches. Like all the big ranches in British Columbia, the Douglas Lake Cattle Company ranch grew out of pre-emptions and land purchases in the early 1860s and 1870s, when the process of reserve allocation had only just begun. By the late 1880s, as shown in Figure 3.2, ranch managers acting on behalf of the company's owners had amassed a considerable ecological base comprising much of the best bunchgrass in the region, leading smaller ranchers to petition the government in 1884 and 1886 to create "commonage" under the provisions of the Stock Ranges Act (discussed in greater detail in Chapter 6).[69] By then there were also eight marginalized Indian reserves in the area, all of which were located around the edges of large corporate and settler cattle ranches.[70]

With ample range and water for irrigation, Interior Native peoples might have developed viable reserve-based ranching economies. As it stood, they had relatively little of either and found it increasingly difficult to maintain their communities. Chief Camille of Canoe Creek was blunt about this in testimony to a Royal Commission on Indian Affairs (the McKenna-McBride Commission) that began in 1912. "All

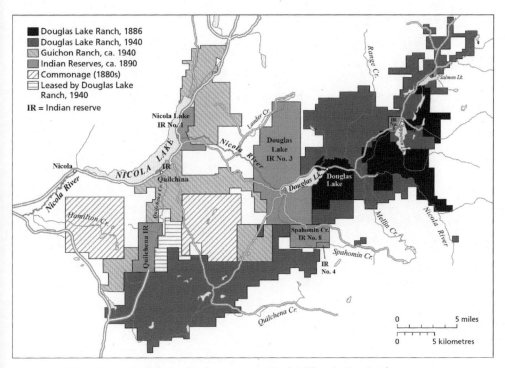

Douglas Lake Ranch, 1886
Douglas Lake Ranch, 1940
Guichon Ranch, ca. 1940
Indian Reserves, ca. 1890
Commonage (1880s)
Leased by Douglas Lake Ranch, 1940
IR = Indian reserve

FIGURE 3.2   Ranches and Indian reserves, Nicola Valley. *By Eric Leinberger*

the land that is marked on the maps as reserves that you passed on the way here is useless," he insisted. "We cannot grow any hay on them, although we grow a little on No. 2 reserve, but the rest is worthless to us. All that is grown for us to live on is grown on this [No. 1] reserve. On No. 3 reserve there is some good land but we have no water and therefore we cannot make any use of it. That is all I have to say, but I want to let you know that we are very hard up."[71] Similarly, at Alexis Creek, Chief Louis of the Stone Band complained that the "land is hardly big enough for us ... It is a very poor ranch. I fence in all what I have on the reserve, and I keep my horses in there, and there is no feed there at all. If I could get some more pasture land, I would like it, and the meadow I got before is not like a meadow, there is no grass in it."[72] Commission transcripts, which were recorded verbatim (often with the aid of a translator) but not included or even referred to in any final report, reveal that virtually every indigenous group in the grasslands faced similar challenges. A 10 July 1914 meeting with the Alkali Lake (Esk'etemc) Band was telling:

Commissioner McKenna: Where do your cattle graze?

Chief Samson: Out here on the open range.

Q: On the open range?

A: Yes, on the open range around mountains.

Q: That is outside the reserve?

A: They on the outside ranges here.

Q: And the horses also, I suppose?

A: Yes.

Q: Do they get plenty of hay for winter feeding their stock?

A: No.

Later in the same meeting:

Q: What use do you make of that [No. 6] reserve?

A: In the winter time they range their horses down there.

Q: And their cattle too?

A: No, they don't use it for cattle.

Q: How many horses run there in the winter?

A: We have taken 100 horses there, and there is not a speck of grass left there in the spring.[73]

At a 31 October 1913 meeting with the Bonaparte Band, the following exchange ensued:

Commissioner McKenna: Are there any horses on this [No. 3] reserve?

Tenas Lapp: Not many.

Q: Do your horses range out all the year round?

A: Some pull through the winter alright but some die.

Q: They die from want of food?

A: They die from hunger.

Q: Have you any cattle?

A: No cattle.[74]

And, finally, this exchange from a meeting with the Ashnola Band:

Chairman White: How many horses are there on the whole reserve?

Chief Ashnola John: I think myself alone, I have 200 head of horses and cattle.

Q: How many horses and cattle do the other Indians own?

A: They own lots of cattle and horses.

Q: Can you give me any idea how many they own?

A: I think there are about 800 head of cattle and horses. You can see for yourself that my meadows to raise sufficient hay to feed that amount of stock is very small.

Q: How much meadow has all the Indians got to feed their stock?

A: I cannot count.

Q: I would like to know about the pasture ranges on your reserves – are they sufficient to keep the cattle and horses the Indians have?

A: It is all rocks. There is no grass there.[75]

Similar exchanges ensued elsewhere as the commission made its way around the grassland. Native people complained that reserves were too small and range resources too few or too poor to make a living raising stock. They also spoke of the declining fish and game populations; restrictive fish and game regulations; conflicts with miners, loggers, and ranchers; and much else. Lack of water was a problem on many reserves because the ranchers controlled the lowlands, which were usually easy and cheap to irrigate; they also had the water rights. Chief Camille reminded the commissioners that this was the situation at Canoe Creek, where arid reserves with little in the way of winter range bordered on large irrigated alfalfa meadows owned by the BC Cattle Company.[76] Others reminded them that this was also the situation at Kamloops, where the Western Canadian Ranching Company (owners of the massive Gang Ranch, among other ranch properties) claimed water from St. Paul's Creek, which ran directly through the Kamloops Indian reserve. Yet, the commissioners remained skeptical. It was widely assumed among settlers and government grazing officials that horses required two or three times more forage than cattle did, and the commissioners knew from questioning and cross-examination that Native people usually had far more horses than cattle. Indeed, at places in commission transcripts, the Native people appear inexact if not evasive about the number of horses on reserves, noting only that they had lots, or not too many, or did not know. At a meeting with people from the Dog Creek Reserve, for instance, the following exchange ensued:

Chairman: Do you raise any horses?

Edward (representing the Dog Creek reserves): No.

Q: Then you buy your horses do you?

A: Most of the horses have been caught from these wild horses that are running in the mountains.

Q: Have you sold any horses lately?

A: No.

A few short exchanges later:

Q: Did they ever have more than eight horses in the Band; say during the last two years?

A: I don't know whether we have sold any horses – I am not the Chief here.

Q: Are you sure there are not more than eight horses here?

A: We run short of water in the lower ditch.[77]

Neither evasiveness nor candour or any other strategy altered the outcome of the meetings, however. As Commissioner McKenna explained in a meeting with the Alkali Lake Band, whose horses outnumbered their cattle by about three to one, "When you come to the government to apply for land, you would have a much stronger case if you did not have so many cayuses, and these men who have hay land on the reserve should make a special effort to get together some cattle, keeping only enough of these ponies as they absolutely need; sell the rest and buy cattle with the money adding to what they got from the sale of their cayuses by working for the white people."[78] Aboriginal people had heard versions of this argument – and its

underlying assumption that Natives did not know how to use land properly
and needed to be shown how – many times before. Chief Camille could
barely contain his incredulity: "How can they raise cattle when we cannot
raise enough [hay] to feed them on? There is nothing to grow there, nothing
to winter them on."[79] Chief Louis of the Stone Band agreed that more cattle
might be desirable but explained how, in the circumstances, keeping more
horses made more sense. "Yes, it would be better to have cattle," he admitted, "but there is no hay on the Reserve. Horses, why they can rustle out
on the open land."[80] Others made much the same point that horses were
better able than cattle to graze out on the open lands and that it was this,
and not some inherent inability to use these lands properly, that encouraged
Natives to keep more horses than cattle. Several Native men, and even a
local Indian Agent, also noted that, despite all arguments to the contrary,
Aboriginal horses in fact had value. Some horses were used in so-called
intertribal trade, while others were sold to settler ranches. Indian Agent
John Smith noted that the Nicola Valley Native people at Douglas Lake
were stock raisers on a large scale, having "over 1800 head of horses, of the
very best class, and some 600 head of cattle." But they needed more rangeland. Their reserves were being overgrazed, he noted, and Native stock
raisers were feeling "their cramped position in pasturage."[81]

Others pointed to similar problems elsewhere in the grasslands. As forest
and range official Owen Sanger observed, the Redstone Indian Reserve in
the Chilcotin region was "a good example of a range which, originally
carrying a good growth of Bunch Grass, with very little Wormwood, now
supports a sparse growth [of both,] which are found in about equal proportions."[82] Similar problems were apparent on the Ashcroft Indian
Reserve, which, "though large in extent is very worthless, the greater part
of it being a horse range, that, owing to overstocking, has been completely
eaten out."[83] By the early twentieth century, it was also clear that some
Indian reserves were becoming infested with weeds. Cheatgrass and Canada
thistle were present on some ranges and Indian reserves as early as 1895,
and were so prevalent in some areas by 1914 that the Department of Indian
Affairs in Ottawa contemplated amending the federal Indian Act – the
legislation that made Native people wards of the Canadian state – so that
"Indians would be liable to a penalty for allowing the growth of noxious
weeds on their reserves."[84] This was both misleading and unfair because
these weeds had been introduced, but it did highlight some of the problems
Native stock raisers faced by the early twentieth century.

Whatever the McKenna-McBride commission made of these matters,
and there is little in its transcripts on which to base a judgment, they

were not persuaded that Native people needed more or better grazing lands. Most requests for more and better grazing land were simply "not entertained, as not reasonably required." In the view of the commission, which no doubt generally reflected that of the Indian Agents, ranchers, and range managers with whom the commissioners had met and corresponded, there was simply no need to make changes to reserve lands because the grazing capacities of these spaces could be significantly increased if Native people simply rid themselves of horses and raised cattle instead. Rather than acknowledge that Indian reserves lacked the specific resources needed to raise cattle, the commission focused on the wastefulness they associated with horses. According to some estimates (considered fair by many), the grazing capacities of Indian reserves could easily be doubled or tripled if used only for cattle, which in any case were more valuable in the marketplace. Significantly, the commission also observed that Native people still had a common right to Crown range, which they shared with settlers.

Certainly, that was the case in 1916, when the commission submitted its final report. Within three years, however, the province had passed its first Grazing Act, making range management a responsibility of the state. Henceforth ranchers would have to purchase annual permits to graze cattle on Crown land, and the grazing fees thus collected would be funnelled into a new range improvement fund. A promotional pamphlet from the province claimed that the immediate benefits of the new system were twofold: on the one hand, it would help reduce conflicts on the range because each ranch would now have well-defined grazing rights; on the other hand, it would enable the province's new Grazing Branch to implement at minimal cost to government a formal program of scientific range management, the core of which would be a system of science-based grazing regulations that altered the timing and intensity of grazing throughout the year in order to maximize the productivity of individual plants while avoiding any irreversible range degradation.

British Columbia was already moving toward state and scientific management of resources when the Grazing Act was passed. Building on a body of ideas, policies, and practices imported largely from the United States, the provincial government embarked on a program of scientific resource conservation in the early twentieth century, creating a Water Branch and a Fisheries Branch in 1902, and a Forest Branch in 1912.[85] In British Columbia, as elsewhere, the point of state regulation was primarily to promote the efficient exploitation of resources, not to restrain it. At the same time, an underlying commitment to utilitarian ideals meant that business activity should benefit society as a whole. Strategies varied in somewhat different national and regional contexts, but the rhetoric of conservation always insisted that resources be exploited in a way that did not ruin them for future use.[86] More generally, the move to manage range resources in British Columbia was indicative of what historian Barry Ferguson and others have termed "new liberalism." Ferguson suggests that the new liberalism of the early twentieth century differed fundamentally from classical liberalism, which promoted the primacy of the individual and the principle of laissez-faire by expanding the role of the state to regulate social and economic development.[87] This demanded not just a more active and interventionist government but also the technical means to accomplish social goals. For many new liberals, it was science and other closely related forms of formal and bureaucratic expertise that facilitated responsible regulation of people and nature. As James Murton writes in a recent book on agriculture and liberalism in early-twentieth-century British Columbia, "New liberals' belief in the ability of scientific experts to understand and manage nature and society gave them the confidence that they could create a better model of the sorts of (social and natural) systems they believed composed the world."[88] The province's new commitment to progressive land reform rested on many of these ideas. Its appeal to range science as the arbiter of rational economic activity fit well, not only with a broader faith in formal expertise but also with the broadly utilitarian doctrine, shared by Canadian and American conservationists alike, that business activities and even nonhuman nature itself need to be regulated in order to benefit society as a whole over the long term.

Nonetheless, the new conservation doctrine created new problems for Native people.[89] The immediate problem was how to acquire and pay for grazing permits; the deeper issue, discussed in greater detail in the next chapter, was that the legal landscape of grazing in British Columbia had suddenly changed. Previously, Native people had a common right to graze horses and cattle on Crown land, a right they shared with immigrant cattle ranchers. After 1919, however, grazing permits were required. This was not quite the enclosure of common lands that some ranchers and government contemplated in the 1890s. Essentially, the Grazing Act created what Louis Warren, in a book on conservation in the United States, calls a "state commons."[90] The result was a regulatory space in which the province directed range management. The new policy of grazing permits did constitute a kind of enclosure, though, because after 1919 access to Crown range was neither open nor free. Significantly, it was now an individual right granted to ranchers at the discretion of the government, and for which ranchers in the province now had to pay. With scientific administration, property rights, and state enclosure of the commons, ridding the range of horses wild and otherwise suddenly became a powerful management imperative.

4

Eradicating Wild Horses

Thomas Mackenzie knew little of British Columbia, and even less about indigenous peoples and their land problems, when he became provincial grazing commissioner in 1919. An Australian by birth, he had dealt with grazing issues in the American West, however, and like James Anderson before him, he was determined not to let horses, wild and otherwise, degrade the range for settler cattle. As for Aboriginal people, well, they could have their horses, but only if these animals stayed put. Echoing arguments made by Anderson and others many years earlier, Mackenzie advocated segregation of Native and settler livestock, in a kind of ecological apartheid. "I understand that the Indians have sufficient hay producing lands on their reserves ... and that they raise sufficient hay for the use of the stock which they own," he observed in a letter to the minister of lands. "If they were to keep to their Reservations, the way would be clear for the proper organization of the settlers to handle grazing lands to the greatest advantage."[1]

By "proper organization" Mackenzie meant well-defined grazing rights for settlers and scientific range management by the state. Well-defined range rights were needed not only to prevent grazing disputes between ranchers – in the new system, each rancher would have permits to graze a certain number of cattle in a particular area – but also to implement a closely regulated system of "deferred-rotation" grazing that moved cattle between ranges seasonally as well as over a period of years in order to maximize the productivity of individual plants while avoiding any irreversible range degradation. Key to this particular arrangement of people, animals, and environment, aside from the construction of numerous fences, gates, and trails, was the close observation and careful management of cattle and range conditions in each grazing area. Initially, the ranchers would do this, but increasingly it would be the purview of range experts trained in the principles of plant succession. The American scientist Arthur Sampson, student of ecologist Frederic Clements and author of several important papers and an influential book on scientific range management in the 1910s and 1920s, had defined these principles. Properly applied, they promised to restore degraded rangelands.[2] As Sampson observed, "Where the vegetative cover has been interfered with more or less seriously ... but where these disturbances have been eliminated or decreased in severity there is a tendency through successive invasions, for the vegetation to become more like the original ... This state marks the climax, or stable type, and is quite in harmony with the world around."[3]

Although Sampson's strategy of moving cattle around to avoid any irreversible range degradation was sound (ranchers had been doing a version of it for decades), in retrospect the science was flawed. Like most early-twentieth-century plant science, Sampson's interpretation of range ecology in the West supposed a single, stable vegetative state in the absence of grazing: the climax. This was what Sampson meant by the "original vegetative state." Plant succession, by implication, was both progressive and predictable, tending always toward pristine conditions. Grazing pressure also produced changes that were progressive, but in exactly the opposite direction. The challenge for range managers in this model was to strike a balance between succession and the stocking rate, allowing just enough animals onto the range to achieve environmental equilibrium.[4] Recent work in range science challenges the very basis of this approach by demonstrating that patterns of succession in western North American grasslands were far more complicated – and ultimately much less linear and predictable – than early-twentieth-century ecologists like Sampson, and administrators like Mackenzie, ever imagined.[5] According to the state-and-transition model, multiple stable vegetation states are possible on rangelands and may persist for long periods. Transient ecological states are also possible. Transitions from one state to the next in this model occur when environmental "thresholds" are exceeded. Ecologists Reed Noss and Allen Cooperrider describe in general terms how this can happen. If grazing pressure at a site is reduced before some critical environmental threshold is reached, the area may well revert to grassland by way of "graminoid-driven succession." But it might not, especially if the previous grass cover had been established under different climatic conditions or if the local fire regime had changed. In either of these contexts, "shrub-driven succession" – evident on many BC ranges by the late nineteenth and early twentieth century – can begin to predominate, ultimately leading to a plant association dominated by woody shrubs such as sagebrush or antelope brush.[6]

Although some ecologists in the early 1920s already suspected as much, those in management usually sided with Sampson.[7] For these men, the challenges of deferred-rotation grazing were more administrative than scientific. Sampson's scientific vision assumed not just an orderly world of nature that never existed but also an orderly world of people and animals that could be created. It presumed the granting of specific rights to Crown range and exposed a kind of panoptic knowledge of landscape in which managers could collect information about exactly where, when, whose, and how many cattle grazed in the grasslands.[8] Government land managers could then begin to manage people and animals, and to some extent even the wider drylands environment, at a distance. Using numbers, tables, and increasingly complex calculations of carrying capacity, they could instruct ranchers to graze only so many cattle on so much range, for only so long, and only at specific times of year as determined by the regulators.[9] Creating Crown range rights for individual ranchers was thus more than a conflict resolution strategy intended to reduce tensions between ranchers, though it was that. It was also prerequisite to scientific land management by the state. In James Scott's terms, over time and space it made people, animals, and ecological processes more "legible" and assumedly more manageable.[10]

Almost by definition, a landscape ordered and made legible by science and property rights for settlers left little room for Native people and their horses (or any other competing claim to grassland, for that matter). Yet, for Mackenzie, that was the point. "The horses of the Indians are responsible for the heavy damage to the range in the early spring," he insisted in a candid letter to William Ditchburn of Indian Affairs in 1924, "and so long as this indiscriminate use continues the damage cannot be prevented."[11] Using the same quantitative logic settlers found so compelling in the late nineteenth century, the new grazing commissioner estimated that horses were at least "three times heavier on the range than cattle, moving quicker, depasturing [sic] closer, and living on the range the whole year."[12] Here was a quick and easy way to increase the carrying capacity of the range that asked little or nothing of settler ranchers. Elsewhere in his writings and public addresses, Mackenzie emphasized the role of settler cattle in degrading the range. In this case, however, cattle were ignored.

To remove horses from the range, and apparently completely unbeknownst to Native people, in 1923 the new grazing commissioner had provincial lawmakers amend three pieces of legislation, the Grazing Act, the Trespass Act, and the Animals Act, effectively making it illegal for anybody to have horses on the Crown range between January and May each year. Essentially, the new range law established a seasonal curfew that horse owners ignored at their peril: any horses caught on Crown land during the winter curfew were to be rounded up by the state, and those animals not sold or reclaimed by their owners or anyone who wanted them at a standard price of $5 per head were to be shot. The Grazing Branch had been also authorized to appoint "special shooters" in remote or sparsely settled areas like the western Chilcotin, where annual roundups and sales were considered impractical.[13] Bounty hunters would receive a maximum salary of $75 a month (for up to four months' work, coinciding with the closed season), plus free bullets, free hay for their horses, and 50¢ for every horse scalp they returned to the Grazing Branch.

Mackenzie's amendments targeted all equines, not just Aboriginal horses. The logic was that settlers and Native people would gather up the all animals they wanted, or could afford to feed without resort to Crown land, leaving just the feral horses and the domestic horses nobody wanted. Nevertheless, the biases of the new law were obvious. Native people usually had far more horses than cattle and relied much more on Crown land for feed because their reserves were small. Strategies varied, but usually, what little winter hay Native people had on hand was set aside for cattle. This arrangement was far from ideal. Every year, Native people lost horses and even some cattle to starvation and cold weather, particularly if the latter came after a drought or grasshopper plague that depleted the grassland. The hope was that horses could fend for themselves during winter months by taking refuge in the uplands. Unlike cattle usually they could paw through the ice and snow to get at the hard grass buried below. Without Crown land, however, Native people would soon run out of range, leaving no choice but to reduce their horse herds or watch their cattle slowly starve to death.

If the biases of the new range law were obvious, according to the Nlaka'pamux Chief John Chilliheetza, so was the legal double standard involved. "Why does the white man oppose to my stock to run on the range?" he asked in a 1924 letter to the Dominion Indian Department. "We the Indians do not oppose to the white men to have their horses and cattle run on the ranges. The Indians say why do the white men want to kill our horses? If we said that to them, we were to kill their horses, would that be well? The white men if his horse was worthless nobody will threaten to kill his horse as it is his horse, he owns it. No one will kill it. It is not well for the white men to say they are to kill the Indian horses because they are worthless. No matter how the horses are, they are the property of the Indians."[14] Indeed, it was against the law to kill these horses. At least, it was hypocritical. Chilliheetza knew exactly what would happen if Native people started destroying settler livestock: pretty soon the police and possibly even the military would arrive, and everyone involved would be arrested and not only fined but very likely jailed. By the same legal standard, the chief reasoned, killing Aboriginal horses, "no matter how they are," must also be illegal. Regardless of what settlers thought about Aboriginal horses, these animals were still Nlaka'pamux property, and under the law, property was protected.

English property law and the state power that lay behind it had done much to dispossess Native people of land, but at times it also provided a means of resistance through appeals such as Chilliheetza's for the rule of law.[15] As legal theorist Joseph Raz explains, invocations of the rule of law assume "that people should be ruled by law and obey it ... and that the law should be such that people will be able to be guided by it."[16] It has nothing to do with the content of any particular law. Nor, as legal historian Douglas Harris explains, does "the rule of law require the rule of good law; it only requires that law provide sufficient guidance so that subjects of the state may know how the latter will react to their actions before they act. In this sense the rule of law is merely an attribute of a functioning legal system, necessary but not sufficient to ensure fundamental rights, justice, and equality."[17] Chilliheetza's appeal to property was in this sense an attempt to remind settler society of the importance they *claimed* to place on law, and property in particular, in order to prevent the killing of his people's horses, which after all were "their property."

Reaction to Chilliheetza's protest letter ranged from indifference to incredulity, but few people in settler society paid much attention to its central argument that Indian horses were Aboriginal property and thus protected by the law. Thomas Mackenzie found it curious that people could claim unbranded horses, which from the perspective of settler law were ownerless and thus open to destruction. He also reiterated his earlier assumption that Indian reserves had enough hay land already, and that it would make range improvement in the province a good deal easier if settler cattle and Native horses could be segregated.[18] He also reminded Indian Affairs that, legally, Native people were wards of the Canadian state under the Indian Act. From this it followed that Aboriginal horses were a

Dominion problem, not a provincial one. As such, it was the Dominion's job to deal with them.

William Ditchburn of Indian Affairs agreed that it would be better if Natives raised cattle instead of horses, and that the administration of grazing lands in the province would be easier if these animals could be confined to Indian reserve lands. But how to do this was another matter. The obvious answer was fencing. The stickier issue was who would pay. Even though Native people and Indian reserve lands were a federal responsibility under the Indian Act, in this case, Ditchburn felt that the cost of fencing should be shared. He agreed that Aboriginal horses were problematic for all the reasons already noted: they wasted and degraded the range through overgrazing and trampling; they polluted better bloodlines; and, compared with cattle, they were pretty much worthless in the market. But on the other hand, they were hardly entirely to blame for the province's range problems because settler cattle degraded the range as well. Moreover, the animal traffic between Indian reserves and provincial rangelands went both ways. According to Ditchburn, there had been numerous instances over the years of settler cattle and horses trespassing onto reserve lands, and as far as could be ascertained, no penalties had ever been enforced. By this logic, the benefits of fencing extended to both levels of government.

Nevertheless, the province refused to pay. The range improvement fund created by the Grazing Act was for provincial problems, not Dominion ones, and for the record, Aboriginal horses *were* to blame, not for everything, of course, but as far as the province's degraded spring and fall ranges were concerned, there was little doubt in Mackenzie's mind that Aboriginal horses were the primary culprits and that it would be all but impossible to restore the grasses in these areas if the horses remained on the range. A few weeks later, Ditchburn countered meekly that there were problems on "both sides," by which he presumably meant federally and provincially, and that therefore it was in the interest of ranchers and the two levels of government involved to split the costs of range improvement in this case. But again the province demurred. Both men appear to have wanted fences for Indian reserves, but even when it came to dispossessing Native people (on which, at the end of the day, there was actually broad agreement between the governments involved), the old political problem of federal-provincial relations could not be escaped.[19]

The deeper problem for the Native people was not that Mackenzie and Ditchburn disagreed on how to pay for fences, it was that they agreed on just about everything else. "The unfortunate feature of the grazing question which we have to face," wrote Ditchburn, "is that the Indians will continue to raise a tremendous number of horses that have no commercial value and that eat up range that might otherwise be used for cattle either of their own or for white stock raisers and it is sincerely to be hoped that they will get rid of these worthless animals."[20] The trouble with Aboriginal stock raisers, he insisted in a meeting with the Allied Tribes of British Columbia (established in 1916 to advance Aboriginal rights and title to land), was that they allowed "their best ranges to be taken up by a lot of Cayuse horses that [had] no commercial value." Indeed, in his view, Native people "would be far better off if they would kill every one of them." "Indians expect the Government of British Columbia to set aside new rangelands for them when their best ranges are being eaten up by horses that have no value," he lectured. "That is a fact." A Native representative at the meeting countered that the horses were necessary for travel and hunting and that Aboriginal people even made a little money from them. Not only were these horses bought and sold by Aboriginal people, but by settlers as well. But Ditchburn scoffed. "There are a few cases, Narcisse and his father Johnny Chilliheetza in the upper Nicola; they raise good stock, not Cayuses; but there are a lot of places where the Indians have these Cayuse horses; and they are eating up to nineteen acres of range where a cow only uses thirteen."[21] Mackenzie might have argued the math in this case. Ditchburn's assertion that horses consumed 1.46 times more range than cattle did was a lot lower than the grazing commissioner had estimated. But otherwise, these men were completely in agreement that the number of horses had to be reduced.[22]

George Pragnell agreed that the number of horses on Indian reserves had to be reduced, but as inspector of Indian Agencies for British Columbia and thus closer to the situation, he had developed a different perspective on how to achieve this. "Matters of this kind often look well on paper and maps or when carried out as an office question," he observed, "but are entirely different when you try to enforce them amongst a people of low intelligence, with other grievances."[23] Closer to the conflict but nonetheless a colonizer and thus imbued with all of the biases and cultural stereotypes of empire, Pragnell had developed a somewhat subtler position on the horse problem. He was deeply concerned that a "great many threats of imprisonment and fines ... have been made toward the Indians, causing a very antagonistic feeling to arise." The ranchers were "talking as though the law was dead set against the Indians in particular," and in a sense they were right because they had more horses than settlers did.[24] Native people thus saw "the new law as nothing more than an attempt to get them off the ranges and did not understand why they should not be allowed to graze their horses, which are their personal property, their argument being that these animals are of money value to them just as much as cattle or sheep might be to other people." In the Nicola Valley, the dispute pitted poor pastoralists against a few large ranches that already controlled range. According to the Nlaka'pamux the complaint against their horses was merely an attempt on the part of Frank Ward, manager of the massive Douglas Lake Cattle Ranch, and Lawrence Guichon, owner of another large Nicola Valley ranch, and perhaps "one or two other cattle owners to corral all the grazing land ... They see no reason why, if one man wants to earn his living from cattle, another should not do the same in the way of horses, and that if they lose their horses they are ruined." Nor, Pragnell continued, were they willing, or able for that matter, to pay $5 a head to reclaim what in fact was their property. Native people had no money, he noted, and the Indian Department would likely be unwilling to pay. The goal was get rid of these animals, not to encourage them. Pragnell agreed that wild horses *were* problematic, particularly in the Chilcotin District, where by all accounts there were more of them. But in the Nicola Valley at least things were different. There were wild horses in the Nicola Valley, as elsewhere, and "worthless" ones too (a reminder that the lines between feral and domestic often were blurry when it came to Aboriginal horses). But Chilliheetza's horses at least had value, and most if not all of these animals were branded. The new range law was thus not only entirely "arbitrary" in Pragnell's view, conflating wild and worthless animals with those that had value, but also possibly contrary to Canadian law because it disregarded Native peoples' property rights. Besides, said Pragnell, "the Indians assure me that they will not allow their horses, which are their property, to be rounded up in this manner." In the inspector's opinion, the only way to avoid "probable bloodshed" in this case was to postpone the roundup long enough to find, and ideally fence, exclusive grazing areas for Aboriginal horses. "If they graze it down with horses they will have nobody but themselves to blame," he wrote paternalistically, "and in that way they would probably see the value of raising cattle instead of horses."[25]

After meeting with Pragnell and a group of Nlaka'pamux people led by Chief Chilliheetza, Mackenzie agreed to delay enforcement of the new law in the Nicola District until suitable grazing areas could be set aside for Aboriginal horses. As always, though, the difficulty was in finding such land. Private property was out of the question unless it was purchased by the Indian Department, but Ottawa rejected this option before any specific purchases were even contemplated. Most of the rest was land under lease or permit, or land set aside as settler commonage under the 1876 Stock Ranges Act. And what was left was generally thought to be too rocky, too full of timber, too mountainous, or simply too far away to be useful as horse pasture. Land held by the National Defence Department was brought up as a possible solution to these problems. It made sense to Pragnell in particular that federal lands should be used for horse pastures, since Native people were a Dominion responsibility under the Indian Act. An added advantage, according to Pragnell, was that the Canadian government might also purchase Aboriginal horses for the military. But Native people were opposed to this. The precise reasons are unclear; perhaps they were uneasy about leaving horses untended in a military area.[26]

Pragnell promised to keep looking for suitable horse grazing areas, but, importantly, neither the Indian Department, nor the provincial Grazing Branch, nor the settler ranching community *actually* believed that Native people needed more and better rangeland. Administrators like Mackenzie and Ditchburn, and to some extent George Pragnell, worried that setting aside exclusive Aboriginal grazing areas would only encourage Native people to raise horses instead of cattle, which was the opposite of what these officials wanted. Like other settlers, they also insisted that the carrying capacities of Indian reserves could be greatly increased, perhaps even tripled, if Native people eliminated or at least greatly reduced the number of horses they kept and raised cattle instead, which in any case were worth more in the market.[27] Lost in these discussions was the fact that most Indian reserves lacked specific resources – water and winter range – needed to raise cattle on anything more than a modest scale. Native people had long said so, but their complaints had gone unresolved.

Also lost in these discussions was how volatile the situation had become, particularly in the Nicola Valley, where the dispute over horses was deteriorating into violence.

A few days after Mackenzie left the Nicola District, the conflict between settlers and the Nlaka'pamux suddenly escalated when, according to Pragnell, "a certain white settler shot four Aboriginal horses and wounded two others" near Douglas Lake. The Indian Agent there suspected a local rancher acting on his own accord, but according to Pragnell, Native people not surprisingly "connected the shootings with the rules of the Grazing Commissioner and there was an uproar immediately."[28] A week later, Thomas Mackenzie returned to the Nicola Valley to "assure the Indians that the shootings had nothing to do with him or his office and that every endeavor would be used by the province to track down those who had done the deed."[29] The Nlaka'pamux remained deeply skeptical about the grazing commissioner's intentions, however, because the alleged shooter was never charged.

Two years later, the wild horse roundup was still on hold in the Southern Interior but was proceeding as planned in the Cariboo-Chilcotin District, where the Grazing Branch had appointed seven special shooters in the early 1920s to do the eradicating. Not much is known about the men who did the hunting, but a telling analysis of their efforts was included in a 1926 report to the minister of lands, reproduced here in Appendix 1. Essentially, it is a public accounting of the costs and carnage involved and a justification for extermination. A table created by Commissioner Mackenzie showed that in total the province elimin-ated 1,950 horses at a total cost of $3,945.80. This broke down to $1,281.03 for wages, $1,950.00 for bounties, and $714.00 for bullets. The total number of bullets fired in two seasons was 5,591; the average number of rounds fired per animal, 2.86; and average cost per animal killed, $2.02.[30] Mackenzie had no idea how much range was saved for cattle, but he did believe these numbers to be evidence of the program's cost-effectiveness for range improvement.

Wild horses may have been the intended targets during these years, but horses owned by Aboriginal people were shot repeatedly near Williams Lake. As Ditchburn explained to Mackenzie, "The Indians had warned a rancher named Henderson not to shoot their horses." But Henderson, or possibly someone else, shot four of their horses anyway.[31] Similar incidents took place at Big Creek, on the middle Fraser River, where Natives lost 13 horses in 1924. The local Indian Agent reported that "they [the Natives] are very indignant about this, since they can prove that there were at least 200 horses [owned by ranchers] on the Big Creek Range, which were not touched by the shooters."[32] They also claimed that the ranges were theirs to use and manage however they liked. But as usual the province dismissed these claims. In response to a similar incident near Clinton, on the middle Fraser River, Grazing Commissioner Mackenzie simply noted that any attempt on the part of the Indians to "interfere with the men employed [in shooting] will be followed by their arrest." They "should [also] under-stand that the Government owns the range and does not propose to be dictated to [by the local chief] in the matter of handling its business thereon."[33]

Back in the Nicola District, where the 1924 shootings were still fresh in the minds of many people, ranchers opted for less aggressive tactics. A December 1926 petition from the BC Stockbreeders Association was typical. Like others, it complained that wild horses were pests that had to be eliminated, and it asked – in ways that thoroughly conflated wildness with race – whether "discriminate compulsory measures can be utilized to rid the ranges of British Columbia of Indian Cayuses." The petitioners acknowledged that settlers had some horses on the range and that in some cases these animals were untended and might even be unbranded. Yet, their altruistic crusade in this case was against Aboriginal horses: "We believe this resolution should be of twofold benefit to the Indian," the petitioners wrote paternalistically. "First it would rid him of his own fond curse. Second it would have a tendency to enforce him to become a cattle raiser."[34] Even though it ignored Native peoples' need for winter pasture, William Ditchburn of Indian Affairs declared the complaint "well founded" and urged officials on the ground to make their best efforts to persuade "the Indians to give up raising useless horses altogether." Like the petitioners, he was sure "the best thing the Indians could do would be to kill all of those [horses] which have no particular use and turn their attention more to cattle."[35]

Of course, it was easy for Ditchburn to make these claims at a distance. But as the inspector of Indian Agencies, George Pragnell had to be somewhat more cautious. Recognizing the pressures placed on Native people by the Indian Department, the Grazing Branch, and even the Royal Canadian Mounted Police (who Pragnell observed had recently become involved in a dispute near Williams Lake in which, allegedly, Natives grazed horses on land allotted to a local rancher), he reiterated his concern that "there will be trouble if a process of elimination is used by the Provincial officials." He had also developed a somewhat deeper perspective on Native peoples' cultural and historic connections to horses. For all the scorn heaped on these animals by settlers, the fact remained that Native people placed "a certain value on these horses," even if he did not exactly understand what that was. He also understood that cattle required winter ranges, "whereas horses can exist after a fashion" by taking refuge in the uplands. At the same time, Pragnell had pretty much had his fill of Native resistance on this issue. He was frustrated that "whenever we suggest any improvements we are told by the Chiefs that they are going to settle at Ottawa or with the King." And he was increasingly convinced that only "a flat refusal of their demands" and a clear statement of what the Indian Department proposed to do "would settle the unrest." Two years earlier, Pragnell had called for compromise in the form of exclusive Aboriginal grazing areas, but now he advocated authoritarianism. In his view, "all these various troubles" would not be settled until "Chief Chilliheetza and his followers" were "finally and firmly dealt with and repressed."[36]

Perhaps not surprisingly in this context, by the late 1920s, the conflict over horses in British Columbia had developed into much broader and more complex claims about Aboriginal rights and title to land. In December 1929, a "large" group of Aboriginal people led by Chief Chilliheetza met with the local Indian Agent, a man named Barber, at the Douglas Lake Indian Reserve to discuss their land and horse problems. "The Indians are afraid that most of the horses will be shot," Chilliheetza explained. "They have no grazing lands [and] not feed enough on their reserves to keep these horses through winter." By his estimate, their hay supply would last at most another week, so the horses simply had to be turned onto the range. For the Nlaka'pamux, it had come down to a Hobbesian choice between the risk of having their horses rounded up or shot and watching their cattle slowly starve to death. The root problem was not ecological but social, for this was a crisis wholly manufactured by the state. Chief Chilliheetza fumed, "None of these horses are outlaws, and none of them should be killed."[37] The message was fundamentally different, however, from the one he had delivered six years earlier, in 1924, which emphasized the inviolability of Aboriginal property rights. Now the emphasis was on Aboriginal rights and title to land. Native people had a *right* to run horses on the range, he argued. The range was theirs as the original owners and occupiers of the land. As Mackenzie's assistant, W.H. Brown, later explained in a letter about the meeting at Douglas Lake, "The Indians strongly object to giving up 'rights' held from 'time immemorial.'"[38]

Mackenzie was frustrated. The "complaint filed by Chief Chilliheetza was in connection with closure of the Nicola ranges to horses for the purpose of getting rid of the useless trespassing and stray horses," he complained, "and dealt with the time worn claim that the Indian should have absolute freedom to run what stock he liked and how he liked on the Crown lands." For ten years, the Grazing Branch had been "encouraging the Indians to get rid of their useless and valueless horses, but without avail," the commissioner lamented, "and it is essential that these animals be no longer tolerated on Crown Lands."[39]

Mackenzie's constituents in the ranching community largely agreed. One rancher put it this way: "There are a lot of Indian horses which do not belong to anybody. Some of them carry the Indian brand, I suppose, but they are practically wild horses. There is no reason why we should pay for forage on the range and have it eaten off by wild horses [whose owners] do not pay anything."[40] Others agreed with this but also recognized that the problem ran much deeper. One rancher related a story in which a local

Indian Agent approached Nicola Valley Native people about not grazing their horses at Marquette Creek, in the Dominion Railway Belt, because a rancher already owned the range there. "The Indian turned around and said 'all of Canada is ours!'" the rancher exclaimed.[41] Clearly, such tales were calculated to irritate and raise the ire of ranchers. And almost invariably it worked. Others not only told similar stories but also insisted in response to these tales that Native peoples were wards of the Canadian state under the Indian Act. From this it followed that Indian Affairs could simply force Native people into submission if only there were the will in Ottawa to do so. One rancher insisted in frustration that the Indian Agent had the authority "to go in there and get rid of those horses, but he does not do it."[42]

Some ranchers suggested, more out of frustration than sympathy, that specific pastures be set aside for Indian horses. One of the most vociferous critics of Aboriginal horses, Frank Ward, manager of the Douglas Lake Cattle Company, actually led the charge at one public meeting, arguing that ranchers had tried in vain to control "these worthless animals" that were eating ranchers "out of house and home." If the horses could not be removed, then perhaps they could be "confined to one place. Then at least you have them under control."[43] Locating suitable horse pastures was more difficult than advocating their creation, however, and as time went on, it became clear that few if any ranchers were actually willing to accommodate Native peoples' grazing needs. Even those who said it should be done made no substantive offer. Thus, the old solution of ecological segregation soon resurfaced. As one rancher put it, Native people "should be forced to keep their horses on the reserves."[44]

Around the edges of this almost uniformly anti-horse and at times simply anti-Indian discourse, a few voices tried to shift attention to the broader picture. A rancher from Riske Creek worried that the ruckus over wild horses had deflected attention away from grasshoppers, which in his view were a much bigger menace. "The most vital improvement to be done in our district is to clean out the grasshopper," he reminded ranchers and range officials. "He can ruin a bigger area in a shorter time."[45] A few others agreed with this, and at least one rancher objected outright to extermination. "There are certainly a lot of valueless horses using good grass," remarked one rancher. "On the other hand I do not approve of going in and shooting horses because they happen to be wild." There had to be a better solution, even if he did not know what that solution was.

Some of the most revealing exchanges between ranchers and officials in the late 1920s and early 1930s revolved around questions of animal classification. Even as they set out to exterminate them, several ranchers rightly asked, "What is a wild horse?" Peter Caverhill, the province's chief forester, admitted that there was a big "difference of opinion" on the question and suggested changing the word "wild" to "useless," but this muddied matters even more. As one rancher asked, what was a "useless" horse? Caverhill's answer sought to establish an objective, material basis for identifying wild and useless horses, yet hopelessly conflated the issue with race. "As near as I can express it," he began, "we have two types of horses, the horse which has never been branded or apparently never claimed, and the Cayuse, whatever you want to call it, which has almost no marketable value and probably is destroying more range in one year than you can get for the whole animal."[46] Rather than confront these complexities, and no doubt to some extent because of them, ranchers fell back on simple solutions to the problems they faced. Ultimately, they agreed that the original 1924 legislative amendments suggested by Mackenzie were right and ought to apply.

In fact, the government would go further. Like Pragnell, Mackenzie and Ditchburn had had enough of Native resistance on this issue. Meeting privately in early 1930, they decided that the shooting and roundups would go ahead as planned. Remarkably, they also concluded that the federal Indian Act – the most important piece of legislation on Aboriginal issues in the country – could be amended if necessary to facilitate greater control of livestock. Taking this step would essentially establish the kind of authority over Native people and their animals that most ranchers wrongly assumed the Indian Department already held. Mackenzie believed that doing so would be unnecessary because ultimately Native people would relent. "The Indians throughout the Cariboo District used to talk about what they would do to anyone shooting horses," he explained in a letter to rancher Harry Tweedle in early 1930, "but we have shot over 3500 head there already and they are still quiet."[47] He was prepared to force the issue, however. In a pithy missive to grazing assistant W.H. Brown, he instructed that "as soon as the time is ready, in other words, when the wild and useless horses are back on the Crown range we will round them up and put men on to shoot. *If any Indian horses are out and destroyed, any complaint [the Indians] make to their department will, undoubtedly, lead to an extension of wardship to control their useless horses.*"[48]

Four months later, in early April 1930, the large group of Nlaka'pamux women and men with whom this story began gathered along with their lawyer outside the government office at Spences Bridge to meet with Mackenzie and to make their fundamental argument that killing horses was contrary to land rights that the Nlaka'pamux and other Native groups had held from time immemorial and that, the Nlaka'pamux insisted, had been confirmed to them by the Queen and thus the power of the British Crown and by their long-standing use of the range. Neither Mackenzie nor anyone else in the government was persuaded by these arguments, but a few within settler society did protest the province's approach to wild horse removal when it intersected with Native interests in the Nicola Valley in the early 1930s. As one settler insisted in a letter to the minister of lands, "If these horses are to be taken off the range, let us do so in a fair way ... and we will fare better in the long run."[49]

The roundup went ahead. Moreover, most Native people eventually relented and reduced their herds. They did so through abandonment, attrition, and sometimes sales to rendering plants – although even this proved problematic when buyers negotiated one price and then demanded a much lower one at the time of the sale. Generally, government officials frowned on this, but then again, they also tolerated it. They insisted in their discussions with Native people that some money was better than none at all, that at the very least their "useless" horses had to go, that Natives should not complain, and that Natives should simply raise cattle instead. In response to reports that Native men were taking part in an Okanagan Valley roundup, one local newspaper even went so far as to applaud them for dropping their "old wealth tradition."[50]

In some cases, Native people not only reduced their herds but also requested hunting permits of their own from the provincial government. It is possible that they simply wanted to control the hunt, yet not all wild horses were Aboriginal horses. On the other hand, scattered remarks and reports from Indian Agents suggest that some Native people continued to contest the province's horse laws into the 1940s. Perhaps not surprisingly, the clearest examples were from the Nicola Valley and middle Fraser River area.[51] A February 1946 report noted that Native people from the Lower Nicola and Coldwater Indian Reserves strongly opposed a plan to remove horses from rangeland on the north side of the Nicola River. Several Indian reserves had been badly depleted by grasshopper plagues in 1944–45, but the immediate problem in early 1946 was cold weather. As the local Indian Agent explained, owing to the "long winter many of the Indian horses are being put out on the range in order to keep the meager hay supply now on hand for the use of cattle."[52] Native people from the Fountain Indian Reserve, north of Lillooet, made similar complaints in 1947 amid renewed commitments to horse extermination along a portion of the middle Fraser River. But the Fountain people resisted.

Chief Sam Mitchell responded that "if this order refers to a certain strip of grazing land we are interested in, we are compelled, each and everyone one of us in this band, to object to such an order."[53]

Away from the Southern Interior, in the East Kootenay Valley close to the Canada-US border, there were similar conflicts between Natives and newcomers over wild horses by the early 1940s. According to one rancher, the ranges there were being "over-run by scrub stallions, belonging to the Indians ... that are very wild, and hard to get close up to." White ranchers and farmers, he continued, had "been trying to raise a good stock of well bred horses" but were hampered in their efforts by "these scrub studs, which go through everything, and take away the mares with them." "This has always been a problem in this vicinity," the rancher complained, "the [Indian] reserve being the cause, and a protection for the horses." Like others, he thought the horses should be removed from the range. He worried, though, that "any action against the Indians" would lead to "retaliation" and acts of "revenge," and the local grazing agent agreed. "I asked would any of the farmers accept the job of shooting the stallions," the agent later reported. But the farmers said no. Apparently nobody wanted to get "mixed up in the matter" as it would cause "a lot of hard feelings" among "the Indians and half-breeds," and maybe even lead to retaliations against settler stock.[54] Photographs from the Kootenay region show Aboriginal horses on "overgrazed" Indian reserves (Figure 4.1).

Back in the Southern Interior, Aboriginal horses continued to be among the casualties of range improvement in the second half of the twentieth century. To give one final example, in 1951, three men were charged with killing three Native horses near Williams Lake. Convicted in the county court, the culprits were acquitted in the province's Supreme Court "on the grounds that they believed that they had a right to shoot wild horses even though no permits had been issued to them."[55] The Anaham Band was "very disgusted at the outcome of this case" and, according to the local RCMP officer at Alexis Creek, they "stated that if anything like that ever happened again they would not come to us for help, but would handle the matter themselves on the range."[56] With this in mind, the officer "respectfully submitted" to the provincial grazing branch "that considering the small numbers of actual wild horses on the Alexis Creek stock range and the hostile feelings of the Indians toward the persons that hold permits to kill any horses found on the range ... that the permits now issued should be cancelled forthwith ... in order to save very serious trouble."[57] The Grazing Branch agreed.

FIGURE 4.1   Overgrazed range and horses, St. Mary's Reserve. *Courtesy of BC Archives, na_12268*

Of course, there were always a few voices of concern at the edges of British Columbia's quiet consensus on killing horses. Even Dan Weir, a Cariboo trapper and hunting guide who had shot hundreds of wild horses in the Chilcotin in the 1920s and 1930s (430 in one winter by his count), eventually became somewhat ambivalent about the ethics of extermination. Like others in settler society, Weir did not consider horses to be wild in the same way as bears and cougars were; nor was he very sheepish about killing them. But he did believe that horses were as hard to hunt as any other wild animal, and that killing them raised basic ethical considerations. Horses were tough animals, as tough as Weir had ever seen, and they took "a lot of killing unless you hit in a vital spot. After they have got warmed up with the excitement of running," he wrote, "they will carry more lead than a moose, and they don't lay down." In Weir's experience, "the lung shot is the surest and most humane. It's a big target and they [the horses] just fall down and die almost before you can get over to them. Anywhere in the lungs and they hardly live a minute."[58]

Others complained that the province's approach to the wild horse problem was simply wasteful. The *Plan for the Reclamation of British Columbia's Wild Horses*, put before the provincial government in the early 1940s, reported that there were still as many as 20,000 wild horses in the grasslands. Although some were "small, disfigured, and useless animals unfit for living," many were strong, rugged animals that should not be indiscriminately eradicated. Killing wild horses, the proposal argued, was wasteful and fundamentally flawed. It "reduced the wild horse bands from the wrong direction" by culling the strong and relatively superior animals as well as the weak and inferior ones. Rather than wholesale annihilation, a program of annual roundups and systematic culling and breeding would instead "rid British Columbia's ranges of the present wild horse nuisance" and at the same time produce "marketable horses for every purpose, turning a liability into an asset." Horses could be sold to local and regional stockbreeders, as well as to the Canadian military. Annual roundups also would attract tourist dollars. "The world-wide attraction of the only wild horse range, where native wild horses could be viewed in the natural course of tourist travel, would be inestimable," the authors of the proposal insisted. "Artists, authors, motion picture producers, and writers, etc. would in the natural pursuit of their own interest assist in publicizing to the world that only in British Columbia, Canada, may such a tremendous undertaking be found."[59] Apparently a few politicians supported the plan, but grazing official R.G. McKee dismissed it outright as "neither sound nor practical." The whole report read more like a "western magazine story than a workable plan," he wrote. And he hoped that the money for it would come not from government but "some private individual" who could "afford to indulge his romantic nature."[60]

The Society for the Prevention of Cruelty to Animals (SPCA) took a different tack on the wild horse program, denouncing aspects of it as barbaric. In one case, the SPCA complained that horses "were being shot through the body [and] in many instances left to die in pain. Mares were killed and their colts left to starve."[61] In another case, twenty-one "scrub range horses" suffocated inside a Canadian Pacific Railway boxcar bound for Vancouver. According to the SPCA, "The horses were found stacked like cordwood and the doors were sealed tight."[62] In 1958, the RCMP stopped a truck at the Canada-US border "after the SPCA complained that 25 wild horses had been kept in the trailer for 36 hours without food or water."[63] When they opened the trailer, they found one horse dead and the rest in poor condition. At least, the SPCA said, the horses had a right to die humanely.

The Canadian Wild Horse Society went even further, demanding that the government end the roundups and create a refuge for wild horses. Established in the early 1960s by Tom Hughes, president of the Ontario Humane Society, and Norma Bearcroft, a court stenographer and self-described horse lover from Vancouver, the Canadian Wild Horse Society, like the SPCA, considered wild horse eradication to be inhumane.[64] Its central plank, however, was not so much an argument for animal rights as it was an origin story in which wild horses provided a romantic link to the colonial past. A story about Bearcroft that appeared in the pages of the *Vancouver Sun* captured the essence of this history. By this account, wild horses descended from Spanish stock first brought to the Americas by the conquistadors sometime in the early sixteenth century. When they first arrived, these horses were simply domesticated animals like any other, but soon a few escaped and spread north, "thriving on the lush grasslands of the prairies and siring great herds of wild horses that are now part of the history of the American west." Decoupled from Native American history, these horses retained only their Spanish roots. As wild animals they ranged across North America's open grasslands more or less at will, subject only to the vagaries of the seasons. But then everything changed. Ranchers with cattle arrived and transformed the horses into pests. Then the extermination began. By the early 1960s, countless thousands of wild horses had been killed and converted to dog food or fox feed each year until, finally, there were just a few wild horses left in the West. "Shaggy and tough," the horses survived on a few small and scattered mountain meadows that ranchers did not want, appearing briefly at lower elevations in April and May just to "taste the first sweet grass of spring." "With a few variations," the article concluded, "this is the story that emerges if one digs deep enough."[65] In all fairness, Norma Bearcroft and her supporters in the animal rights community were probably the first in settler society to seriously question the rule of ranchers in the grasslands. And for that they were labelled horse-loving sentimentalists. Had they dug a little deeper, however, elements of another story might have emerged. They might have understood the centrality of horses in Aboriginal history, and they might have discovered that killing horses had had something to do with colonialism; at least they might have realized that some wild horses in the province had more common origins as feral outcasts or lost or abandoned pack animals. Efforts to establish a sanctuary for wild horses drew from a radically simplified archive of North American history.

So, in their own way, did official accounts of wild horse extermination. As H.K. Debeck observed in a mid-century presentation to the American Society for Range Management:

After horses first escaped from the early Spanish explorers in Mexico, they soon spread northward throughout the western ranges of this Continent. These new grasslands were not unlike the steppes of Asia where horses were first domesticated, and the Mustangs prospered and multiplied in their new home. Three hundred years later, in 1811, when David Thompson descended the Columbia River, horses were already an established part of the landscape in British Columbia. A few bands in remote areas have been untamed for several generations, but all so-called "wild horses" on this Continent are escaped domestic horses. They have served man well in the development of this western frontier, but our range plants have not evolved along with domestic animals and many of the open ranges in British Columbia have suffered as a result of yearlong grazing from an unnecessarily large "wild" horse population. For the protection of the Crown ranges, it therefore became imperative to eliminate the excess and unwanted ones. Naturally enough, any such program would be violently opposed by the parties wishing to leave their useful horses at large on Crown range ... To a great extent the ranges have been saved from abuse and the extra forage available has been grazed by more useful kinds of livestock.[66]

Even the most passionate resistance to eradication by non-Natives had the effect of reinforcing dispossession, however. As Louise McFadden, one of Norma Bearcroft's strongest supporters, lamented:

They are nearly all gone from British Columbia now, these wild horses of our quiet valleys and hills – the blacks, greys, sorrels, roans, duns, appaloosas, and palominos – once seen in great herds described as a sight as beautiful and life-fraught as any the grassed earth ever showed. Like the buffalo, they eat grass; and like the buffalo, that is their only crime. Each horse eats about twenty-five pounds of grass a day, enough to support one cow or five sheep; and in a society that values everything in dollars and cents, the wild horse must go. In the interests of the stockmen ... legislation was passed for their extermination and under profit incentives men flushed the horses from every hidden valley and canyon. In B.C. they were slaughtered by the tens of thousands until now only a few hundred are left ... We have killed many species such as the passenger pigeon and we have others such as the whooping crane on the brink of extinction. Then too late we become interested and realize the loss. With his unlimited powers for destruction man has found that the easiest way to overcome anything that competes with him is to kill it. While this is the easiest solution, it is not the most civilized.[67]

Nature writers, too, effaced the connections between colonialism and wild horse extermination in their accounts of environmental change. Reflecting on the changing environment around his parents' McIntyre Creek ranch in the early 1940s, Henry Parham observed that:

A few years earlier the range had been full of wild horses; some of them wild for generations; others, horses that had been broken in, and then, when turned out again, had joined some wild band. When first I had come to the dry belt it was quite unusual to drive from Penticton to Fairview without seeing one or two of these bands. Under the leadership of some little stallion they would come near enough to get a good view of us and our horses – the latter of course being the attraction – and after a short inspection, with arching necks and tails held proudly, they would wheel round and gallop out of sight over some hill. There were still a good many on the ranges to the south of us after we made our home at Vaseux Lake, but the growing demand for light as well as heavy horses on the prairies made it worthwhile for a few cowboys to build corrals and guide-fences in suitable places, and into these traps they gradually ran them all, afterwards shipping them by car-loads to Calgary and other prairie towns ... After they had all but gone it was a great relief to the rancher to feel that he could turn his horses and mares on the range without losing them in a wild band, or of having "scrub" colts from his well bred mares.[68]

In detail these passages differed. So did the people who wrote them: Bearcroft and McFadden were urban animal rights advocates; Debeck was a provincial land manager; and Parham was a rural nature writer. And yet all of them recalled a past that no longer existed, if it ever had. In doing so, they constructed what historian William Turkel calls an "archive of place" (although with less emphasis on "material traces" and artifacts in the land) in which Aboriginal people never mattered.[69] Decoupled from Aboriginal history and the cultural politics of colonialism, the war on wild horses – which at times was little more than a proxy war on Aboriginal people – appeared far less violent than it actually was.

No refuge was ever created in British Columbia, but roundups became fewer and far smaller after 1930 as the number of wild horses in the province dwindled. Between 1955 and 1959, the province paid bounties on 1,001 wild horses, and small-scale roundups in 1974 and 1980 removed 68 and 47 horses respectively. A somewhat larger roundup in 1988 shipped 129 horses from the Chilcotin region to Williams Lake, where they were sold and then turned into pet food. By the early 1980s, the reasons for wild horse removal had grown somewhat more complicated. All the old arguments against these animals persisted. Horses were now seen as "taking food away from wildlife," but as regional wildlife branch manager Marty Beets told the *Vancouver Sun* following a 1988 roundup, "They're also competing for food with cattle." Wild horses posed a greater problem in 1987 than at any time in recent memory, said Beets. "It's getting more critical," he insisted. "We've got less water, so there's less forage and the competition may get even more severe. The water table is rapidly dropping and potholes are drying up that haven't run dry since the 1930s."[70] Range manager Lyle Resh agreed that feral horses posed considerable problems for wildlife and range management. Unlike cattle, horses "occupy the range all year, they overgraze and cause erosion to the Chilcotin's side hill country, and they graze the sedge, grasses and shrubs that provide food for cattle, deer, moose, and wild sheep."[71] Protecting wildlife and preventing soil erosion were new rationales for ridding the range of wild horses, but the underlying logics of eradication had not changed much since the late nineteenth century. In the arithmetic of management, "feral horses" – the preferred terminology of biologists and range ecologists by the 1980s – were a detriment to the production and careful utilization of more valuable animals, including "native" animals like deer, moose, and bighorn sheep.

Just how many wild and feral horses were exterminated in the late nineteenth and twentieth centuries is impossible to say. Records held by the Grazing Branch indicate that 13,420 horses were exterminated between 1924 (when the eradication program was first enacted) and 1955 (when it began to slow down), and that perhaps another 1,500 wild horses were removed between 1955 and 1980.[72] Likewise, the fates of the individual animals are impossible to determine, though archival records from the early twentieth century do point to a number of grim possibilities. A chemist from Britain heard there were approximately "one million stray and disabled horses available for disposal" in British Columbia and wanted to know how much it would cost to have these animals shipped regularly overseas to a rendering plant that would turn them into fertilizer and various "other useful products."[73] A group of businessmen from Manitoba had a contract to ship some 50,000 horses annually to Antwerp, Belgium, and several other European cities for use as horsemeat. "The horses must be healthy," they wrote, "but may be old and crippled."[74] Robert Ballard, son of veterinarian William Ballard, wanted horsemeat for his rapidly expanding Vancouver-based dog food business.[75] Similarly, a group of businessmen from Port Alberni wondered whether they could secure wild horses, which they intended to slaughter and grind up into fish food, for less than $5 a head.[76] And two medical doctors from Vancouver were interested in studying the "suprarenal gland, especially the cortex" and explained "that horse glands were most suitable for this study because they were richer in active hormones."[77] Then there were the Russians. In the late 1920s, the Soviet government agreed to purchase 4,000 Canadian horses for agricultural, and possibly military, purposes on the semiarid Russian steppe. According to one report, as many as a thousand of these horses could be rounded up on the ranges of British Columbia.[78] Sales records were impossible to locate, but representatives from the Russian government did visit the Kamloops and Nicola Valley Indian Reserves in 1927. Most wild horses had simpler fates, however. Some were loaded into railcars and sent to the United States or Alberta, where they were rendered as fertilizer, dog food, and feed for fox farms, but it appears that most were simply shot by bounty hunters and left, minus their ears, which were needed to collect the cash for killing them, to rot on the open range.[79]

PART 2
Grasshoppers

5

Grappling with Grasshoppers

The war on wild horses was part of a wider campaign against creatures considered to be pests, and as battle plans developed against the equines, a second, related conflict erupted over grasshoppers. Like wild horses, grasshoppers were highly mobile herbivores that competed in various ways with cattle for grassland. In almost every other way, though, the war on insects was different. Partly this was because of the animals involved. Unlike wild horses, grasshoppers possessed a remarkable capacity to periodically increase their numbers, giving rise to what settlers sometimes called a "locust plague," and were a pest only when they swarmed. Mainly, the war on insects was different because obviously nobody owned grasshoppers, whereas people did own horses, even wild ones. Nor did anybody ever defend grasshoppers. There were complaints when nontarget species, including people, were inadvertently poisoned. But nobody cared about killing grasshoppers, whereas killing wild horses eventually raised ethical questions.

Nevertheless, my argument in this chapter and those that follow is that grasshoppers were no less connected to the human communities that tried to exterminate them than wild horses were. Indeed, in some ways they were more connected, making them much harder to exterminate. To elucidate these connections, and assess their implications for people and nature, the chapters in this section offer an insect's-eye view on ranching history. Cattle ranching came to British Columbia in the 1860s with the Fraser Canyon and Cariboo gold rushes. An extension of the American range cattle frontier (of Hispanic origin), it arrived, as geographers Cole

Harris and David Demeritt observe, "just after Native populations had been decimated by smallpox, and at a time when the government of British Columbia offered land for purchase or lease for next to nothing."[1] Ranchers with cattle and property rights quickly took over the grasslands and cattle competed there with creatures that ranchers and range managers soon considered pests. Among the many animals that ranchers attempted to eradicate, or at least control, were several species of grasshopper. Working closely with federal entomologists, provincial grazing experts organized a poisoning campaign that failed to eradicate grasshoppers but wrought havoc in the grasslands. As the chapters in this section show, killing insects exposed unwieldy (and in many ways impossibly intertwined) social and ecological realities that considerably complicated and even undermined these efforts. It also created new realities that nobody anticipated and made other problems in the grassland much worse.

Current science tells us that grasshopper irruptions are part of grassland ecology, but tracing this history in any detail is impossible because apart from a few faint traces in plateau indigenous tradition – that in any case only confirm that irruptions happened, not when they happened, how large they were, or how long they lasted – we lack records for all but the most recent of these irruptions.[2] There is evidence that a grasshopper irruption occurred in 1886, nearly twenty-five years after the first settler ranches were established. But the first swarm to be recorded in any detail occurred four years later, in the summer of 1890. Nobody knew what caused the 1890 irruption, or even what species of grasshopper was involved. Many ranchers worried it was the Rocky Mountain or "hateful" locust that began harassing Great Plains farmers and ranchers in the early 1870s. But agricultural officials were dubious. The Rocky Mountain locust was known to be a relatively large insect, whereas the insects involved in the BC plague seemed, on the basis of second-hand accounts from settlers, to be much smaller. The hateful locust was also commonly confused with the common red-legged locust (*Melanoplus femurrubrum*), which was at the time considered a different species. Most likely this was a case of mistaken identity fuelled by dramatic reports of locust destruction from the Great Plains. Nevertheless, and no doubt in light of lingering uncertainties about the insect's true identity, one provincial official echoed entomologists working on the Rocky Mountain locust, urging every settler in the grasslands to be "on his guard and at once report any unusual increase in the number of grasshoppers and to send specimens for identification."[3]

Not that being "on guard" actually mattered. Effective means of dealing with insect pests, especially highly mobile grasshoppers that migrated in countless numbers when they swarmed, were still largely undeveloped. Late-nineteenth-century entomologists advocated a number of natural controls for pestiferous insect populations.[4] One report noted that black-birds, meadowlarks, and several species of grouse consumed large numbers of grasshoppers "and should be jealously protected." In some parts of Canada and the United States, game laws had been revised for just this reason, but not in British Columbia, where ranchers and agricultural officials were more interested in using birds that might also be eaten or sold. For the common red-legged locust and for other species, wrote Dominion entomologist James Fletcher in one report, "large broods of poultry are particularly useful in keeping down the numbers and should form a part of the equipment of every prairie farmer."[5] In a similar vein, an 1891 report from the BC Department of Agriculture suggested that the "high bench lands" of the Interior country were "conveniently suited" for raising poultry, which in turn were useful in "keeping down" insect pests including grasshoppers.[6] Another report added that turkeys would be immensely profitable and that where grasshoppers were numerous, "fowls have been found to be of great service in reducing their numbers."[7] On the other hand, blackbirds and turkeys could eat only so many grasshop-pers, and by the end of the nineteenth century, entomologists were also advocating more direct means of insect control. One of these tactics involved the use of hand or horse-drawn traps called hopperdozers. Catching grasshoppers "alive in a machine or trap which is drawn over infested fields" was a popular and effective method of insect control else-where in North America and had the added benefit of providing farmers with "valuable winter feed for poultry," claimed one report.[8] But like chickens and turkeys, machines and traps could remove only so many grasshoppers from the range and, in any case, were deterrents only *after* the insects had swarmed, whereas the goal was to control them before this happened.

A more direct and less laborious approach to insect control was the use of poison bait, usually some combination of Paris Green arsenic, manure (or bran), and molasses (or sugar). Compounds of arsenic have a long history as domestic pesticides, but their use in agriculture likely dates to eighteenth-century France.[9] They first appeared in North American agri-culture in the 1860s, when they were used to combat potato beetles. Before long, arsenics were employed against other insect pests, and by the turn of the nineteenth century they were directed at grasshoppers and locusts as well. A mixture of arsenic, bran, and sugar (a slight variation on the manure and molasses-based mixture mentioned above) was recommended for use in British Columbia as early as 1895, and by all accounts it effectively killed insects, though one report claimed that it also occasionally killed birds, cattle, chickens, and dogs and was harmful to humans, so settlers had to be careful. The bigger problem was distribution. Spreading arsenic bait over fenced winter ranges or relatively small parcels of cultivated land, as was being done by farmers in eastern North America, for instance, was one thing. Applying it to extensive and sparsely settled grasslands connected more by cattle trails and pack trains than by roads and railways was quite another.

Grasshopper populations irrupted again in 1898, not only in the Nicola Valley but also on the Riske Creek range, located at the junction of the Fraser and Chilcotin Rivers, and further south near Lillooet, where according to one resident ranchers had "to feed out a lot of hay on account of the grasshoppers leaving pasture short."[10] One rancher noted that this was the second time the grasshoppers had appeared in the Nicola Valley. The first time was in 1890, when "they made complete havoc" on the valley's hay crop. In both cases, those grasshoppers deposited countless eggs "on sandy and gravelly hillsides, about an inch from the surface," and the rancher was convinced that unless "something happened to destroy them before they hatched, it will be very little use putting in a [hay] crop next spring." Another rancher from the Nicola Valley similarly lamented that he "could not grow enough feed to keep any quantity of hogs." The grasshoppers were "very bad last summer and laid their eggs," he reported, "so that we are expecting our crops will be all eaten by them next year." Rather than build a hopperdozer or ask the government for arsenic bait, he decided to adapt his agriculture by planting "very little wheat or oats, but principally peas and potatoes, as they [the grasshoppers] do not bother these crops so much." A Lillooet farmer agreed that this was a good grasshopper control strategy and even recommended that the government plant decoy crops in the grassland – mainly wheat and oats, but also some barley – so that the next time the insects swarmed, they would perhaps avoid settlers' cultivated fields and fenced winter pastures altogether. The decoy crops could also be harvested in years when there were no swarms, to offset the costs involved. The government demurred, however, because grasshoppers were pests only when they swarmed. Moreover, the location of the swarms could not be predicted. Thus, the cost of planting and maintaining decoy crops could not be justified.[11]

Like others before, the 1898 grasshopper plague eventually passed. One rancher reported, no doubt with some relief, that "nearly all the grasshoppers have disappeared and a great many have died."[12] Whatever solace

ranchers took from this was tempered by lingering questions about where
the insects had gone and, perhaps more importantly, why they had
returned. Settlers frequently used the term "locust plague" to describe
grasshopper irruptions. As the scientist and historian of entomology Jeffrey
Lockwood has noted, this terminology invoked "the same terror used by
God to punish the Egyptians," and its use in British Columbia might
suggest that some people regarded grasshopper irruptions as the work of
an angry deity.[13] But many settlers simply assumed it was the nature of
these insects to appear occasionally in large numbers, do damage to crops
and pasture, and then to all but disappear. Writing in 1891, a rancher
reported, on the basis of his experience raising stock at Williams Lake,
that grasshoppers "only do damage two years in thirty."[14] Others saw the
"natural" ecological determinants of the irruptions even more clearly. Thus,
E.P. Venables, head of the Dominion Entomology Laboratory at Vernon,
reflected toward the close of 1901 that grasshoppers "were numerous at
some places, and although no damage was done, some people are anxious
lest there be a repetition of the plague of three years ago." Fortunately,
some of their natural enemies were also "in evidence to an equal extent
with the grasshoppers." The grey spotted blister beetle, for example, was
"very abundant" and it was hoped that their larvae would help out if they
kept up their "good name for destroying the eggs of grasshoppers."[15]
Essentially, this was the prevailing scientific explanation of insect irruptions
in the nineteenth century.[16] Thus, Dominion entomologist James Fletcher
attributed the 1898 plague in British Columbia to a temporary absence of
parasites and disease-bearing fungi that together usually tempered the
insect's reproductive ability.[17] By this logic, the 1898 irruption had been
nothing more than a minor blip in the overall balance of nature. Whatever
the precise ecological mechanism at work – and it would be a number of
years before entomologists offered a fuller explanation – settlers were
increasingly convinced that both the scale and the frequency of grasshopper plagues in British Columbia had increased.

Grasshoppers irrupted again in 1907 and 1914. Moreover, the nature
and scale of these events was reflected in the language settlers used to
describe them. Some settlers likened these swarms to tornados because the
damage they did, while significant, bore no discernible pattern: some fields
and ranges were levelled or "rendered bare" while others were left
untouched. Dominion Inspector of Indian Orchards Tom Wilson thought
the 1914 swarm more "resembled a snow-storm." It was impossible to know
how many insects were involved, but clearly their impact was considerable.
Hay crops of clover and alfalfa had been "much injured" by the swarm,

Wilson wrote, "so much so as to bring about an appreciable shortage in weight per acre." Meanwhile, and moving northeast into the Nicola Valley, the grazing grounds around Minnie Lake had been "severely attacked" and "many thousands" of acres of open rangeland had been "rendered useless." A later report noted that nearly 200,000 acres of bunchgrass had been "laid waste" in 1914 alone.[18]

In this context, property lines and other human borders were meaningless: mobile nature made a mockery of both. Grasshoppers even disrespected the international boundary when a 1914 outbreak in southernmost British Columbia spread into northern Washington State.[19] The cause of these outbreaks was unclear, but there were clues that weather conditions were involved. Hot, dry conditions early in the spring and fall appeared to favour grasshoppers, whereas cool, wet conditions during these times did not. A lingering question was whether ranching and grasshopper abundance were related: some ranchers noticed grasshoppers depositing eggs on gravelly hillsides that were overgrazed and trampled by cattle.[20] Likewise Wilson had begun to suspect that "injudicious grazing" had "forced the locusts to places where they could obtain the requisite amount of nutrition."[21]

Grasshopper populations also irrupted on ranges along the middle Fraser and lower Chilcotin Rivers in 1914. In these cases, the primary insect involved was probably the clear-winged or roadside grasshopper, but at least one rancher reported that the swarm comprised several species, with clear-winged insects dominating. The exact cause of the irruption was as unclear as ever, but echoing Tom Wilson's assessment from the Nicola District, one government grazing official explained that if there "happens to be no cold rains during June to kill their young, the grasshoppers will multiply at an alarming rate, with the result that they do more damage to the range than the stock who are feeding there." This was the case in 1914, he reported, and as a result the grasshoppers were "particularly plentiful" that year. As in the Nicola Valley, the insect's impact on crops and rangeland was considerable. "In many places," according to one account, the Riske Creek and Beaumont ranges "were almost completely denuded of grassland."[22]

Such accounts, although suggestive and accurate in some ways, were nonetheless potentially full of hyperbole and bias. The word "plague," for instance, was loaded with religious significance but said little or nothing about the grasshopper irruptions themselves and even less about why these events had occurred. Similarly, when Wilson and others said that ranges and hay crops were "severely attacked," they imputed to grasshoppers a decidedly ill intent – indeed, an almost human maliciousness – that the insects actually never possessed. It also seems highly unlikely that entire ranges were "laid waste" or "rendered bare" or "completely denuded" by grasshopper swarms, though the insect's ability to graze over large areas was considerable. In any event, contrary to settler rhetoric, grasshoppers were never as destructive as cattle were, even when they swarmed. For one thing, individual plants usually survive these swarms; for another, the nitrogen-fixing crust of mosses and lichens that surrounded them was also left undamaged. The same simply could not have been said of heavy grazing by range cattle, which not only overgrazed and damaged individual plants by removing the parts that produced new seeds but also trampled and destroyed them, while creating cracks in the microbiotic crust, enabling weeds and woody shrubs to take hold.

Moreover, it never occurred to these observers that grasshoppers might do more than simply "damage" or "destroy" the grassland. Yet, recent ideas in range ecology suggest a more complicated relationship between insects and the wider landscape they inhabited. It is true that the introduction of cattle and horses altered the historical-ecological context in which grasshopper irruptions occurred, so that even small outbreaks after domestic grazers arrived could leave large areas looking barren or denuded. But given what we now know about grazing effects in semiarid environments, it also stands to reason that by heavily grazing individual plants without destroying them, grasshopper irruptions probably benefited bunchgrass ecosystems, at least at the local scale, by stimulating a fresh new growth. At least, a fresh growth of grass might have benefited native grazers like bighorn sheep. There may be even more to the ecological story, however, because current science also tells us that patchy landscapes with unevenly aged plants and a relatively diverse mix of species are more robust – in other words, are less susceptible to disease – than uniform landscapes with evenly aged plants and very little species mix, the interesting implication being that grasshopper irruptions were ecologically beneficial for the grassland before large numbers of exogenous grazers arrived.[23] Along with floods, fires, and other natural disturbances, at the landscape level, grasshopper irruptions would have helped to create a naturally patchy grassland environment.

The way settlers wrote about grasshopper irruptions also tended to obscure the fact that insect swarms affected some groups of people more than others. The impact of these irruptions frequently bore a discernible human geography. Indian reserves often suffered the most because they lacked the natural and economic resources needed to endure sudden, disruptive changes in the environment. The 1890 outbreak is a case in point. Ranchers already discouraged by the dry summer of 1889 and the following harsh winter that killed many cattle and horses for want of winter pasture now had an insect problem as well. Yet, the situation was worse on many Indian reserves, where, according to British Columbia's chief inspector of Indian Agencies, the combination of drought, grasshoppers, and cold weather the following winter, along with an "insufficiency of fodder" in the first place, "killed very many of their cattle and horses."[24] Just how many Aboriginal horses and cattle died that winter is impossible to determine, but clearly the inspector blamed nature for what in many ways was a social problem. "Natural" disturbances were always more difficult for Native people to endure because Indian reserves had such narrow ecological margins. As noted in Part 1, few if any Indian reserves had sufficient winter range or the water needed to irrigate hay crops, and this made them especially vulnerable to things like drought, cold weather, grasshopper irruptions, and other changes in the environment. Any one of these disturbances had the potential to prove problematic or even disastrous, but drought, grasshoppers, and bitterly cold temperatures arrived in *succession* in 1889–90. Settlers also lost livestock that winter. Yet, for reasons that were as much social as environmental, the situation on Indian reserves was worse. Aboriginal horses and cattle fell victim not just to the vagaries of nature in 1889–90 but also to the ecological inequities of an Indian reserve system that left their owners with too little land and far too few of the resources needed to raise livestock. Such was also the case in 1907–08. Indian Affairs attested that the grasshopper plague that summer seriously depleted the hay crop. Some Native people in the Kamloops-Okanagan Agency were running short of winter feed and had to be given relief in the form of winter hay purchased by the Dominion government. The situation was less severe in the Williams Lake District in 1908, but a few years later, in 1914, the local Indian Agent reported that a grasshopper plague, in combination with drought and overgrazing by horses and cattle, had left some reserve lands badly depleted. This was just the beginning, however, because grain and root crops on reserves were "almost a complete failure" that year, with many not even being planted.[25]

Many small-scale settler ranchers also suffered from a lack of winter pasture following the 1898, 1907, and 1914 grasshopper plagues, but here too the reasons were as much social as ecological. It was common practice for the smaller ranchers to purchase additional hay supplies from the larger and more productive operations, but even the spectre of a swarm convinced some of the these ranchers not to sell. This left some small ranches short of hay during the winter months when cattle had to be fed, and in some cases forced them to turn their cattle onto open spring ranges before the bunchgrass was ready to be grazed (possibly putting the cattle in direct conflict with wild horses). Admittedly, grasshopper irruptions affected large ranches as well as small ones. Nonetheless, the largest family-owned and corporate cattle ranches in the grasslands fared relatively well during bad grasshopper years because they had more water and land at their disposal and far larger hay supplies. The largest of these ranches, the Douglas Lake Cattle Company, even found ways to profit, albeit indirectly, from grasshopper plagues by purchasing adjacent cattle ranches that folded in the 1910s and 1920s under the combined and related pressures of changing environmental conditions, including drought and range degradation, and deteriorating economic conditions culminating in the Great Depression.

Less clear than the "damage" grasshopper plagues did to crops and rangeland was what to do about them. Poison was one option. According to the American entomologist Charles Lounsbury, the "various arsenicals" were being used to great effect in his new home of South Africa, and in the late 1910s, Lounsbury recommended arsenic to British Columbia's new grazing commissioner, Thomas Mackenzie, a reminder that even after formal European empires had faded into the background, colonial elites and scientific experts, now part of dominant settler societies, continued to interact with each other by way of well-established social, administrative, and scientific networks.[26] Colonial British Columbia presented particular difficulties, however. Initial experiments with arsenic indicated that only two of the forty or so species of grasshoppers found between Merritt and Riske Creek would take the bait, and, as it turned out, not the right two. The insects whose population irruptions were "devastating" the province's rangelands turned out to be *Camnula pellucida* and *Melanoplus atlantis*, not the hated Rocky Mountain locust after all, but both insects refused the arsenic bait. Perhaps more molasses was in order, or maybe a little lemon, as was called for in the "Kansas Mixture." But even if entomologists got the recipe right, there was still the considerable problem of distribution.[27]

The experience of the First World War suggested another line of attack. In August 1919, amid reports that grasshoppers were "laying bare" an area of some several hundred square miles in the Chilcotin District, Grazing Commissioner Thomas Mackenzie wrote to the Canadian military with what he thought might be a "visionary idea": he wanted to gas the grasshoppers. At certain times of the year, he explained, grasshoppers congregated in the "shallow swales" of the open range, where the grass was greener than in other places, and "it would appear that at that time the gas could be used with good effect."[28] The military was receptive to Mackenzie's idea, and a military official told him that the information he required could be obtained from one J.A. Hall, a resident of Vancouver, who was also "one of the senior officers employed by the Imperial Authorities on munitions work" and whose "duties during the War pertained almost entirely to poisonous gases."[29]

It is not clear whether Mackenzie followed through with his experiments, but his appeal to the army is a Canadian reminder that the means, methods, and metaphors of war permeated North American understandings of and approaches to insect control in the late nineteenth and twentieth centuries.[30] In British Columbia, as elsewhere, words of war not only surrounded insect problems but also suggested ways of solving them. Newspapers regularly described how "armies of grasshoppers" swept the landscape, "wasting" ranges and field crops alike.[31] Military imagery also powerfully shaped scientific descriptions of grasshopper irruptions. As Edmund Russell and others have observed, entomologists in North American tended to see themselves as being at war with insects: the last and perhaps only line of defence against a rapidly advancing and recalcitrant "natural enemy." Thus, the cover page of an important 1924 report from British Columbia, coauthored by Dominion entomologists R.C. Treherne and E.R. Buckell (in Canada, entomology was a federal responsibility[32]), depicted a horde of grasshoppers about to advance across an open, even undefended, and obviously pristine bunchgrass range. Plans to control "outbreaks" – itself a word that by the early twentieth century had taken on military connotations – also frequently turned on military imagery and metaphors. Faced with the overwhelming task of spreading arsenic bait on British Columbia's open rangelands, entomologists noted the "strategic" importance of "narrowing the frontline" before beginning "operations" or initiating a poison control "campaign."[33] There was always utility in depicting pest control this way. As Russell writes, "Describing pest control as war helped entomologists portray nature as a battlefield," which in turn helped to "elevate the status of their profession, and mobilize resources."[34]

Science spoke with many voices, however. In British Columbia, entomologists promoted better land use and carried out basic taxonomic and habitat studies even as they experimented with arsenic and organized poison control "campaigns," and considered gassing the grasslands. Indeed, a central conclusion of early entomological research in the province was that, in a sense, poor land-use practices caused the irruptions. Reporting the preliminary results of studies initiated by Dominion entomologists in the summer of 1919, Grazing Commissioner Mackenzie explained: "Owing to heavy grazing the growth of forage is so sparse that grasshoppers are forced to travel far for food. Under such conditions it is impossible for their ordinary enemies to keep them down to normal numbers. In consequence they have rapidly increased."[35] This was also entomologist R.C. Treherne's message to the BC Entomological Society in the spring of 1919; at the same time, E.R. Buckell prepared for the first full summer of fieldwork on British Columbia's relatively remote Riske Creek range. To be sure, the entomologist elaborated, it would be "contrary to reason" to imagine that the grasshopper's "ordinary enemies" would cause the complete extermination of the grasshopper, "otherwise on what would they themselves feed?" Moreover, even under what Treherne called "strict natural conditions," climatic and other factors could prove "more fatal to the parasites than to grasshoppers," thereby enabling the latter to expand beyond expectations in a "normal" year. By the same token, "a certain scarcity of grasshoppers in some years could cause a certain number of the parasites to die without performing their special function in life." Such were some of the vagaries of nature, the entomologist explained, and some of the situations in which a given population of grasshoppers could quickly add to its numbers. Such perturbations meant little in the larger balance of nature, however, because when environmental conditions returned to normal, ecological stability in the grasslands would be restored.

The only thing that would upset this natural tendency to balance, according to Treherne, was "the unnatural interference of man," including poor grazing practices that forced grasshoppers to migrate away from their natural controls in search of food. Indeed, the entomologist averred, "almost invariably do we find the host insect more active on the wing than the native parasites. What chance do you suppose a bacterial or fungous disease, whose only hope of proving effective is under congested conditions, has of becoming established when the host insect is scattered in all directions over an open range? What chance has a predatory beetle, whose larvae actively move through the soil, feeding upon egg-cluster after egg-cluster, to reduce the numbers of the host insect?" The answer, of course, was no chance at all. This explained why, when one considered the historical record of grasshopper plagues in the province alongside the ecological record of ranching – with outbreaks evident on increasingly overgrazed range – it was possible to discern a pattern of increasingly widespread and severe population explosions. Viewed in this light, the solution to the grasshopper problem was perfectly clear: land-use practices that would "reestablish the natural order of things." According to Treherne, it should be the goal of all "range conservation" to "re-establish" the natural grasses so that the grasshoppers would remain "more or less localized." This would give what he called the "beneficial insects" of the range (by which he meant all the insects that preyed on grasshoppers) an opportunity to accomplish their "purpose" in the world and maintain the balance of nature.[36] The discourse of war was pervasive in entomological circles, but science suggested less aggressive and arguably more robust approaches to environmental problems as well, amounting, in a sense, to a strategy of ecological containment.

Clearly, much had changed in entomology since James Fletcher speculated in the late nineteenth century about the roles of parasites and disease-bearing fungi in regulating grasshopper populations. As historian of science Stéphane Castonguay explains, Fletcher's entomology fit "within a tradition of inventory science" that sought to count and classify species. By the turn of the nineteenth century, however, entomologists had begun to build on Darwin's ideas to think historically about the relationship between insects and their environments. To be sure, "their post-Darwinian understanding of the natural world still relied on a teleological metaphor – the balance of nature – to explain the regulation of animal populations." But the use of "applied experimental and quantitative methods in their studies of the relationships between organisms and their environment provided a dynamic and evolutionary interpretation of the balance of nature."[37] In short, new ideas yielded new methods as well as new and deeper understandings of relationships between human activity, insect population dynamics, and the natural vagaries of particular environments.[38]

The analysis of grasshopper outbreaks that Treherne offered to the entomological society clearly exemplified this shift. "It must be realized," he argued, using a racialized anthropological analogy, "that in the same way as man, animals, and plants have developed definite traits and characters in accordance with their surroundings and environments, so grasshoppers separate into species as regards their habitats." The "first object" of study for the entomologist, therefore, was to "segregate and to classify the various types of country that may be found." The next step was to determine the various species that inhabited that country "in order to find out if there is any relationship between the insect and its environment."[39] Elements of the older entomology – a strong emphasis on taxonomy and belief in the balance of nature, for instance – remained important. Yet, new emphases in evolutionary theory, and their diffusion throughout the sciences, sent research in novel theoretical as well as empirical directions.

Much of this emerging analysis and interpretation of grasshopper populations in British Columbia followed from fieldwork by Buckell on the Riske Creek range.[40] Located at the junction of the Fraser and Chilcotin Rivers, the Riske Creek range is a broad, undulating plateau bounded by two steep, deeply incised river valleys. Historically, this was indigenous territory. Tsilhqot'in and probably Secwepemc people hunted, fished, gathered, and eventually grazed horses there, though the precise nature and scale of these activities, which were far from static in any case, is exceedingly difficult to determine. Written records are nonexistent for this period, and nineteenth-century accounts are sparse and difficult to interpret. All of them were written after Native populations had been devastated by European disease, and at a time when Native land-use practices were being curtailed and confined to tiny Indian reserves. In consequence, they probably tell us more about Native peoples' attempts to adapt to changing circumstances (to say nothing of the cultural assumptions of those who wrote these accounts) than about Aboriginal land use over the long term. This much is clear: the indigenous population in the territory that became Riske Creek, like indigenous populations throughout North America, was far larger before resettlement than after.[41] This, combined with what is known of precontact land-use practice in the surrounding area, suggests that when European settlers arrived in the mid- to late nineteenth century, they found not some unsullied "wilderness," but rather a partially humanized landscape: a subtle hybrid of history, ecology, and changing human geographies.[42] Beginning in the late 1860s, however, a new order was imposed, and when that happened, a new environmental history emerged. In the process, as noted earlier, Native people were confined to Indian reserves, and ranchers with property rights in winter range (whether it was lowland or meadowland) erected fences and spread cattle (and to a lesser extent sheep and horses) across grasslands they increasingly called their own. Backed by the administrative power of an ascendant, albeit distant, colonial state, and beginning with strategically located winter ranges, ranchers with cattle and property rights claimed the grasslands for themselves.

Cattle, to borrow historian Virginia Anderson's phrase, were clearly "creatures of empire." But as "animals of enterprise" they were also creatures of capitalism.[43] By the early 1870s, remote Riske Creek had become a resource-producing periphery, a place where commoditized animals commoditized grass, which humans cannot eat, by converting it to meat, which they can. By North American standards, most of the ranches were relatively small, but one of them was enormous. Indeed, with almost 50,000 alienated acres in 1920, and access to a million more in the form of leases and grazing permits, and sheer force of cattle numbers, the British-owned Gang Ranch dwarfed every operation in the region. Unlike most ranches in British Columbia, which relied largely on family labour, the Gang Ranch was an industrial ranch with a workforce. Run by managers, overseen by foremen, and worked by wage labourers, the "home ranch" was a 16,000-acre tract of lowland located on the west side of the Fraser River north of Churn Creek. The company owned another 5,500 acres of lowland at Big Bar, 14,000 acres of lowland on the Riske Creek range, and numerous meadowlands, all of which were kept in reserve for winter pasture. The remainder of the Riske Creek range was grazed in common the rest of the year by some 6,000 head from surrounding ranches, including the Gang Ranch.[44]

The rise of ranching at Riske Creek changed the indigenous grasslands there in many ways. By the time Buckell arrived in the early 1920s, elements of this new ecology and the intertwined environmental effects of colonialism and capitalism were everywhere apparent. "The open range" that Buckell believed had originally been "covered with a fine stand of Bunch-grass (Agropyron spp.), often from two to three feet in height" had been "practically destroyed" by overgrazing. In contrast, the "bunchgrass slopes" that formed the winter ranges, "having been fenced many years ago, and all cattle kept off them except in winter," still produced "a fair stand of bunchgrass."[45] Like the rest of agricultural North America, Riske Creek had become a propertied settler landscape – in William Cronon's words, a "world of fields and fences."[46] Indeed, even simple fence lines set in motion significant ecological modifications. In Buckell's assessment, the geography of fields and fences and the population geography of grasshoppers were actually closely connected. On the open range, where bunchgrass was heavily grazed, he found innumerable grasshoppers grazing shoots of new grass, though not usually bunchgrass. In contrast, in areas where tall stands of bunchgrass still grew "in profusion," grasshoppers were relatively hard to find, except for the odd few always found lurking along cattle trails and fence lines. There was "little doubt" in Buckell's mind that the most destructive species of grasshopper were those whose natural habitat was a "dry, bare, closely grazed range." Although abundant on overgrazed range, these grasshoppers were "practically extinct" on ranges at higher elevation, where the grass was in much better condition, and were never encountered on fenced winter ranges (though a few could be found along the fences themselves, suggesting a natural preference for disturbed landscapes).[47] Buckell's central conclusion that understanding habitat changes over the past half-century was crucial to understanding the recent history of grasshopper outbreaks clearly echoed that of his supervisor, as did his conclusion that better land use was in order. But the details of his analysis differed significantly. The recent severe grasshopper outbreaks in British Columbia were caused less by habitat loss that forced grasshoppers abroad in search of food, there free to reproduce at will, than by habitat creation. By overgrazing the range, ranchers inadvertently created breeding grounds for the very grasshoppers they now wanted to exterminate.

But the analysis went deeper. Overgrazing not only created good breeding areas for grasshoppers but also appeared to be changing their feeding and breeding habits. Consider what was known about the feeding and breeding habits of *Camnula pellucida*, "one of the main injurious species." By all accounts, it had a "habit of remaining together in swarms and of migrating over the country in summer, often entering the long grass and grain fields which are quite unsuitable for oviposition." Usually, the females fed there until it was time to lay eggs, at which point they left the swarm for "special egg laying grounds situated on flat, dry, alkaline pieces of ground covered with close cropped grass, or on dry gravelly knolls," just as some ranchers had observed in the 1890s. Although distributed over hundreds of square miles when feeding, female grasshoppers usually found "comparatively few acres of ground" that were suitable for breeding. At Riske Creek, however, *Camnula* "did not keep at all rigidly to the so-called typical habits mentioned above." It did not migrate in dense swarms but instead spread out from innumerable small egg beds scattered all over the range, and it was never observed exhibiting the "typical" migratory habits of swarms.[48] Some of what Buckell observed at Riske Creek went against the grain of existing knowledge. It seemed that habit and habitat were being reworked to form new ecological relationships.

In many ways, Buckell's work on the Riske Creek range reflected shifting emphases in the environmental sciences. As Sharon Kingsland and others have shown, by the early twentieth century, the study of natural fluctuations in animal populations was becoming an important part of scientific research.[49] Charles Elton was already doing important work on the population history of fur-bearing animals in the Canadian subarctic, and it was partly on the basis of this work that Elton later insisted that the "balance of nature" never existed.[50] This was an important moment in the history of ecology, as Kingsland and others have noted. But the basis for Elton's argument had in fact been laid much earlier by oceanographers working on fishery problems in the North Sea. Working with statistics from Norwegian herring fisheries, for example, in 1918 scientist Johan Hjort was able to show that more than half of the herring harvested between 1907 and 1913 came from an unusually large cohort born in 1904, and he suspected that similar natural fluctuations occurred in North Sea cod and haddock stocks.[51] Although trained in the tradition of descriptive, inventory science, Buckell was familiar with this new work in population dynamics and sought to apply this knowledge to the grassland of British Columbia. It appeared that fluctuations in grasshopper populations, unlike those in North Sea herring stocks, were more cyclical than irregular, occurring approximately every six to eight years. Similar periodicities in locust and grasshopper populations had been recorded elsewhere, particularly in Africa.[52] What set Buckell's work apart from Hjort's, and to a lesser extent Elton's, was its central conclusion that natural fluctuations in animal populations were significantly shaped by human factors.[53] The core of his analysis focused on the ways that ranching had remade the grasslands: overgrazing did not cause so much as dramatically amplify grasshopper irruptions by creating favourable feeding and breeding areas across an enormous geographical area. Unlike the histories of ecological variability uncovered by Hjort and Elton, the changes Buckell described were as much social as they were natural.

This exposed a deeper problem, because in truth Buckell had no baseline for assessing changes in grasshopper population dynamics in British Columbia before cattle ranching arrived. His analysis tacitly accepted the commonly held assumption that grasshopper irruptions had become both larger and more frequent after 1890. All research makes assumptions, of course, but this one was particularly important because inevitably it fuelled notions that these insects had to be controlled. The problem in the 1920s was that entomologists like Buckell actually had no idea how grasshoppers behaved before ranching arrived, or to put the problem another way, whether these insects were hardwired, as it were, to act only one way in nondisturbed landscapes or whether their natural response actually depended on context. Nor for that matter did entomologists know how many grasshoppers there were during "normal" years or how many there were during outbreaks. Ultimately, the image of insect irruptions increasing in size and frequency over time was impressionistic, not empirical, and based on limited historical experience. There was a lot about the history and geography of grasshopper population dynamics that entomologists did not and probably could not know.[54]

This was important, not in the philosophical sense of trees falling in forests, but in the material sense of putting arsenic, and later more harmful chemicals like DDT, in the grasslands. As we will see, settlers put these and other poisons in the grasslands for a host of political, economic, and perhaps even psychological reasons. Always in the background, however, was the assumption that both the scale and the frequency of grasshopper irruptions increased significantly after 1890, and that this in turn caused new problems for the province's ranching economy. Insects did cause new problems for people, particularly in areas that had been heavily trampled and overgrazed. But the story of grasshoppers was more complicated than even the most astute observers, men like E.R. Buckell, ever realized.

In recent years, as new ecological perspectives have been developed, many older assumptions have been abandoned. This has enabled entomologists to produce more complicated and presumably more accurate accounts of grasshopper population dynamics.[55] Clear-winged grasshoppers, for instance, are now known to show wide variations in abundance and distribution reflecting a range of environmental variables, including weather, grazing, predation, parasitism, and disease.[56] Elements of this much more nuanced account were anticipated, if not clearly understood, as early as the 1890s, and in the 1920s, plans to address them comprised a sort of scientific to-do list. Thus, Buckell, now leading the BC investigation, reported to the Ontario Entomological Society in 1922 that insufficient data precluded any "definite statement" as to the effect of "natural control agencies, such as parasites and weather conditions, upon a locust outbreak under range conditions." Buckell assumed that weather conditions when the nymphs emerged from their eggs were the most important influence on survival in the short term. Birds also undoubtedly destroyed "large numbers." But the extent to which disease, parasites, and predation affected grasshopper populations still needed "further study."[57]

The list of unanswered questions about grasshopper population dynamics was long, and for various reasons most would remain unanswered. Ironically, one of the most important reasons was the research itself: widespread evidence of overgrazing and, more importantly, increasing indications that certain species of grasshopper – including those doing most of the "damage" in British Columbia – preferred closely cropped grasses to uncropped ones, tended to overwhelm other lines of inquiry and focus attention narrowly on the ecological effects of grazing. But so did funding problems. Money and personnel were constant problems in British Columbia, but the 1920s were especially difficult for entomological research because large-scale grasshopper irruptions also plagued the prairie provinces of Alberta and Saskatchewan during this decade. As Treherne explained to Thomas Mackenzie, it was impossible to direct more resources to British Columbia because there were larger insect problems on the prairies, where much of Canada's agriculture was concentrated."[58] Ultimately, the work was left for Buckell. It was a daunting task for one researcher to undertake, and ranchers complained vigorously about what they understood to be an unfair allocation of national agricultural resources. But such was the political economy of pest control in Canada by the early twentieth century. Privately, even Mackenzie conceded that prairie grasshopper problems were more important because of their far greater impact on the Canadian economy. Social factors strongly shaped the course of scientific research. Meanwhile, easy if not inaccurate connections between range degradation and grasshopper abundance tended to obviate a deeper scientific analysis.[59]

Framed largely as a consequence of unregulated grazing run amok, the grasshopper problem came to stand for much of what regulators considered wrong with the province's cattle industry by the early twentieth century. Disregarding wild horses and Aboriginal people altogether, Mackenzie stressed that the "destruction wrought to the ranges" was "due entirely" to poor land use on the part of ranchers, in particular their tendency to concentrate grazing in just a few favoured areas close to their ranches rather than spread their stock around. Low elevation forests, for example, were often excellent for grazing, yet ranchers rarely used them. "In the course of time they will probably realize this but it is a difficult matter to educate them," he wrote with considerable condescension, "and I feel that no opportunity should be lost to impress these facts upon them." Remarkably, there was no mention whatsoever of wild horses in this correspondence. According to Mackenzie, cattle were to blame. The province's ranchers had completely "lost sight of the fact that all the most important operations of their business take place on the open range and that these operations go on each year without any attention on their part."[60] The result was a much altered and degraded grassland environment and, apparently, widespread and increasingly severe grasshopper irruptions that further depleted the range. A story about unregulated grazing gone awry, however, would hold out hope of redemption in the form of conservation practices that would restore the grassland.[61]

Even though the best science available indicated that better land use would eventually solve the province's grasshopper problems, ultimately, ranchers and range managers opted for poison. They chose this strategy for several reasons, one of which was time. It would take decades to complete a close survey of provincial grazing resources and to acquire the expertise, experience, and empirical data necessary to calculate carrying capacities for each range. Poison was quicker. At the same time, changes in ranching economics in the 1910s and 1920s also favoured poison control. After the railway arrived, many ranchers enjoyed impressive profits as demand soared and prices for cattle hit record highs. But by the early 1920s, the boom was over and ranchers were caught in a cost-price squeeze stemming from declining beef prices and deteriorating environmental conditions – including grasshopper plagues – that further increased production costs.[62] A full economic history of ranching in British Columbia remains to be written, but financial records for the Douglas Lake Cattle Company underscore in many ways the severity of the situation and the changing ecological and economic context that ranchers and range managers confronted in the 1920s. Established in the early to mid-1880s when a handful of influential settlers, including Indian Reserve Commissioner Peter O'Reilly, banded together to control the sale of beef to railway construction crews, by the early twentieth century, the Douglas Lake Ranch was among the largest of its kind in the Canadian West. The scale of its operations was indeed impressive. The ranch itself was a massive block of about 150,000 acres of prime bunchgrass pasture, but it controlled hundreds of thousands of additional acres by way of leases and grazing permits (and practically by virtue of its large cattle herds). Like the Gang Ranch, its closest competitor, the Douglas Lake Ranch was a corporate operation. It had a manager; several working foremen; numerous cowboys; a support staff of cooks, blacksmiths, and sawmill operators for its onsite sawmill; and a small army of seasonal labourers, including Native men and boys from nearby Indian reserves. Beyond attending to the herds, the most crucial job on the ranch was planting and harvesting the hay needed to carry cattle and horses through the winter.[63]

In his book *Industrial Cowboys*, environmental historian David Igler shows how Miller & Lux, a large California-based cattle company, was able to guard against certain kinds of environmental problems and disturbances by engaging in what he calls "horizontal consolidation" of land and water resources. For large, vertically integrated ranching operations like Miller & Lux, he argues, "monopolizing land and water resources provided an insurance policy against the West's drought and flood cycles and its complex natural environment."[64] This was the Douglas Lake Cattle Company's strategy as well, and it usually enabled the ranch to absorb economic losses associated with fluctuating markets and changing environmental conditions. It even enabled the company to absorb adjacent ranches when these folded. Yet, in his April 1925 report to shareholders, ranch manager Frank Ward struggled to put a positive spin on the company's financial situation, lamenting at the outset that operations resulted in a net loss of $11,520.91. Prices were, in Ward's words, "the lowest on record," averaging $56.18 per head as compared with $113.79 per head just seven years earlier, in 1918. Moreover, and perhaps more importantly, the number of cattle available for sale had been simply "too small to realize a sum of money sufficient to cover the company's operating costs." Ward noted that this was because of a reduction of the herd in 1918, "which was done owing to the run-down condition of the range at that time," the combined result of drought, overgrazing, and grasshoppers.[65] The grasshoppers showed no signs of abatement, he reported, but experiments were being undertaken by the provincial government to exterminate the pest. Meanwhile, he would attempt to rebuild the herd to about 10,000 head. Doing so would enable a yearly brand of 2,400 to 2,500 animals, which, even at low prices would generate up to $60,000 in revenue for the company without any meaningful increase in operating costs. He could not declare a dividend, however, and he doubted very much whether the next year would be different, despite expectations of a small profit. Admittedly, Ward may have been duplicitously blaming nature for some of his own bad decisions, including the decision to increase the cattle herd when markets were strong, water was more plentiful, and range condition was better. As ranch manager he might have done more to guard against an economic downturn or an unfavourable change in the environment by keeping cattle numbers steady, or even reducing them somewhat (though this might have been hard to explain to shareholders). Nevertheless, his comments provide perspective on the changing context of ranching in the early 1920s. Reflecting on this context in a 1925 letter to the provincial Grazing Branch, the politically influential Nicola Stock Breeders' Association, of which Ward was a key member, urged the provincial government to provide relief: *We realize that range conservation is a means of controlling the grasshopper but with the scarcity of grass caused by this pest on all ranges, this work is practically impossible unless we greatly reduce our herds, which at present prices would spell ruin to the industry."*[66] Not surprisingly, in this context, sympathetic government officials were reluctant to impose new land-use practices. It was simpler, probably cheaper, and far more acceptable politically to kill insects.

Economic considerations and political expediency powerfully shaped British Columbia's approach to range and pest problems in the 1920s, but these were not the only factors that pushed the province toward poison control. The acute nature of grasshopper outbreaks also powerfully influenced policy. An account written by entomologist E.R. Buckell from the Nicola Valley suggested something of the scale and severity of grasshopper irruptions and why the federal and provincial governments ultimately embraced poison control as a solution. In the summer of 1922, Buckell reported that migrating swarms of grasshoppers were seen moving off the open range in "countless numbers." In many cases, "separate swarms covering an area of a quarter of a mile in width" were seen "crossing roads from 8 am until 6 pm for a week at a time." Even the flow of water across the landscape slowed as irrigation ditches piled up with dead and drowning bodies of grasshoppers too young to fly. "Their numbers were beyond estimation," the entomologist wrote with awe. The swarms resembled a "thick snowstorm," individual insects appearing as "minute shinning specks" against an otherwise bright blue sky.[67] The persistent spectre of such outbreaks and the periodic, often chaotic, arrival of grasshoppers tended to suggest short-term emergency measures. At one point, the Department of Agriculture even considered introducing thousands of turkeys, rushing them as needed from one part of the grassland to another, but apparently some politicians considered the plan too expensive. They also worried that "thousands of turkeys gobbling and trotting all over the country, blocking country roads as they moved from district to district, would prove a nuisance." If the plan seems laughable now, it also suggests the considerable uneasiness, even anxiety, that surrounded grasshopper problems in the late nineteenth and early twentieth centuries.[68] The spectre of a large-scale grasshopper outbreak was always on the horizon, leaving ranchers already worried about debt, range degradation, and other problems to wonder what the future held. In this fraught context, more benign approaches to insect control, such as range restoration and travelling turkey armies, failed before grasshopper outbreaks that impelled ranchers and land managers to pursue one set of emergency measures after another.

Meanwhile, life history and habitat studies undertaken in the early 1920s convinced entomologists that there were primary breeding areas in the grassland, essentially large egg-bed base camps from which outbreaks originated.[69] At this point, Buckell later recalled in a typically military turn of phrase, "the whole policy of attack on the problem changed" – another reminder that military metaphors powerfully shaped the science and practice of insect control during this period.[70] Entomologists could now – to push the military metaphor a little further – organize pre-emptive strikes, the purpose of which would be to pepper grasshopper egg beds with arsenic bait at hatching time. Initial experiments on egg beds proved promising, so range managers readied themselves and ranchers for a war with insects. According to grazing official W.H. Brown, "teams of men" had to be ready "at a moment's notice" to mix the various materials in their proper proportions and then spread the resulting bait on the egg beds.[71] Local newspapers also picked up on the rhetoric of war, if not always the actual plan of attack. "British Columbia will fire the opening gun of a war against grasshoppers and locusts this week," reported the *Victoria Daily Times* in 1924. "An invading army numbered in the billions will soon sweep down upon the Okanagan and other Interior districts eating every blade of grass and other vegetation as it goes." But ranchers and farmers were "preparing desperately to meet the threat" with "enormous quantities of poison," which were "to be strewn in the path of the insect hordes. In this way," the article concluded, "literally tons of them will be destroyed" before they reached the region's winter ranges and cultivated areas.[72]

Egg beds became the front line in British Columbia's battle with grasshoppers, but mobilizing a poison control campaign proved much more difficult than officials had expected. The first challenges were on the Indian reserves of the Nicola Valley. Provincial grazing officials had identified weedy, overgrazed Indian reserves as possible source areas for grasshopper outbreaks, and they pressed local Indian Agents to secure Native cooperation with poison control. As W.H. Brown put it, "I explained to [the local Indian Agent] the absolute necessity of cooperation with the Douglas Lake Indians and ... that this I thought could be accomplished because there was ample time before next spring to thoroughly canvass and explain to them that only with their cooperation could we possibly hope to finally exterminate the grasshopper and restore the depleted ranges to their 'old time' carrying capacity." But when Native people from the Nicola Valley refused to put poison on their reserves and blocked others from doing so, grazing officials realized that matters were more complicated than anticipated. As far as can be ascertained, members of the Douglas Lake Band were concerned about human illness and the loss of livestock, as well as rights of access to land. The Nlaka'pamux at Douglas Lake were in no mood to cooperate because the province's new range law prohibiting winter grazing by horses had just been announced. But apparently the arsenic issue ran deeper than this. As one account declared, a decade or so before the government's poisoning campaign was announced, an Indian Agent in the area put poison on the reserve but with "very poor results, as the death of a few chickens and cattle and sickness of the children caused the Indians to look with great disfavor on any more poisoned bait being placed upon their lands, so that the matter had to be dropped."[73]

The stiffest challenges, however, came from the ranchers. "We are doing all we can, including baiting," Buckell explained to Mackenzie in the summer of 1924, "but very little cooperation has been received from the ranchers themselves, each man appearing to think that the work should be taken over by the government[,] entirely losing sight of the fact that with its limited forces in the field, it can do little more than furnish the poison, and assist in every way to organize and advise the stockmen."[74] Perhaps some ranchers did want the government to do the work, but many self-styled smallholders countered by suggesting that if overgrazing was causing the grasshopper outbreaks, the burden of control ought to be on those whose animals had done the damage, namely the large corporate and family-run ranches who controlled the range. As we will see in the next chapter, this critique meshed neatly not only with existing entomological science but also with pre-existing community fault lines in the Nicola Valley, where Frank Ward and Lawrence Guichon were among the most powerful ranchers. Smallholders had for decades disputed access to winter pasture and water rights in the valley. The war on grasshoppers had folded into a longer, class-based confrontation over who controlled resources. The next chapter traces the roots of this conflict to the earliest days of resettlement.

6

Resisting Range Monopoly

As environmental conflicts often do, the Nicola Valley dispute drew heavily from its own history. Already in 1886, just one year after the Douglas Lake Cattle Company was incorporated, the region's smaller ranchers protested the company's seemingly insatiable appetite for rangeland. In just a few short years its owners had amassed more than thirty-five square miles of prime bunchgrass range, with plenty of water and winter pasture, and the valley rumour mill suggested that they were about to acquire more. Rather than wait for this to happen, in May 1887, the smaller ranchers resorted to the law to protect their interests. Fifty-three locals petitioned the provincial government to set aside a twenty-five-square-mile block of bunchgrass range as commonage under the 1878 Stock Ranges Act. The government granted this request, creating the Lundbom Commonage, and by 1889 a second commonage of similar size, the Hamilton Commonage, had been established as well. Still concerned about the concentration of range resources in the region, ranchers successfully petitioned for a third commonage to be known as the Meadow Marsh Commonage, comprising some twenty-nine square miles of bunchgrass between Douglas and Chapperon Lakes. These were victories but, ultimately, grazing reserves did little to ease tensions because, under provincial land law, commonages were inalienable but also not off limits to any rancher. Although a board of overseers was elected to manage the land, as allowed by law since 1879, Douglas Lake cattle, as well as cattle from the Guichon Ranch, another large ranch in the area, ranged more or less at will across the regional commons.

Nor did the Douglas Lake Ranch quit acquiring water and land in the area. By the early twentieth century, many of the best open ranges had already been fenced, but the company still found ways to expand the scale of its operations. In addition to absorbing small adjacent ranch properties whenever they came up for sale, which was the ranch's official policy by the early twentieth century, it even managed to acquire 10,000 acres of land when the province opened the Marsh Meadow Commonage to purchase and pre-emption in 1890. Under provincial land law, individual settlers were entitled to one 320-acre land title per application, but like many other cattle companies in the North American West, the Douglas Lake Cattle Company discovered a legal, albeit underhanded, way around this problem. Ranch historian Nina Wooliams notes, "By enrolling individuals to sign as preemptors, and so avoiding the technicality of being limited to preempting only one title at a time, J.B. Greaves [one of the ranch's owners] copied a technique which many cattle and land companies had used." Many ranchers in the valley protested this move, but apparently the province "turned a blind eye to this abuse" of the law by the cattle company.[1] Nor was the cattle company the least bit discouraged from attempting similarly controversial land purchases in the future. Early in 1903, it offered to purchase the 16,000-acre Hamilton Commonage from the provincial government for $2.50 an acre, as did one of its competitors, the BC Cattle Company. In this case, the government balked. The reasons are unclear, but selling commonage could be disastrous from a political perspective. Discouraged by this decision, but determined to acquire land, the owners of the Douglas Lake Ranch still found ways to expand the scale of their operations. During the Boer War, the BC government passed the South African War Land Grant Act entitling "any Canadian who had been on active service in that war to a land grant of 160 acres." But according to Wooliams, "many young soldiers had no wish to go on the land, and eagerly accepted offers from [$]1.00 to [$]2.25 per acre for their negotiable scrip." These purchases alone added nearly 8,000 acres.[2] Less than two decades after incorporation in 1886, the owners of the Douglas Lake Ranch had amassed some 85,000 acres and, by 1915, the total had increased to 125,000 acres, making it the largest private landholding in the province and one of the largest ranches in the West. But this was only a partial accounting of the ranch's massive landholdings, because like the Gang Ranch and other large cattle operations it also controlled hundreds of thousands of additional acres of Crown range. Much to the chagrin of small-scale ranchers, in 1900 the Douglas Lake Ranch also raised some 10,000 head of cattle and horses. A few other large ranchers, including the Guichons, whose considerable land holdings (in 1920, fully 40,000 acres plus leases and grazing permits on half a million acres of Crown land) were also a source of tension, had large cattle herds as well.

Most ranches were small by comparison and relied almost exclusively on family labour, as noted above, and on more marginal landholdings to produce a commodity for market. A typical smallholder ranchstead in the late nineteenth and early twentieth century "might comprise several small log buildings – house, root cellar, hay shed and barn (for calves, a few horses, a milk cow or two and chickens) – and simple corrals located at the edge of a small, natural hay meadow or amid a few acres cleared for hay fields."[3] Not much is known about the year-to-year operation of these small ranches because generally they left few or no records. The largest smallholder in the Aspen Grove area in 1914 was probably Richard Guildford, with 2,300 acres (including alienated land and land used under a grazing permit) and 109 head of cattle; the smallest was likely Art Roberts, with 160 acres and 22 head of cattle. So, clearly, the province's "smallholders" were a somewhat more diverse economic group than their name implied. A partial list of grazing fees owed by Nicola Valley ranchers in one year for which there are records (ca. 1920) provides additional perspective on the disparities between big and small ranches in the region (see Appendix 2), as well as on some of the economic differences among so-called smallholders.[4]

By the early twentieth century, not just small-scale ranchers and mixed farmers but also a few within government had begun to look somewhat askance at the Douglas Lake Cattle Company and other large cattle operations because their massive accumulation of land and water resources challenged an idealized, even romantic, vision of agriculture in which numerous smallholder ranches and mixed farms spread across a quaint, albeit economically productive, pastoral landscape. The author of a 1913 report nicely encapsulated the cultural importance placed on agriculture when he remarked that small-scale ranching and farming would cultivate in British Columbia "the very best kind of population."[5] The roots of these visions ran to the earliest days of European resettlement and reflected the cultural preoccupations of an industrializing, staples-oriented society still committed to the social and moral virtues of agrarian life.[6] But this emphasis on preserving smallholdings in the face of range concentration was very much a modern problem. To understand this problem, we need to resituate the rise of ranching in the larger story of resettlement.

It was axiomatic among colonial theorists, and even among settlers and colonial authorities in British Columbia when their coffers were full of mining taxes from the gold rush and other staples exports such as timber, that agriculture was the proper basis of wealth and social order. But in colonial settings especially, it was much more than this. Land remade in the image of agriculture, land "improved" or "reclaimed" from what the British political and property theorist John Locke (among others) called the "state of nature" was land relocated squarely within the sphere "civilization."[7] It was equally assumed that Native people were uncivilized precisely because they did not practise agriculture.[8] From this it followed that Native people were an anachronism that had to be removed (as well as reformed) lest they impede the upward path of European progress and improvement.[9] In these ways, as Cole Harris and David Demeritt have argued, agriculture in early modern British Columbia, as elsewhere in the age of European imperial expansion, was "a complex social and ecological introduction with subtexts tied to colonialism and the creation of an immigrant society."[10]

The manner in which the first colonists wrote about the grassland environment revealed traces of these subtexts, as well as of the way in which newcomers to the drylands adapted older agrarian values and expectations to fit an ecologically unfamiliar environment. An 1860 description by James Douglas observed that the "hillsides were mostly covered with trees formed into groups, or growing with park-like regularity, widely apart, and free from brush or underwood. The peculiar feature of the country," he continued, "is the profusion of grass that covers both woodlands and meadow, affording rich pastures for domestic animals, a circumstance which gives to this district an extraordinary value, as every part of the surface, whether hill or valley, may be turned to account and made available either for tillage or stock farming."[11] Likewise, in 1872, George Grant, secretary to Sanford Fleming's survey of Canada for the Canadian Pacific Railway, wrote of the country around Fort Kamloops that "the only timber in the district is a knotty red pine, and as the trees grow widely apart, and the bunchgrass underneath is clean, unmixed with weeds and shrubs, and uniform in colour, the country has a well-kept park-like appearance."[12]

Douglas and Fleming were not alone in describing the drylands they encountered this way. Around the world in the age British imperial expansion, colonial administrators, surveyors, and naturalists often observed that open, park-like landscapes seemed particularly well suited, even naturally adapted, to British agricultural settlement. In doing so they not only invoked the picturesque parklands of Britain, thus making distant landscapes seem familiar to a distant imperial audience, but also adapted them culturally and ecologically to fit new environmental circumstances. Generally, "parkland" referred to fairly open landscapes with trees dotted about – a sort of Capability Brown, English-landscape park idea, but without the necessary oaks and English meadow grasses. In colonial settings, however, such landscapes took on multiple and sometimes contradictory ecological meanings as settlers encountered quite different kinds of ecologies: savannah with thorn trees in South Africa; the eucalypt open woodlands or tropical savannah of Australia; and the aspens and open grasslands of the Canadian prairie. Settlers like Douglas also adapted the parkland aesthetic socially, essentially stripping it of some its elitism in order to accommodate the general project of settlement and agricultural development of newly colonized lands. As Simon Ryan writes of British parkland aesthetics in the settler colonies of Australia, "Whereas in Britain the parklands often were purely for pleasure – an ostentatious display of surplus wealth – in Australia, the functions of pleasure and production are seen to be combined."[13] So too in early British Columbia parkland aesthetics were combined in various ways with the practical challenges of settlement and agricultural production to produce a hybrid cultural landscape. Parkland imagery, while accommodating quite different ecologies, could be adapted socially and culturally to meet the practical economic needs of a nascent settler society at the far edge of empire: in early British Columbia, as elsewhere in the age of European imperial expansion, parklands could be places of respite as well as places of work.

Ideas linking a broadly British parkland aesthetic to pragmatic plans for agricultural production and the more general project of (re)settlement were particularly potent in the grasslands of colonial British Columbia, where the land itself seemed to suggest the presence of an English peasantry. As Matthew Begbie, British Columbia's first judge, wrote imaginatively, and somewhat misleadingly, of the grassland environment in the summer of 1860:

> The face of the country is not unlike the Downs near Brighton with rich bunchgrass however and dotted with timber and occasionally higher hills and woods ... Throughout this country in its width and breadth there is scarcely a tree or an herb identical with that on the West of the Cascades. It may be said there is but one tree, the Columbia Pine; but one herb, the bunchgrass. On the banks of streams and lakes, there are cottonwoods, willows and alders. There are mountains too but the bunch grass grows everywhere with a universality and an exclusiveness that is quite surprising. The beauty and cultivated aspect of many parts of this country, which have

the appearance of being tended with as much care and taste and labour as any part of Kent or Surrey is scarcely to be believed ... I could not believe that instead of snug farmhouses and cottages with a numerous peasantry there was probably not a human being of any description within many days' journey of the delightful grass field where I was lying down from which I could scarcely turn away. But in all the country, larger I suppose than the length and breadth of England, there are no magistrates, no laws, and no surveys will be there for years.[14]

Begbie's "landscape" can be interpreted many ways. As visual ideology, it assumed production for the market and bore the class-based assumptions of elite British colonists; as a way of seeing, it anticipated the arrival of European science and standards of law; and as an act of colonial erasure, it assumed that North America was *terra nullius* when Europeans arrived.[15] Begbie's landscape was a "text" like any other: built on assumption, layered with meaning, and marked by culture.[16] But there is more than this embedded in his observations. Read ecologically – also a cultured "way of seeing" – Begbie's account suggests, albeit faintly, elements of a material landscape shaped not just by the labour of Native people, whose presence Begbie ignored, but by the labour of nonhuman nature as well. His pastoral vision hinged on the presence of extensive bunchgrasses born of semiaridity and encouraged by periodic burns of natural and cultural origin.[17] Cottonwoods, willows, and alders bounded the wetter, infrequently burned areas around lakes, rivers, and creeks; ponderosa pine defined the bordering forested uplands. Admittedly, the area's ecological history was much more complicated: obviously, there was more than one type of tree and more than one type of grass in the drylands. Yet, even a quick and partial sketch of this history serves to underscore the ways in which Begbie was unintentionally correct when he described some parts of the Interior country as being "tended with as much care and taste and labour as any part of Kent or Surrey." Stretched out over many centuries, Aboriginal burning practices and nonhuman natural processes had produced Begbie's pastoral landscape as a dynamic, park-like environment. If the Interior country appeared to Begbie to be partly cultivated, it was because in a sense it had been.[18]

Be that as it may, Begbie's imagined agricultural geography never developed to the extent that he and later officials had hoped. Partly this was because most of the province's arable land was limited to the lower Fraser Valley, which left the Interior to cattle ranches adapted to the challenges of semiaridity. Lax land laws made it exceedingly easy for men with capital to acquire huge tracts of land. But changes in transportation and markets also mattered. "Ironically," writes historian Alan Seager, "when the transcontinental railway arrived, it checked the growth of the cattle kingdom." BC ranches in the 1890s now competed not only with cheaper beef from Alberta but also with that from the United States. In this context, "the significant enterprises that persisted tended toward even larger units of production, [which] picked up the holdings of their weaker competitors."[19]

The railway itself was a powerful force for consolidation in the grasslands. Canadian Pacific Railway (CPR) construction camps created an instant market for cattle, but the lasting effect of the railway was to encourage expansion and consolidation in the cattle economy by creating better and faster connections between rural producers and urban consumers. The CPR was already heavily investing in the transportation of live cattle. According to economic geographer Ian MacLachlan, "The CPR made such a large investment in rolling stock for cattle that they balked at the refrigerated shipment of carcasses in reefer cars for many years."[20] The post-railway period was thus one of rapid expansion in British Columbia's cattle economy as ranchers and investors set out to capitalize on the "time-space compressions" and new marketing opportunities created by the railway.[21] A few numbers help to tell this story. In 1876, one estimate put the number of "horned cattle" in the entire grassland at 35,000, but a decade later, there were more than 30,000 head of cattle in the Thompson-Nicola District alone, a third of which were controlled by just one or two ranches.[22] By 1893, some 70,000 cattle were in the grasslands, and by 1897, the herd had increased to at least 109,000 head.[23]

Expansion and consolidation in the cattle economy involved more than simply adding cattle to the range, however. It also involved adding the right kind of cattle, and this required capital. Geographer Terry Jordan notes that the cattle that came to British Columbia with the gold rush were probably predominantly California longhorns, although midwestern shorthorns from Oregon must have been in the mix as well.[24] But by the 1880s, BC ranchers began introducing Herefords (of eastern and midwestern origin) and Hereford-shorthorn crosses because they calved easier, fattened better on bunchgrass, and were better able than other breeds to withstand long, cold winters. Ranchers with capital especially valued Herefords because they matured faster than other breeds, allowing for quicker turnover in cattle herds and faster profits for ranchers. Improved breeds of cattle of eastern and midwestern origin thus played a crucial role in the late-nineteenth-century modernization of western North American ranching economies.

Expansion and consolidation in the cattle industry was also made possible by basic changes in economic organization. Before the railway arrived, there were few large ranches in the grasslands. Many raised fewer than 250 head of cattle, and all of these small ranches relied on family labour to do so. A typical small ranch included a house, barn, fenced winter rangeland, and several small corrals. A number of these ranches would persist (albeit not entirely unchanged) into the twentieth century. However, after the railway arrived, ranching also corporatized and industrialized: the massive Douglas Lake Cattle Company was incorporated by BC investors in 1886; the equally enormous Gang Ranch was incorporated by a London, England–based investment agency in 1892; and the BC Cattle Company was incorporated in 1900. Unlike most ranches in British Columbia, corporate ranches relied on wage labour. The Gang Ranch was also vertically integrated: in addition to large rural ranch properties, it owned butcher shops in Vancouver and Victoria and eventually a rendering plant that turned animal by-products into fertilizer. Collectively, these corporate ranches controlled the beef trade.

If expansion and consolidation in the cattle industry involved important changes in economic organization, they also rested on a fundamental reorganization of the environment. Ironically, the very natural factors that made lowlands good winter range, especially low annual snowfall, also made the grazing capacities of these areas relatively low compared with grasslands at higher elevations, where precipitation was greater but where harsher winter conditions precluded ranchers from using these areas as winter range. Initially, ranchers responded to this problem by trying to limit, as best they could based on conditions, the amount of time their cattle grazed on lower grasslands. Increasingly, however, they addressed the low carrying capacity of winter range by shifting water from the uplands. Sometimes they redirected old gold miners' ditches, but more often they dug new ditches and embraced simple irrigation technology. The large corporate ranches used Chinese labour to construct these works. In one case during 1891 and 1892, as many as forty Chinese irrigators lived around the edges of the Gang Ranch, digging ditches for a dollar a day.[25] One former ranch manager supposed that this is how the ranch got its name, "because there was such a gang of Chinese labourers up here digging the irrigation ditches."[26] The result, by 1900, was about 800 acres of irrigated lowland, mostly sown with alfalfa and a little timothy.[27] Most irrigation works were relatively small, involving family labour and often much less than a hundred acres. But all helped to remake lowlands in ways that increased the productivity of ranches. In the short term, irrigation insured ranchers against the vagaries of weather. If a winter was hard or long, or if local bunchgrass ranges crusted over with ice and snow, ranchers could feed their animals until conditions improved. In the long term, irrigation enabled ranches to keep larger herds during the winter months, and this, along with the railway, was key to meeting the rising demand for beef in the province's rapidly urbanizing lower mainland.[28]

Rather than give rise to Begbie's numerous rural "peasantry," the grasslands were dominated first by cattle barons and then by a few large family- and corporate-owned cattle ranches. By the 1890s, Okanagan Valley rancher Thomas Ellis alone had amassed over 30,000 acres; the Western Canadian Ranching Company, owners of the Gang Ranch on the middle Fraser and Chilcotin Rivers, had over 50,000 acres. A few other large ranches – including the Douglas Lake Ranch, Alkali Lake Ranch, Empire Valley Ranch, Guichon Ranch, and the BC Cattle Company Ranch – controlled large parts of the remainder. Unlike the majority of ranches in the province, the corporate ranches that dominated the cattle industry by the late nineteenth century employed boards of directors, business consultants, accountants, wage labourers, and professional ranch managers whose job was to manage people, land, and cattle in order to minimize costs, maximize profits, and pay out dividends to distant shareholders. These were not the rustic family farmhouses that colonial officials envisioned in the early 1860s. Nor were they industrial ranches in the modern sense of "factory farms." They did rely on wage labour, however, as well as on urban finance capital, extensive irrigation works, comparatively large cattle herds, and massive landholdings to produce a commodity for market. It was this decidedly lopsided distribution of cattle and range among newcomers, and the way it conflicted with deeply held agrarian ideals, that concerned so many settlers and eventually led to political action that had as its goal the development of an alternative agricultural modernity based on small-scale commodity producers. Ultimately, there was little or nothing in nineteenth-century range law that smallholders or sympathetic government officials could use to combat corporate concentration of range resources. Commonage could not be purchased or pre-empted, but nor could any particular rancher be excluded from these spaces; ranches with large herds could still dominate land use there. By the early twentieth century, however, antimonopoly, and even anticorporate, sentiment extended to the offices of government, where, eventually, it informed plans for land reform.

According to government official R.R. Benedict, provincial land policy, historically based on a mix of pre-emptions, purchases, and leases, was largely to blame for the monopolization of range resources by a few large corporate and family-run ranches. These policies had the considerable disadvantage, he rightly argued in a 1911 report on grazing rights, "of making it possible for the individual to acquire large tracts of land and consequently to monopolize the resources of the province." This had already happened in the Nicola Valley and Chilcotin District "in the cases of the Douglas Lake Cattle Co., and the Guichons in the former, and the Gang Ranch in the latter." Indeed, in Benedict's view, the Douglas Lake Cattle Company offered a prime example of the "injurious" effects of large landholdings on community development. Whether he thought private ranch properties should (or could) be expropriated by the provincial state and then redistributed to smallholders is unclear. Probably he did not. He did note, though, that if the Douglas Lake Cattle Ranch, which by the early 1910s supported some 12,000 head of cattle, were to be divided up it would support as many as "60 stockmen with 200 cattle each."[29]

Benedict's position was praiseworthy in some respects, but the arithmetic was nevertheless full of practical problems. Resources at Douglas Lake were widely dispersed, so the company's 10,000 head of cattle were constantly on the move. Open grasslands at lower elevations provided winter, spring, and fall range, but cattle spent the summer grazing (and getting lost) in forested uplands, where a mix of forbs and grasses grew in the understory of relatively open stands of ponderosa pine and Douglas fir. All this movement required considerable infrastructure and labour. In 1911, the home ranch comprised as many as thirty-five buildings, including two large barns with haylofts, a piggery, a company store, homes for company foremen and their families, bunkhouses for cowboys and seasonal hands, and a sawmill. There were also separate, fenced pastures for beef steers, breeding stock, and sick animals. A vast network of dams, canals, and ditches channelled water to the company's extensive alfalfa fields. Perhaps ninety people worked on the ranch year round. Many more were hired during the all-important haying season. Animal labour was also critical, and included as many as four hundred riding horses and an unknown number of heavy horses for hauling plows and hay cutters. In short, the Douglas Lake Ranch had an ecology and corresponding economic geography of production that did not divide neatly into sixty separate ranches (Figures 6.1–6.3).[30] Benedict was basically correct, however, when he complained that agricultural lands were "not being placed under cultivation, population was at a standstill and schools were lacking." He continued, "all evidence of what is understood to be a normal farming community" was wanting. "The wealth and the social life of the [Nicola] district" were severely restricted by range monopoly, and much the same,

FIGURE 6.1   Gang Ranch, winter hay. *Courtesy of BC Archives, f_01092*

FIGURE 6.2   Gang Ranch. *Courtesy of BC Archives, f_01087*

FIGURE 6.3   Gang Ranch. *Courtesy of BC Archives, i_22381*

he suggested, was "bound to occur in the Chilcotin if the Gang Ranch is allowed to increase their holdings of the bunchgrass range and hay producing lands."[31]

Others in government shared Benedict's vision of diversified agricultural development in the grasslands and made efforts to express it in policy, including the province's minister of lands, William Ross. In his annual report for 1912, Ross noted that the province's first priority was "to render [the rangelands of the province] available to the settler who is without capital to buy large tracts of land outright." To that end, a permit system was to be instituted whereby ranchers paid per head of cattle rather than per acre of land. "By this system," Ross said, "the rancher is able to start his business with a minimum of capital, while the government receives a fair revenue, and by limiting the number of stock grazed to the actual carrying capacity of the land," estimated to be one million cattle or five million sheep, the province would save land "from the serious and lasting results of overgrazing."[32] From the perspective of prospective settlers and government authorities concerned with the broader project of colonization, this was a marked improvement over previous, classical liberal approaches to allocating rangeland. As one government paper promoting the minister's "new and progressive policy of grazing" rightly explained, the old order had tended very strongly toward "range monopoly" and social stagnation.[33]

Ross was at heart a moralist. Among other things, he ignored the economics of ranching and the way in which market pressures, environmental factors, and the railway, in addition to lax colonial land laws, had encouraged range concentration in British Columbia. He also obviously knew very little about ranching or the carrying capacity of rangelands. Evidence of overgrazing was already apparent and widely acknowledged in the Interior, so some ranchers and grazing officials were less sanguine about the prospect of expansion. The idea that the cattle herd could be doubled to about 240,000 head – let alone increased eightfold to one million head – left many people unconvinced, even with the implementation of judicious grazing practices and extensive use of forested uplands for summer grazing. Ross also misunderstood the nature of range science. It would take years or decades to acquire the expertise and experience needed to estimate the carrying capacities of the province's grasslands, which were not only ecologically complex (in ways that are poorly understood even today, after decades of observation) but also spatially extensive, particularly when forested lands were included. Moreover, ranchers required more than cheap, ecologically undifferentiated acreage to raise livestock. What they needed were the same natural resources Aboriginal people needed: lowlands that could be used as winter range, and water that could be used to irrigate hay crops. But the best winter ranges and water resources were already alienated when Ross instituted his policy. Ranchers and mixed farmers also needed common lands that could be used as spring and fall range, but barring changes to the province's commonage legislation, the largest ranches – Douglas Lake Cattle Company, Western Canadian Ranching Company, BC Cattle Company – would continue to dominate grazing in these areas simply because of their much larger cattle herds.

The Big Bar range, on the middle Fraser River, was a case in point. In 1914, according to Owen Sanger of the provincial Forest Branch, there were just over 2,800 head of cattle there, nearly 60 percent of which were owned by just two corporate ranches: the Gang Ranch had roughly 700 head; the BC Cattle Company had around 1,000 head; and the Alkali Lake Ranch (another large corporate operation) had 350 head. The rest were variously distributed among several much smaller ranchers: the Hance brothers at Big Bar had 75 head (horses); Charlie Wilson from Crow's Bar had 45 head (horses); William Grinder of Big Bar had 200 head (cattle); Charles Costering of Big Bar had 325 head (cattle); and an unknown number of settlers from Big Bar Creek had 100 to 200 head (cattle and horses). Sanger observed that the range in many places was "badly over-grazed and carrying a much larger number of cattle than it presently should." This was, he said, because cattle and horses were kept on the range for pretty much the entire year: cattle from about March until November, and horses all year long. The smaller ranchers around Big Bar proposed to establish a common there and manage it collectively by removing cattle for up to five months each year in order to give the grasses a chance to grow again. Sanger estimated that doing so would double the carrying capacity of the range, although admittedly it was difficult to determine stocking rates in the abstract. Nevertheless, it was "evident" to Sanger that if the lands were not set aside as commonage, "in a very short time the more powerful stockmen will control all of the good range and watering places and the smaller stockmen and new comers will be entirely without range for their stock, which means that they will have to abandon their preemptions or other lands."[34] The old legal problem was that land set aside as commonage, though technically manageable collectively under the 1876 and 1879 Stock Ranges legislation, was only inalienable and not off limits to any individual rancher. In Sanger's view, the outdated commonage law needed to be amended to allow for greater local control.[35]

Drawing from these perspectives, a 1915 report by government official Percy Lemare argued that corporate concentration of resources along the middle Fraser and Chilcotin Rivers was a detriment to good range management in the area and, moreover, also basically undemocratic. According to Lemare, all ranchers were engaged in an open range system of land use involving the seasonal movement of cattle between fenced winter lowlands, which the ranchers owned outright, and open or Crown ranges at higher elevation, which the cattle grazed in common at no cost. Contrary to later assessments, however, the range during this period was not entirely unregulated. In some cases, a rancher had a "superior right" to certain ranges because it was customary for him to put cattle there. In other cases, ranchers set spring turnout times for cattle and sought to balance stocking rates and grazing capacity against the grazing needs of individual ranches.

Even breeding was somewhat regulated, as some ranchers tried to manage the number and quality of bulls turned onto the open range. In short, said Lemare, "There had grown up a system, very imperfect to be sure, of range rights and control." The qualification was important. It never occurred to Lemare (or anybody else for that matter) that Native people had been unfairly excluded from these arrangements, or that informal regulation by ranchers ultimately rested on and was made possible by dispossession. But he did believe that, overall, the regulatory landscape was uneven, and that this in turn had important implications for range use. Rules that applied to one range did not necessarily apply to another, he noted, or even to the same range in a different year. The result was a hodgepodge of common grazing regimes, some of which were well organized, and others that were not. It was also true that many ranges, including some of the informally managed ones that Lemare generally held up as exemplars of smallholder cooperation, had been heavily overgrazed. However, the bigger problem, in his view, was that the largest ranches in an area – the Gang Ranch, Empire Valley Ranch, and BC Cattle Company – determined decisions about range use simply by virtue of their far larger cattle herds. In these cases, Lemare observed, a few large ranches effectively, and to his mind unfairly – even undemocratically – got to decide whose cattle grazed where, when, on what, and to what extent. It also forced some smallholders to graze lands they might otherwise avoid. Therefore, the province's land laws, particularly its badly outdated commonage law, should be reformed to allow for more democratic forms of range allocation and thus more sustainable resource use (to borrow a modern phrase). Indeed, "if no attempt is made to divide the range between the users, and the land is merely opened to lease or purchase, the more progressive and wealthier stockmen would be able to secure all the range and this would drive out the weaker man." The only alternative, Lemare continued, was to "legalize present customs and practices" that favoured smallholders.[36] Government officials trained in plant ecology could offer scientific advice about range use, and perhaps help to resolve disputes. But land use would largely be determined locally and democratically by way of voting. Exactly where and how Native stock raisers, who also needed range, fit into this arrangement is unclear. Probably they did not.

Smallholders in the Nicola Valley area also returned to the principle of commonage, but with an important legal twist. Early in 1914, thirty-five ranchers from Aspen Grove, some twenty miles southwest of the Douglas Lake Ranch, appealed to the government with a list of grievances against Ward and Guichon, who, the petitioners said, "habitually" drove thousands of head of cattle onto crown ranges to which the large ranchers had no right. On these unfenced ranges there was "hardly a blade of grass to be seen." But even fences were "no protection" against the cattle from the large ranches. In several cases, the petitioners complained, "our hay stacks have been eaten and we can ill afford to lose any hay on account of our long winter."[37] Another problem was that Ward's cattle (allegedly) introduced blackleg, a debilitating and usually fatal livestock disease, into local cattle herds. (For his part, Ward insisted that the infected animals had been imported from Alberta and that his animals were disease-free.) The principle of commonage provided only a partial answer to these problems, however, because although commonage was inalienable, it could not be withdrawn from any particular cattle rancher. In this context, the only way to prevent Ward and Guichon from encroaching on local rangelands (and possibly spreading blackleg) was to create what the smallholders called community pastures (basically, commonages), from which Ward's and Guichon's cattle would be legally – and with proper fencing, physically – excluded.

Another smallholder plan proposed to exclude large landholders from the Hamilton and Lundbom Commonages (created in the 1870s) by granting twenty-one-year leases to small-scale stock raisers. Significantly, a portion of the range would be set apart for sheep, which had been excluded from the range by legislation dating back to the late 1870s. But sheep were also cheaper than cattle and thus more accessible to smallholders with little in the way of working capital. The next step was to divide the range on the basis of how many cattle or sheep a rancher had, but clearly the classification system itself reflected smallholder social values: Class A ranchers having fewer than 100 head would have their range allotment made first, followed by Class B ranchers with 100 to 500 head. Any range leftover at this point would be allocated to Class C ranchers, the large family-owned and corporate operations with more than 500 head, in order to raise the stocking rate to the "carrying capacity" of the commons as determined by a local management board working in concert with grazing officials from the Forest Branch.[38] Obviously, this proposal strongly favoured smallholders. Moreover, any additional regulations would be determined locally and "democratically" by voting at the local livestock association. The largest ranchers were politically influential to be sure, but they were also relatively few in number, so it stood to reason that elections on land use were the way to go.

Smallholders tabled several more commonage proposals in the 1910s and early 1920s, but the so-called large men had their own ideas about how to protect and develop the range. In the 1910s, Frank Ward and few other large-holders recommended that long-term (twenty-one-year) pastoral leases be reintroduced throughout the grassland in order to encourage investments in range improvement and to prevent Crown ranges from being overgrazed. One proposal, presented to the provincial government in 1914, was that long-term grazing leases be based on the number of cattle a ranch had on hand or was in a position to acquire; significantly, sheep would be excluded on the grounds that they were "ruinous" to range quality. Here too the class biases of the proposal were obvious because, under this arrangement, ranches with large numbers of cattle (or the capital needed to acquire them) would be eligible for potentially enormous long-term leases, whereas ranches with few cattle or that lacked the capital to buy more would be eligible for small ones only.

Rather than open the range to lease or purchase, according to one self-styled smallholder, the provincial government should instead create commonages and community pastures. Long-term leasing would be good only for men like Ward and Guichon, he observed, because both men had the cattle and the capital needed to acquire large tracts of land. But allowing them to do so would squeeze out the smallholder. "Big men will lease up all the land leaving none for others," he wrote in 1914. "I know from experience that as soon as the big men get a lease of certain ranges they employ riders to chase off all stray cattle and if a smaller man happens to have a few head that get on a leased range they will find that their poor cattle will be driven from the Rockies to the Himalayas – I have seen this happen when the Dominion Government leased their winter ranges."[39] In the early 1880s, in an effort to control common grazing lands, the Dominion government introduced legislation enabling ranchers with capital to acquire massive, 100,000-acre lots on twenty-one-year leases, leaving smallholders with inadequate resources.

Grazing Commissioner Mackenzie used these disputes to illustrate the wider problem of range concentration in a few large settler ranches. In many places large herds of cattle like those owned by the Douglas Lake Cattle company roamed at will on spring and summer rangelands, leaving little forage for livestock owned by smallholders. The cattle were then herded onto large fall and winter pastures that were fenced. The unfortunate result was that the "small settler, who should have range protected alongside of his ranch," was forced to use up his hay supply earlier than would be the case if he had sufficient spring/fall range (very often the same areas were used for both seasons) and natural winter range.[40] Still, there needed to be a balance: "The plan the settlers wish this office to carry out would give everything to them but would give no consideration to the rights of the Ward and Guichon interests."[41] The settlers claimed that Ward and Guichon had "no right" to graze cattle around Aspen Grove but in fact they had permits and leases to about 40,000 acres.[42] Perhaps not surprisingly, it never occurred to Mackenzie, or to anybody else involved in these discussions, that Native stock raisers living on tiny, resource-poor Indian reserves might have rights to land as well.

Leases and customary use rights were important but probably not entirely determinative when it came to evaluating proposals for community pasture. The deeper issue was that Mackenzie doubted the very principle of common grazing. By the early 1920s, both commonages in the Nicola Valley area were in bad ecological condition. Weeds were prevalent in many areas, soils were eroded in others, and the range was generally overgrazed. According to UBC botanist Andrew Hutchinson, whom Mackenzie had commissioned to do a study of range types and conditions in the province, both commonages were also badly infested with grasshoppers. In the summer of 1926, he noted, the insects were quickly "spreading to other properties."[43] In Hutchinson's view, however, the commonage problem was as much political as ecological. The present commonage law was "simply unworkable," he argued in a letter to Mackenzie, because it required a general election in the area before any actions could be taken to improve land use. Usually this meant long periods when there was little or no management in these areas. The commonage law, therefore, "should be simplified to place the management of each common in the hands of the actual users under government supervision and to facilitate the appointment of a local board of overseers."[44]

Although this was a praiseworthy plan in many respects, Mackenzie had his own ideas. Rather than open the commonages to purchase or lease, or amend the commonage law in order to enhance local management of resources, Mackenzie decided to demonstrate instead the benefits of government range management. Beginning in 1920, Nicola Valley commonages would be regulated by the state. Mackenzie even ordered the construction of a mock commonage landscape showing proper land management that could be shown at agricultural fairs and meetings with livestock associations. Built by Mackenzie's assistant, W.H. Brown, the 4-by-4 painted plywood and plastic landscape depicted the seasonal distribution of cattle on the Lundbom and Hamilton Commonages, as well as their annual movements under scientific management. Rather than serve as a symbol of smallholder cooperation, the province's commonages would be used to illustrate the ills of unregulated land use and the advantages of state management. Thus, Mackenzie rejected the smallholder request for community pasture. Instead, he ordered that several fences and cattle gates be built in the area to keep Douglas Lake and Guichon cattle off Crown range allocated to other ranchers. But the barriers did little to resolve the situation. As small-scale rancher Richard Guildford complained, "Ward's cattle are in there by the hundreds and have it eaten off ... We think it is not right to pay the government for range only to have his cattle eat it off."[45] At this point, and several times later, the smallholders simply stopped paying their grazing fees.

When small-scale ranchers balked at grazing fees or poison control campaigns, scientists accused them of being irresponsible and unprogressive. The entomologist E.R. Buckell, among many others in the government, was certain that if the smallholders had done "their fair share" in terms of identifying egg beds and distributing the poison, the infestations of the mid- to late 1920s almost certainly could have been controlled.[46] Grazing Branch officials held similar views. Even Thomas Mackenzie, who earlier defended smallholders' rights to rangeland, complained that the grasshopper "emergency" in the summer of 1925 developed "when it became apparent that Ward and Guichon could not control the main infestation and the flights were getting away from the territory tributary to their mixing stations." Mackenzie believed that this "emergency" arose because smallholders in the area "neglected to render assistance at the time the hoppers were hatching."[47] For the smallholders, however, insects were in the long term less important than equity and responsibility in the use of range resources. At the same time, it never occurred to these ranchers that there was anything inequitable about the distribution of land and resources between Natives and newcomers or about the dispossession this entailed.

Rather than address the social and economic inequities raised by the grasshopper problem, Mackenzie opted for legislation that would compel ranchers to use poison. His familiarity with the range and the events of the previous season had convinced him that grasshopper infestations could be "practically eliminated" if all the stockmen did their part in poisoning efforts: "Some action must be taken to require those who should be interested and whose welfare is dependent upon the control of the grasshoppers to contribute assistance in some way," he insisted.[48] Nothing in federal or provincial law could compel ranchers to use poison, but there was the South African example. In 1911, the Union of South Africa drafted legislation that its agricultural officials hoped would facilitate a fight against locusts and migratory short-horned grasshoppers. Under the new locust law, white ranchers and farmers, as well as indigenous people living on reserve lands (to be set aside in 1913), were required to report the location of egg beds and any apparent increase in the number of insects in the veld (the local name for grassland), and when necessary to assist the Union government with poison control. It also spelled out the penalties, ranging from fines to compensation for costs and damages, for failing to do these things.[49] Mackenzie strongly favoured the legislation enacted by South Africa, by which, he claimed, the swarming of grasshoppers and locusts in that region had been "rendered impossible."[50] The South African range law was tantamount to a union-wide draft in which everyone was required to serve.[51] Mackenzie wanted to adopt similar measures in British Columbia, so he worked with legislators to craft a grasshopper control act under which ranchers or specially appointed poison control committees would spread poison baits provided by the province.

Still, there were problems, not the least related to human health. Some grazing officials were aware that "men have suffered arsenical poisoning through working with the powder." Coverage of ranch hands under the Workmen's Compensation Act was optional. Claims would be heard if the government paid the wages of those distributing the poison, but Mackenzie worried that making such payments in every other case would set a bad precedent, since nearly all the expenses associated with insect control had "heretofore been borne by landowners."[52] In the government's calculation, ranch owners should pay the wages of workers distributing poison and provide compensation for any associated injuries or illnesses because the ranchers ultimately benefited from the poison control program.

When large ranchers also withdrew support for a grasshopper control act, the government tried to demonstrate the program's potential effectiveness with a test project near Minnie Lake on Crown lands that were either used in common by big and small ranchers or leased to the Guichon Ranch and the Douglas Lake Cattle Company. By the late 1920s, these experiments seemed highly successful, though at least one small-scale rancher in the area lost five milk cows and two steers to accidental arsenic poisoning. On the other hand, "countless" grasshopper nymphs also died during these experiments and, according to Buckell, an outbreak was probably prevented. Grazing official W.H. Brown went so far as to suggest that "the scepter of power" was now in their hands, especially when the more powerful ranchers renewed their support for a grasshopper control act.[53] As Lawrence Guichon (owner of the Guichon Ranch) put it in 1927, "This has been a very favourable season for grass, and the rains we are having now are an insurance for next season. The grasshoppers are still with us, however, and from all accounts may be a serious menace next year. It looks as if we're in a fight again. Would it be possible to quarantine this district compelling all landowners to fight or pay?"[54]

Ultimately, they would fight *and* pay. Officials at the Grazing Branch drafted grasshopper control legislation that envisaged an annual tax proportionate to total deeded acres. This would cover the costs of poison control but also place a significant share of the tax burden on large ranchers. Several smaller ranchers still argued that they should be taxed at a lesser rate, as their rangeland was less valuable than that of the larger ranchers. Others argued that many outbreaks began on overgrazed and weedy Indian reserves and that therefore Indian Affairs should pay part of the bill, or that the federal government should pay because the largest egg beds were in the Dominion Railway Belt. Consensus had eluded the Grazing Branch, so the province passed legislation enabling the creation of grasshopper control zones and simply let communities decide for themselves whether they wished to create a control zone and participate in poison control.[55] This strategy seemed more democratic, but in practice the wishes of large landowners still carried the day. Commissioner Mackenzie concluded after a meeting with ranchers in early 1930 that because there was "antagonism at the Nicola meeting between the large and small owners of land ... the establishment of a grasshopper control district [should] be based upon the wishes of the owners of at least 60% of the acreage to be included ... rather than upon a 60% vote of the number of land-owners in such a district."[56] Framed this way, this Grasshopper Control Act passed later that year strongly favoured large landowners, thereby ensuring that the Nicola District would become a grasshopper control zone.

As historian Richard White reminds us, "Spatial arrangements matter a great deal in human history. They reveal the social arrangements that help produce them."[57] By the end of 1930, the administrative power of the state and the economic power and political influence of the large-scale rancher had created a legal space, the Nicola Control Zone, comprising 1,163,595 acres, within which it was illegal to refuse to cooperate with poison control.[58] Mackenzie lamented that the new law would not apply to Native reserves, a federal responsibility under the Indian Act, but William Ditchburn of Indian Affairs assured provincial officials that his department would lobby Native people to participate in poison control.[59] Elsewhere within control zones, the act enabled public officials in search of egg beds "to enter upon lands within the control area or lands adjacent thereto, without consent of the owner or of any person having any estate or interest in the land."[60] Ranchers in control zones did not have to apply poison to their properties, but they could not stop others from doing so. Moreover, according to section 8 of the act, "no action shall be brought against the committee in its corporate capacity, or against any member of the committee, or against any servant or workman of the committee for damages occasioned by an act or thing done by it or him in good faith in pursuance of this Act and its regulations."[61] Sections 16 and 17 spelled out penalties for offences: "Every person who obstructs, hinders, or prevents a committee or any member, servant, or workman of a committee engaged in the exercise of any power or in performance of any duty conferred or imposed by this Act or the regulations shall be guilty of an offense against this Act." Further, "every person who is guilty of an offense against this Act or who violates any provision of this Act or the regulations shall, on summary conviction, be liable to a fine not exceeding fifty dollars."[62] To put these fines in perspective, it helps to know that a $50 fine in 1930 would be roughly equivalent to a $600 fine today. This was probably a significant penalty for most people in British Columbia at the beginning of the Great Depression, but it would have been especially burdensome for smallholders facing uncertain markets with limited financial resources. Grasshopper irruptions exposed these inequities but certainly did not create them.

7

New Enemies, Enduring Difficulties

Insect poisoning began in earnest in the Nicola Valley in the early 1930s, and as the decade wore on and grasshopper plagues subsided, entomologists and range officials declared victory over their insect enemies. Even Buckell was impressed by the apparent success of poison control, though better range practice was still in order. The spreading of bait should be "only one phase of the problem," he told the province's chief forester in 1935, and much more could be done to prevent the occurrence of outbreaks by "certain practices in range management," provided of course that such practices were "not detrimental" to the cattle industry.[1] This, of course, was the problem with range management in the late nineteenth and early twentieth centuries: political economy and the short-term needs of the cattle industry almost always prevailed. This was why poison control carried the day relative to slower, but also more benign and arguably more durable, conservation practices that emphasized range restoration. New land-use practices were implemented in some areas, and a good deal of experimental and survey work was done. But rather than form one part of a multipronged effort to maintain the cattle industry – as originally envisioned by Buckell and Mackenzie in the early 1920s – poisoning egg beds became a kind of technological panacea for the problems people faced.

There was still the old problem of spring turnout times. In 1932, provincial grazing official George Melrose worried that in many cases stockmen were placing herds on the range in advance of the dates allowed by their grazing permits, "thus injuring the forage" and reducing range capacity.[2]

Likewise, a 1935 grazing manual from British Columbia indicated that grazing too early in spring bore serious long-term or cumulative consequences for range condition. For one thing, it tended to shorten the root system of individual plants, making it hard or impossible for them to obtain enough moisture after the spring runoff was gone. Thus damaged, individual plants were more likely to die during the dry summer months. Grazing too early in the year also prevented plants from storing sufficient energy for future growth, which meant that valuable perennial and herbaceous plants were replaced by "inferior annual plants that are of lower nutritional value or unpalatable due to their downy or hairy nature."[3] Not only was there less forage overall, but it was also less nutritious, which in turn affected an animal's health, and even more importantly, its weight. Smaller animals ultimately meant less money in ranchers' pockets. Simply put, spring turnout times mattered.[4]

In ways that only became apparent over time, grazing was remaking the range in ways that made it decreasingly useful for cattle. In the early 1930s, a study carried out by federal range ecologist L.B. Thomson reported, on the basis of two years of field studies and data provided by the former grazing commissioner, Thomas Mackenzie, that the carrying capacity of some ranges was probably only one-tenth of what it had been just two or three decades earlier. Of course, such estimates were fraught with uncertainty and masked considerable regional variability. But as far as could be ascertained from records and fieldwork and conversations with ranchers, the range in many places was indeed badly depleted. In the Nicola Valley, the carrying capacity on spring, fall, and winter ranges varied from 15 to 20 acres per head of cattle; for summer ranges, from 20 to 30 acres per head of cattle. In the Cariboo District, carrying capacity varied from 20 to 35 acres for spring and fall range and from 20 to 30 acres for summer range. Thomson had little in the way of historical data, so a precise comparison with nineteenth-century estimates was impossible. Nevertheless, the decline "was quite marked." The worst areas were in Chilcotin, where it was estimated that "under present conditions," fully 80 acres of rangeland were now needed to raise just one animal.[5]

A closer examination revealed not just that some ranges were more depleted than others but that the process of degradation had a distinctly human geography to it. It was clear to Thomson that spring and fall ranges – the so-called Crown range that ranchers usually used in common – were especially depleted, whereas fenced (or alienated) areas "were not so seriously affected." Conditions varied, of course. Some fenced areas were somewhat overgrazed, and not all Crown ranges were equally depleted.

Nonetheless, the differences in range quality on fenced and unfenced ranges were notable. Where ranchers were using "common grazing grounds" – by which Thomson meant Crown range, not commonage created under the Stock Ranges Act – there was "a tendency to overgraze it and obtain all the possible use without considering the perpetuation of the resource." But in areas that were fenced, and where "sound management practices" were followed, there was "no real serious damage done by overgrazing."[6]

Rapidly declining carrying capacities were partly a reflection of the region-wide drought that began in the mid- to late 1920s. "During the past three years," Thomson noted, "the light rainfall and practically snowless winters have resulted in a much reduced growth of grass." Another problem was that many of the natural water holes where, usually, cattle could have a drink, were either low or empty. This was likely more problematic than many people realized because it meant that grazing was becoming concentrated in areas that had at least some water, placing greater pressure on individual plants and leading to ever greater grazing- and trampling-related range degradation. Drought was important but not determinative. "One of the main sources of water supply is the beaver dam," Thomson noted. "The beaver has in the past constructed enough dams to adequately water many ranges."[7] Thanks to beaver dams, even during droughts the water supply was usually adequate to meet some ranchers' needs. But now things were different. An open season on beavers established many years earlier (the precise date was impossible to determine) meant a steady decline in the number of dams, "until now there are few remaining." It stood to reason that if these animals were protected or even reintroduced the water supply on the range would be improved. But beavers alone were not the answer. The deeper issue for Thomson was poor land management going back to the earliest days of ranching in the grassland, the cumulative effect of which was to remake and degrade the range.

An unacknowledged but plausible ecological possibility in the BC case was that the common grazing areas that Thomson identified as being badly overgrazed had a lower overall carrying capacity to start. But in any event, the deeper issue in early British Columbia was not that the "open" range was completely unregulated, but rather that it was not regulated enough, or in the right way: Aboriginal people were often excluded; local control by smallholders was limited; and large cattle owners mostly did what they wanted. The state did at times take steps to address some of these problems. The 1876 Stock Ranges Act and the 1879 Act to Protect Winter Stock Ranges, William Ross's land reforms, and efforts to amend the commonage law were examples. But the social order established in the nineteenth century mostly persisted, even after the provincial Grazing Act was passed in 1919 and range management became a formal responsibility of the state.

This was perhaps most evident on the Riske Creek range that E.R. Buckell observed in the early 1920s. In the mid-1930s, the province asked Thomson and ecologist Edwin Tisdale to study range conditions there and report back to the government. The results were discouraging. About 20 percent of the 20,000-acre "prairie" had "been reduced to the weed stage," producing "very little palatable fodder." Some areas were "so badly depleted" that even with protection and reseeding range recovery "was bound to be very slow." The quickest route to range recovery was to reseed these areas with another species, such as crested wheatgrass or something similarly "hardy" in nature and thus able to stand up to heavy grazing. Otherwise recovery could take up to fifteen years. Fortunately for ranchers, the remaining 80 percent of Riske Creek was in much better condition, but there was still "very little" bunchgrass left. "June grass" was perhaps most common across the remainder of the range, but they also found sizable patches of "spear grass" in some areas. Both grasses were good feed for cattle, but under current grazing practices these too of course would be depleted. With these observations in mind Thomson and Tisdale recommended that the range be "so regulated that the grass has a chance to make a fairly normal development and produce seed in the wetter seasons." They also suggested, more concretely, that at the end of fall grazing there should be a "carry-over of at least 25% of that year's growth." Not only would this carry-over of older grass afford new plants protection from early grazing; it would also "furnish a more balanced feed" for livestock.

How to regulate for grazing capacity, estimated at 2,700 head, was a different challenge, since there were some 6,000 head of cattle in the area. Managers either had to adopt a shorter grazing season, or prohibit grazing in some areas to allow the range there a chance to recover. Both solutions would force ranchers to find other places for their animals and absorb the added expenses that the more frequent (and distant) moving of animals inevitably entailed. Over time and "under improved proper methods of handling," however, "the improved condition of the cattle, [and an] earlier and larger calf crop should pay for the additional expenses involved." For Thomson and Tisdale, it was imperative that these issues be addressed before any additional degradation occurred. The depletion and mismanagement of this range, they wrote, "has reached a point where a definite grazing program, backed by strong administration, is necessary if the area is to retain its value among grazing lands in the Province."[8] This was exactly the rationale that led to the passage of the Grazing Act in 1919 in the first place, but nearly twenty years later, many regulatory problems persisted.

Photos of Riske Creek from the 1920s to the 1940s provided perspective on environmental problems during this period and were widely circulated. One especially striking photograph taken in 1941 depicted the badly depleted range in the Riske Creek area (Figure 7.1). A close-up put a finer point on the problem by including a small ruler that served to emphasize the scale of depletion (Figure 7.2). The ruler on bare ground vividly depicted the degree of range degradation in the region but also showed how important photos were for documenting abstract ideas such as succession and depletion. Pencils, rulers, people, fence posts, and animals were commonly used by scientists and grazing officials for scale and to give interested audiences – ranchers, politicians, other range managers – a better sense of ecological conditions at particular sites. Hats also worked, as shown in another photograph depicting heavily grazed rangeland at Riske Creek (Figure 7.3). These areas were indeed overgrazed, but here too we need to keep in mind that overall carrying capacity in these areas was lower compared with areas with creeks and rivers that were fenced.

FIGURE 7.1   Badly depleted range, Riske Creek area. *Courtesy of BC Archives, na_12576*

FIGURE 7.2   Overgrazing at Riske Creek, with ruler for scale. *Courtesy of BC Archives, na_12577*

FIGURE 7.3   Overgrazing at Riske Creek, with hat for scale. *Courtesy of BC Archives, na_12580*

Some of the richest evidence of ecological change and degradation in the grassland came from photos of experimental plots known as exclosures. As the name implies, exclosures were areas that had been fenced to prevent cattle and other large herbivores from grazing in order to study "natural" patterns of succession and association in regional plant communities, even though historically there were no such fences in the grassland. In other cases, exclosures formed part of a deferred-rotation grazing experiment in

FIGURE 7.4   Exclosure on Nicola Range. *Edwin Tisdale Summary Report*

which the timing and amount of grazing pressure associated with cattle and sheep were deliberately manipulated and carefully managed. The most impressive image of an exclosure came from the Lundbom Commonage, in the Nicola Valley. Taken in 1935, it shows the remarkable – indeed almost unbelievable – recovery of a small patch of bunchgrass in just four years (Figure 7.4). Note the barren, tabletop landscape in the background. Similar photos were widely circulated among ranchers in order to demonstrate the wisdom of state management. The photo works in almost Hobbesian fashion to conjure contrasting images of an irrational and unregulated past (the badly degraded area outside the fence) and a rational and fully regulated future (the completely restored area inside the fence, corresponding to the space of state management).

On the other hand, some rangelands did not revert to bunchgrass when grazing pressure was completely removed (a result consistent perhaps with the predictions of the state-and-transition model of range succession discussed in detail in Chapter 4). Overall, range results inside exclosures, just like results outside them, were usually modest and mixed. This suggested to some scientists and managers that range recovery would take some time – perhaps even twenty to forty years according to a study from British Columbia completed in the early 1970s – if it happened at all. A photo of an exclosure constructed on the Riske Creek range in the early 1920s provided an instructive example (Figure 7.5). Taken in 1931, it shows the slow

FIGURE 7.5 Riske Creek exclosure, 1931. *Courtesy of BC Archives, na_05938*

but apparently relatively steady recovery of a patch of bunchgrass, and several other palatable plant species, inside an area that had been fenced.

Conditions varied throughout the grasslands, of course, and not all areas were as "deplorable" as the worst parts of Riske Creek or the Lundbom Commonage. Still, many settlers felt that the problems identified there fairly represented problems elsewhere in the grasslands, even in the Nicola Valley, where after 1930 the grasshopper problems had become less severe. Even Lawrence Guichon and Frank Ward, with all their water and range, worried that the grass on which ranchers relied would not last. For his part, Ward thought that the future of range management might be in reseeding programs using introduced species. In the early 1930s, he started two experimental plots at the Douglas Lake Ranch, one seeded with crested wheatgrass, the other with western ryegrass. As grazing official George Copley later explained, the results were promising. The crested wheatgrass plot was originally good bunchgrass range but was "eaten out by moles which ... turned over the soil until it was in a highly cultivated condition." Before the moles came, though, the crested wheatgrass had averaged eighteen inches in height and was in "a very healthy condition," with blossom heads of two and a half inches long, which many ranchers would have considered a pretty good hay crop. The western ryegrass results were even more encouraging. Although the plants averaged only sixteen inches in height, they produced "almost twice as much leafage as the Crested Wheat" and provided "a much better forage grass." The Grazing Branch also experimented with introduced plant species. In the 1920s and 1930s, it cultivated impressive stands of Kentucky bluegrass and crested wheatgrass (Figures 7.6 and 7.7). Despite these promising results, Ward and Copley felt it would be many years or even decades before ranchers benefited from such work, even if the provincial government took up the task on a large scale. Weeds and woody shrubs were obstacles in many areas and probably would have to be removed before the range could be reseeded.[9]

FIGURE 7.6   Reseeded and protected stand of Kentucky bluegrass. *Edwin Tisdale Summary Report*

FIGURE 7.7   Crested wheatgrass on reseeded and protected area. *Edwin Tisdale Summary Report*

Photos from the mid- to late 1930s illustrated the changes Ward and Copley had in mind. One showed "depleted" lower grassland on the Tranquille Range near Kamloops and asked readers to "note the abundance of sagebrush and sparseness of bunchgrass vegetation," both signs of heavy overgrazing (Figure 7.8). Another showed four-year-old sagebrush taking over an area that had been heavily overgrazed (Figure 7.9). Another photo showed "bunchgrass range" in the background and a thick growth of cheatgrass in the foreground (Figure 7.10). According to Copley's colleague, George Melrose, it was entirely possible that depleted bunchgrass ranges colonized by cheatgrass could be restored with a proper grazing plan. It

FIGURE 7.8   Depleted lower grasslands on Tranquille Range. *Edwin Tisdale Summary Report*

FIGURE 7.9   Four-year-old sagebrush seedlings on depleted range. *Edwin Tisdale Summary Report*

FIGURE 7.10   Cheatgrass/downy bromegrass in foreground on overgrazed area. *Edwin Tisdale Summary Report*

was also conceivable that the process could be accelerated with controlled burning if it were done at the right time of year (in other words in spring when conditions were wetter and therefore safer for setting fires). But some studies also suggested that unless it was severely burned, cheatgrass would simply come back stronger the next year. This was problematic because a severe burn would destroy not only the weeds but also the soil needed to regrow the bunchgrass. This much was clear: *Bromus tectorum* was becoming a serious issue in many areas, and as such it warranted "considerable study and attention."[10]

By the early twentieth century, it was obvious that forest encroachment and ingrowth was occurring in many places. As early as 1918, in a report to the federal Commission of Conservation, foresters H.N. Whitford and R.D. Craig observed that fire-made grasslands occurred across the dry Interior. In the Peace River country bordering northwestern Alberta, these areas were extensive, but in other regions, "their areas cannot even be approximated." Nonetheless, the woods were slowly expanding their range. Whitford and Craig had no doubt whatsoever that the province's grasslands had been "much extended through the complete destruction of forest by fire," and that where the fires had ceased, the forest was "again invading the places it once covered, especially on northern slopes."[11]

What to do about this problem, if anything, was another question. As early as 1921, a rancher from Kamloops warned the members of the Dominion Dry Belt Commission that "the whole of this district stands

on the very verge of ruin attributable to the so-called forest preservation
and fire control policy of the forestry department," which, among other
things, had "heaped up to our very doors such a mass of inflammable
material that our lives and everything belonging to us are in jeopardy."
Having been in the Kamloops area for many years, the rancher remembered a time when the range had been open and park-like. Likewise, a
rancher from Grand Forks recalled a time before the provincial Forest
Branch arrived, when fires caused by "lightening and other sources" were
allowed to burn and the range had an "open, park-like appearance." In
those days, he remembered, one could ride a horse through the woods,
and even graze cattle there, but "to attempt it today would result in an
entanglement in brush and scrub trees that absorb all the moisture."
Another self-styled "old-timer" recalled that in the early days, "the Indians
burnt off [the lower forests and grassland] in the spring and fall" and the
result was better and more open range. That was the "old order," he said.
But now things were different. Government "autocrats" in Victoria passed
fire laws that ruined the range by allowing shrubs and scrub timber to
come up. A rancher from Merritt noted, "It would be best to light a fire
and let it go in order to win [back] the range." Not all ranchers were as
enthusiastic about burning as these men were; nonetheless, a good many
of them agreed that the province's fire policies were in many ways
misguided.

Publicly, the provincial Forest Branch portrayed fires as universally
destructive, but privately, opinion was somewhat divided. The fact
remained that not all fires were exactly alike in terms of their ecological
effects. Context mattered. Large fires produced landscapes that were
reminiscent of war zones. There was evidence, however, that frequent
light burning was actually good for range quality. As forester Owen Sanger
observed in 1916, "Before the enforcing of the Forest Fire Laws, it was
common practice among the ranchers to set fire to the Jack Pine upon
every opportunity." The result was "the creating, in many areas, of an
impassable abatis of fallen logs, and the destruction of what soil there
was before the fire." On the other hand, Sanger remarked, "on those
comparatively rare areas where the soil was good, and the fire occurred
early in spring, followed two or three years later by another which burnt
up the debris and occurred at the same time of year, the result has been
a great improvement in the quality of the feed on the area burnt." Perhaps
because he was a forester in a province strongly committed to fire control,
Sanger tended to focus on the destructive effects of forest and grassland
burning – the aforementioned impassable abatis of jack pine. But there

was also evidence that light burning in certain environmental contexts had beneficial effects as well.[12]

Sanger's colleague, Percy Lemare, agreed that context mattered when it came to forest and range burning. Reflecting on the role of fire in 1917, he observed that where the soil was "light and thin[,] fire will destroy it and leave only a barren waste for many years so that no good would result in burning in regard to the improvement of forage on these areas." But where the soil was "good and of sufficient depth to withstand the fire, the forage crops were much improved by burning of the timber." Timing and elevation were crucial. These fires should be set "as much as possible in the spring just after the snow has left the ground," he wrote, "the fire then burning off the old accumulations of dry grass litter, and windfalls etc. without burning down into the soil which at that time is generally frozen." Summer fires at low elevations were dangerous and ecologically counter-productive in any case because the soil would be rendered useless for range plants. At higher elevations, however, it was often possible to burn, "without endangering the country adjacent[,] up to the end of July." The result would be more and better forage for livestock. "From an examination of the lands it is proposed to burn over," Lemare wrote, "it is believed that such a policy, if properly restricted, will prove of public benefit."[13]

Sanger and Lemare were not alone among North American foresters in recognizing the potentially beneficial effects of fire for grazing, but they were very much in the minority on this issue.[14] Since the late nineteenth century, British Columbia's forest policy had been premised on fire sup-pression. Moreover, some administrators saw grazing as part of that policy. Minister of Lands William Ross noted as early as 1912 that grazing in mountain forests prevented "the accumulation of grass and leaves, increases the rapidity of decomposition of dead material, and also makes trails, all of which decreases the fire hazard."[15] Like others of his generation, Ross did not realize that fire suppression also unleashed undesirable environ-mental changes, including encroachment and much larger fires in the future. Yet, in the first half of the twentieth century, fire suppression could easily be justified on ecological grounds. Prevailing scientific theories generally held that any burning was an unnatural disturbance that pre-vented grassland ecosystems from achieving their ultimate or "climax" form, which was usually a forest.[16] From this perspective, forest encroach-ment reflected purely "natural" processes of plant succession. Fire-free grasslands became forests because that was what nature intended.

Even without science, however, fire suppression could be justified on economic grounds for, as environmental historian Stephen Pyne observes, "fire competed openly with the axe."[17] Forests were making British Columbia a wealthy province, and as ecologist John Parminter has noted, the "province's forest revenue and the equity represented by the standing timber demanded a fire protection force second to none."[18] According to the Royal Commission on the Timber Industry in 1910, private investments had to be protected, provincial wealth had to be husbanded, and the principle of public ownership of forests had to be nurtured. From this perspective, fire protection was much more than simply sound forestry: it was a moral responsibility of the state. Science mattered, of course. But economics was reason enough to prevent and extinguish fires, especially given that benefits of burning were unclear. As one government official explained in response to a 1916 request for burning permits, it was precisely because of this uncertainty, not to mention the "tremendous" area of land involved, that a decision on the issue had been delayed. Put another way, the province needed evidence, not anecdotes, that burning was best possible practice. What was required, he suggested, was "a thorough investigation to ascertain whether timber growing or pasturage will give the highest permanent use value on 20 or 39 million acres of land." Of course, this did little or nothing to alleviate ranchers' grazing problems in the short term. But he added that "inasmuch as a mistake of classification" would "require a generation and more to correct," it was crucial that the province develop a policy that would "stand the test of time."[19]

Fires continued to burn, of course, but on balance they became less frequent in the late nineteenth and twentieth century with both the decline of Aboriginal burning and the rise of state fire protection. These changes had profound and lasting consequences for people and nonhuman nature alike, one of which, paradoxically, was more destructive fires in the future.[20] By allowing forests to become denser and thus full of "fuel," fire suppression dramatically increased the likelihood of massive stand-replacing conflagrations. From a strictly grazing perspective, however, the new fire regime of larger burns occurring at greater intervals resulted in a slow, steady reduction of rangeland. On north-facing slopes and sites with ample water, fire suppression allowed pine and fir seedlings to take root, whereas on drier sites, fire-intolerant shrubs such as sagebrush and antelope brush expanded greatly.[21] Meanwhile, many old-forest grazing areas became impassable because of forest ingrowth. Although impossible to quantify, it stands to reason that these processes placed additional pressure on an already strained grassland environment.[22]

By the early 1940s, there were problems in the uplands, where increasingly ranchers ranged their cattle in summer. One report claimed that beetle-killed trees were falling down by the thousands, crashing down on and across fences and stock trails. Bark beetles (genus *Dendroctonus*) were as much a part of Interior forest ecology as were the forests themselves, but the tiny black insects had remained invisible to ranchers and range officials, much as grasshoppers had until they became a problem. The first signs of infestation emerged in the 1890s around the ranching community of Princeton. By the early 1930s, "clumps" of dead and dying ponderosa pine trees called red-tops could be seen throughout the Southern Interior. Although difficult to tally precisely, the impact of these beetles appeared considerable. Entomologist Ralph Hopping estimated that about 150 million board feet of pine had been "killed" in the Princeton area alone, and an earlier examination by Dominion forest entomologist J.W. Swaine of beetle-infested areas near Merritt revealed that 40 to 90 percent of the timber "was absolutely killed on large areas." In the early 1930s, Hopping warned that at least 150 million board feet were about to be lost in the Coldwater area south of Merritt, where a "very active infestation is now in progress." Indeed, it was "evident that the yellow pine in this whole forest between Princeton and Kamloops is threatened with ruin by these outbreaks and that control operations [directed by provincial and Dominion Forestry officials] offer the only hope of saving it."

Hopping's understanding of bark beetle "outbreaks" and how to control them strongly paralleled the account of grasshopper problems by Buckell and Treherne. His starting point was the then centuries-old assumption that nature in the absence of human interference tended toward stability and balance. Simple and confined sporadic outbreaks were part of forest history, yet the amount of timber lost to them, though impossible to calculate, was probably considerable when added to what Hopping referred to as the "endemic or 'normal' level of infestation that existed in all forests." Under certain conditions, these events could develop into "epidemic outbreaks" consisting of a single or primary species, as well as several secondary species that could "devastate a whole countryside." Weather was also critical. Warm, dry breeding seasons, for example, favoured bark beetle development; wet and cold did not. The number of "natural enemies" at work in a forest also mattered for beetle populations. Parasites, disease-bearing fungi, predaceous insects, and several insectivorous bird species – in other words all the usual "ordinary enemies" of economic entomology – had a direct impact on maintaining smaller and more stable bark beetle populations. But none of these natural controls was determinative. Hopping believed that epidemic outbreaks followed not from seasonal variations in temperature and precipitation or from "minor" perturbations in enemy insect, parasite, and bird populations but from those disturbances that upset the "natural order" over large areas and for extended periods: namely fires, windstorms, and, most important, forestry.

In a series of papers presented to BC forestry officials from the 1920s to the 1940s, Hopping emphasized that each ecological disturbance, but especially the latter, created ideal bark beetle breeding habitat for an epidemic outbreak. "In windfalls and fires we have conditions produced in which the bark beetles are not hampered by the resistance of healthy trees." But in logging operations, he insisted, "we have a much more prevalent cause of epidemics. The immense amount of fresh slash, in the form of tops and cull logs, affords an ideal breeding ground for the most destructive beetles." Winter forestry – the only kind of forestry possible in Interior British Columbia at the time, given the difficulties of moving wood to the railway at any other time of year – was "especially favourable to attack upon the standing timber." Hopping explained that the "beetles, completing their life-cycle in the freshly cut material, emerge, and, having no new supply of cut material to enter, for they will not breed in dry logs, enter the living standing trees and kill them within a year. They then spread from year to year throughout the timber stand leaving devastation in their wake." Viewed in this light, the clear solution was to establish forest practices that restored the "natural balance." The most important, Hopping suggested, were fire suppression, which would eliminate beetle habitat; the removal or spring burning of timber slash, and thus any bark beetle eggs that the slash might contain; and the systematic removal of "overmature" pine and fir trees, which entomologists and forestry officials considered weak and prone to infestation.[23] Meanwhile, and for many years to come, ranchers and range officials had to deal with the deadfall (Figure 7.11).

Hopping was convinced that poor forestry, particularly the recent buildup of slash, was responsible for the province's bark beetle problem. But there was an alternate explanation: that bark beetle infestations "were caused by keeping fire from the forests." Many ranchers made this argument in the 1910s and 1920s; in the 1930s and 1940s, some ranchers even illegally burned these areas in order to deal with the deadfall. But for various reasons, Hopping dismissed this argument. For one thing, entomologists knew "absolutely that tremendous epidemics occurred before fire was ever kept out of the primeval forest." The fact that bug epidemics predated fire suppression was evidence the two were unrelated. Nevertheless, there was a connection between beetle epidemics and fire because the quantity of bug-killed timber on the forest floor often determined "the

FIGURE 7.11   Deadfall from bark beetles. *Edwin Tisdale Summary Report*

degree of destructiveness of a fire." There was also evidence that beetle populations benefited from such fires because of "the large amount of partly killed trees" that were the result, and that in turn afforded "ideal conditions for the multiplication of the injurious species." In other words, "fires and insect infestations react": beetles kill trees; dead trees lead to larger fires; larger fires create more beetle habitat; more beetle habitat leads to larger beetle populations; and so on. Light burning – which Hopping defined as "burning under conditions whereby the timber stand is not materially injured – had been suggested as a means of controlling bark beetle outbreaks. The idea was that by reducing or eliminating the endemic infestation present in every forest, light burning would also prevent an epidemic from occurring. But Hopping objected. Partly this was because bark beetles only bred in "fresh down timber," not dead timber. But under normal conditions fresh down timber formed only a small part of any forest, thus limiting outbreaks. In fact, only a "severe conflagration" would "kill out an epidemic of beetles." But such fires would also destroy the timber, whereas light burning would likely only encourage beetles by expanding their "ideal" habitat – in other words, partly dead and freshly downed timber. Hopping thus concluded that there were "two great menaces to our forests – fire and insects."[24] Rather than work at odds, ranchers and grazing authorities should work together with entomologists to get rid of both.

Bark beetles, forest ingrowth and encroachment, range degradation – by the early 1940s, according to Frank Ward, there was simply no gainsaying "the seriousness of our grazing problems, for the writing is on the wall. To those of us with very heavy investments in the stock business our position becomes more critical as time goes on. We see the range slipping, forcing us to reduce our herds, while [competitors outside the province] are increasing theirs." Ward may have been exaggerating for effect or simply to defend his decisions over the years as ranch manager. But there was no question that twenty years after the Grazing Act was passed, many range problems persisted. One of the biggest problems that ranchers, and perhaps Ward in particular, faced in the early 1940s was that recent increases in production costs, associated mainly with investments in irrigation over the last two decades, were not being matched by corresponding increases in cattle production. Overall, according to one study, the size and quality of the province's "calf crop" had not changed much since the early 1920s. Indeed, sales figures from some ranches showed that the average weight of individual cattle had *decreased*. Admittedly, another report noted that the reason for the decline in cattle weights was complicated. Changes in breeding practices – particularly a shift on the part of some ranchers to naturally lighter breeds of cattle – were probably partly responsible for the decline. But others believed that range degradation was also to blame. Overgrazing not only favoured less nutritious plant species but also potentially meant that cattle had to move around more to find suitable and sufficient forage, which some ranchers speculated naturally translated into weight loss.

The economic problem in this case was that ranchers were price takers, not price makers, so simply charging more for their animals to compensate for the economic losses associated with declining cattle weights and rising costs was impossible. More valuable cattle breeds might fetch higher prices in the market, but these animals were also more expensive to acquire in the first place. The obvious way out of this dilemma was for each rancher to raise a few more animals. But this provided only a partial solution to the issue of declining cattle weights, and in the long term was deeply problematic because it would require even more invest-ment in irrigation and entail even greater grazing pressure in the grass-land. Usually the only solace offered to ranchers and range officials in the early 1940s was that the province's grasshopper problems appeared to be a thing of the past.[25]

The approach to grasshopper control developed in the Nicola Valley in the 1920s *did* appear to working – so well, in fact, that in the 1930s, ranchers created four more control zones – at Riske Creek, Clinton, Midway, and Osoyoos – covering most of the open rangeland left in the province. A 1936 article in the *Vancouver Province* newspaper reported that BC-style control zones were even being created in Africa: "Africa, which has been plagued since biblical times by swarms of locusts has come to British Columbia for a method of controlling the ancient pest," the story boasted. "At a conference of the world's leading entomologists in Cairo, the method of grasshopper control developed in the Nicola Valley was adopted as the most efficient ever discovered according to advices received by the department of agriculture here."[26] This was partially true. Buckell had presented several papers at the Cairo conference, one of which dealt with methods for controlling "non-gregarious" (non-swarming) grasshopper populations. In it he briefly explained the control zone concept and its underlying biological logic – that poisoning grasshopper egg beds before they hatched was essential to grasshopper control. In another paper, Buckell suggested that the success of this strategy in British Columbia confirmed the Russian entomologist Boris Uvarov's ideas about solitary and gregarious phases in locust populations (addressed in greater detail below), and the fact that it was easier and ultimately more effective to poison solitary populations in their breeding areas before swarming occurred. Although British Columbia's rangelands were relatively large, concentrating on the breeding grounds meant attending to fewer than 2,000 acres.[27]

Certainly, other assessments were less judicious. In a 1938 newspaper article, agricultural official W.L. Talbot described how a "dramatic battle for control of the Nicola Valley ended in triumph within a few yards of defeat." On "some battlefields the dead lay as thick as four hundred and better to the square yard over large areas." Armed with thousands of tons of arsenic bait and simple maps showing the location of egg beds, entomologists set out to subdue their insect enemy and, by August 1938, a once "vast" grasshopper "army" – a "huge" insect "armada" – had been "reduced to a skeleton force."[28] Talbot's bellicose rhetoric and rampant exaggeration aside, the moral of his story was obvious: "man" had waged a war with insects and won.

In fact, entomologists' hold on the grasslands was far more tenuous than Talbot realized. Grasshopper plagues approaching "biblical" proportions descended on Interior rangelands during the summers of 1943 to 1946.[29] No range was left untouched. Grasshoppers ravaged even the famous Nicola Grasshopper Control Area. According to the annual report of

Indian Affairs, "The grasshopper pest did a great deal of damage to ranges and crops."[30] Nicola Valley rancher Joe Coutlee had "seen nothing like it in sixty years riding the range."[31] Frank Ward noted that the grasshopper plague lowered the average weight of cattle and meant smaller profits for ranchers already contending with wartime regulations on food production, including an embargo on the export of cattle to the United States. This deprived ranchers of much bargaining power. Moreover, the purchase of cattle for slaughter in Canada had been confined to "certain interests." Dressed beef was now subject to government grading, with prices pegged to grade. At the same time, beef rationing reduced consumption by a quarter, while increased labour costs associated with the war and an "exodus of Indians to the orchards and berry fields of Washington" only made problems worse.[32] All of these changes affected the cattle company's bottom line, but what happened at the Douglas Lake Ranch also affected smaller ranches. Ward frequently purchased surplus cattle from other ranchers and sold them surplus hay, but now he was reluctant to do either because of his own shrinking margins. As Ward explained in a report to company shareholders, "Conditions were such that hundreds of beef cattle which ordinarily would have been shipped off grass were carried into winter and placed in the feed lots to be marketed off grain, all of which had to be purchased."[33]

Even Buckell bowed before the power of nature in 1944. Never before had "an outbreak quite like the present one been encountered," he observed in *Canadian Entomologist*. Usually outbreaks involved several species of grasshopper, with *Camnula pellucida* usually predominating. But the 1943–44 "plague" consisted of just the lesser migratory grasshopper. Nothing stopped them, not even in the Nicola Valley, where public officials had been dumping poison on egg beds since the late 1920s. It was "a new enemy," wrote Buckell, with new habits and a well-documented history of devastation. "This species is known to be the most injurious species in the northern United States and Canada, and the great outbreaks of 1874 when the Rocky Mountain locust devastated the Northwestern United States from Montana through the Dakotas to Minnesota and thence into the Canadian prairie, is still one of the landmarks of North American history."[34] Buckell was right about having to confront a new enemy with new habits, but the insect in question was not western North America's old adversary, the Rocky Mountain locust.[35]

The roots of this taxonomic confusion lay in a paper written by South African entomologist Jacobus Faure and published in the *Journal of Economic Entomology* in 1933.[36] Faure suggested that the now infamous Rocky

Mountain locust, which many entomologists believed had gone extinct, was alive and well after all, but incognito. He based his argument on Uvarov's influential phase theory of 1927, which held that locusts had a remarkable capacity for physiological change.[37] Working on the semiarid Russian steppe, Uvarov had observed locusts changing in physical form as they transitioned between solitary and gregarious phases. When this happened, the insects changed colour, grew longer wings, and exhibited various behavioural differences. Uvarov's colleague, entomologist V.I. Plotnikov, had recorded similar changes in a study of central Asian locust populations, and Faure noted these as well while working on locust problems in South Africa. Neither entomologist, or any other working at the time, knew precisely what prompted the changes, though environmental factors and population density seemed critical. In many ways, the direction of this early theorization was basically correct. Locusts did change form in certain circumstances, and both environmental change and crowding associated with population increase were critical factors, even if the exact mix of mechanisms at work differed according to context.[38] Faure believed that his phase theory explained the sudden disappearance of the Rocky Mountain locust early in the late nineteenth century: it was merely the gregarious phase of another insect, most likely *Melanoplus mexicanus* or the lesser migratory grasshopper, which was still common on western grasslands.[39] Thus, the hateful Rocky Mountain locust, also known as *Melanoplus spretus*, did not so much disappear from North American grasslands as disguise itself.

The so-called evidence for a *spretus/mexicanus* split personality was far from convincing, however. Faure did not observe these changes in the field and never succeeded in inducing phase transformation in migratory grasshoppers in the laboratory, yet, in his view, enough work had been done to justify the conclusion that *spretus* was the gregarious phase of *mexicanus*. Entomologists generally accepted Faure's assertion, although as scientist and historian Jeffery Lockwood points out, usually with considerable caution, qualifying claims with statements such as "believed to be the migratory phase" in the case of *spretus,* or "thought to be similar or perhaps identical to the Rocky Mountain locust" in the case of *mexicanus.*[40] This was wise. Subsequent taxonomic comparisons of *spretus* and *mexicanus* genitalia, and later their DNA, revealed that Faure had been wrong about the reappearance of *spretus* in *mexicanus* form. *Spretus* and *mexicanus* (renamed *sanguinipes* in 1967) were different species.[41] The tests also revealed once and for all that the Rocky Mountain locust had gone extinct sometime very early in the twentieth century, most likely, as Lockwood argues, because of irrevocable alteration of key breeding areas and refuges by ranchers and farmers in the 1880s and 1890s.[42] The Canadian entomologist Norman Criddle unknowingly collected the last living specimens, a male and a female, in the grasslands of Manitoba in 1902.

Mexicanus was not *spretus*, but believing that it was surely helped Buckell explain the 1944 outbreak to ranchers and renew their commitment to the control zone concept, which, he worried, might be waning. He conceded that from "the enormous numbers of grasshoppers present over the entire range in the Nicola it is possible that some of you may think that your control zone operations, which you have carried on so faithfully for a long period of years with such gratifying success are, after all, a failure," but this was "definitely not the case in spite of the fact that in 1944 you experienced one of the worst outbreaks of grasshoppers in the history of your rangelands and may be quite seriously affected again in 1945." The insect had caught everyone off guard, not least because it was the first *mexicanus* outbreak in provincial history. A shortage of men, machines, and chemicals associated with the war made matters worse, but *mexicanus*'s intractable biology also made it an exceedingly difficult insect to beat. It did not have well-defined egg beds; eggs hatched over a very long time; nymphs and adults refused to eat arsenic bait; and both appeared completely immune to fungi, though the effects of parasitism did show on some adults. In these ways, Buckell observed, *Melanoplus mexicanus* was essentially different from British Columbia's old adversary, *Camnula pellucida*, the roadside grasshopper. This bore deep implications for pest control because strategies devised to deal with the one insect did not work on the other – an enduring theme indeed in the history of economic entomology. This did not mean that the control zone concept ought to be abandoned. Buckell insisted that in "matters pertaining to insects it is never safe to prophecy anything[,] as so many factors influence their numbers." The *mexicanus* plague would soon "pass into history," probably not to return for many years. Already, crows and blackbirds and "at least 10 kinds of parasitic flies" were gorging on the grasshoppers, the latter slowly eating them alive from the inside out. Meanwhile, science would develop better methods for managing these pests. When and if the Rocky Mountain locust or lesser migratory grasshopper returned, the entomologists would be ready.

Buckell adeptly anticipated and eased ranchers' worries, but basic uncertainties festered over the exact cause of the 1944 outbreak. "For some reason which we cannot explain at present," he confessed, "the insect has increased beyond all imagination."[43] Several factors seemed in play. Favourable weather for breeding was probably important. A dry summer and warm autumn in 1943 and again in 1944 likely enabled females to lay far more eggs than usual. The dramatic geographic expansion of *Melanoplus* breeding areas because of overgrazing by cattle and "the loosening of the surface soil by an enormous increase in the number of pocket gophers in recent years" was another factor.[44] Indeed, the ecological connections between cattle, gophers, and grasshoppers ran deeper than perhaps Buckell realized. Northern pocket gophers are burrowing herbivores that inhabit a wide variety of environments, but they thrive in disturbed areas, especially irrigated alfalfa fields, where they find ample food and easy digging.[45] Thus, it stands to reason (but is difficult to prove) that the increase in pocket gophers was partly an effect of environmental changes associated with the rise of winter feeding by ranchers after 1890. To be sure, weather, disease, and other factors were at work in shaping the gopher population.[46] But the sudden jump in pocket gopher numbers also coincided with a significant decline in the badger population, due in large part to habitat loss associated with resettlement of the grasslands, and badgers were among the most effective predators of pocket gophers. A decline in one animal population may well have contributed to an increase in the other, and there was indeed a rapid increase of pocket gopher populations in the late 1920s and 1930s.[47] This posed a considerable problem for agricultural production. Pocket gophers damaged irrigation works, ate crops meant for cattle, and carried ticks that caused a kind of paralysis in livestock.[48] What ranchers and range managers did not know at the time but may well have suspected was that extensive burrowing by pocket gophers also created additional breeding areas for *Melanoplus mexicanus*.

Buckell's analysis, buttressed by informed ecological speculation and then-recent research in entomology, suggested that solving the *mexicanus* problem entailed much more than merely achieving a proper mix of institutions and pesticides. But a new class of powerful chemical poisons was already in the air when the *mexicanus* outbreak occurred. In November 1944, Buckell informed University of British Columbia zoologist George Spencer about a recent conversation with a colleague concerning chemical poisons. A few days earlier he had had a long talk with Paul Marshall, an entomologist from the Dominion entomology branch, who gave him the address of two firms, one that made dinitrocyclohexylphenol dust, and another that produced dinitro-ortho-cresol dust. In light of the recent "*mexicanus*" outbreak in British Columbia, Marshall thought that Buckell and Spencer "should get dinitro dust, which is on the market and is 40% strength, and then dilute it to find the minimum

strength to kill hoppers using pyrophyllite or bentonite as a dilutant."
Marshall maintained that these pesticides were extremely effective against
insect pests but also harmful to human health. Thus, he warned Buckell,
anyone "using these chemicals *must* wear respirators, rubber gloves, and
tight overalls as it is very dangerous in any strength."[49] Spencer agreed
but hated the idea of having to wear respirators, rubber gloves, and
overalls when using this dust. "It will be like boiling under our range
conditions," he complained.[50]

These were extreme measures undertaken by intelligent people, with
little or no regard for the wider grassland environment, to say nothing of
their own health and well-being. But science did offer less toxic approaches
to grasshopper control. An important, albeit minor, line of research
revolved around what Spencer called "ecological" approaches to insect
control. As early as 1935 he had spoken to Nicola Valley ranchers about
modifying areas used as egg beds in ways that made them unsuitable for
oviposition. Perhaps the most interesting line of research followed from
life history studies conducted at Riske Creek and in the Nicola Valley in
the 1940s. It involved controlling grasshoppers with fertilizers. Noting that
in late summer, grasshoppers created bare patches in which to lay their
eggs, and that the following spring young hoppers fed on the tender tips
of new grasses, Spencer suspected that if these patches were treated with
ammonium nitrate, and the grasses grew tall, dense, and tough, young
grasshoppers would starve. An experiment confirmed his expectation "that
their mouth parts are apparently too weak to chew the sides of grass leaves
so they crawl up and eat the tender tips. The larger ones can eat the sides
of grass leaves and by the third stage they begin to cut down the grass and
move off the egg beds." A new line on insect control was at hand "to treat
Camnula beds well before the eggs hatch with ammonium nitrate so as
to have a very heavy stand of tall, strong leaves by the time the baby hoppers come out so that they find tough stems and dense shade instead of
short and tender leaves and much sunshine." There were other benefits as
well. Tall, dense grass had a "great tendency" to develop a fungus that
attacked grasshoppers and, of course, the increased growth would be
"exceedingly attractive to stock, so that even if the hoppers fail to die in
it the extra growth will benefit range animals."[51] Spencer's results were
promising indeed and strongly echoed his elder colleagues' conclusions
about range restoration going back to the 1920s, but chemicals were
quicker, cheaper, and far more acceptable politically than changes in land
use that might increase production costs – better to have the government
put poison on the grasslands.

Reflecting on the rise of chemical pesticides in a 1952 paper titled *Fifty Years of Entomology in the Interior of British Columbia*, entomologist E.P. Venables lamented that the control of insects had "lost the human interest, which it had in the early days." Back then, he recalled, "remedies were far more heroic ... and could be applied, in most cases, without referring to the chemist, who, today, hovers in the foreground and almost excludes the entomologist. The control of insects now seems to be in the hands of the chemical engineer, and universal destruction is the order of the day."[52] Nostalgia is never good history. The implied sharp division between chemistry and economic entomology was more imagined than real. The two endeavours were always more closely related than Venables realized or was willing to admit. Venables also ignored the negative, if unquantifiable, impact that arsenic, itself a chemical, had on local plant and animal populations. Every year arsenic poisoning claimed a few horses and cattle, and there was anecdotal evidence that many other animals were killed as well. Several naturalists suspected that grasshopper baiting killed honeybees and "musical birds," producing an early-twentieth-century silent spring.[53] To what extent other wildlife was affected by arsenic is unclear. There were clues, however, even in 1952 when Venables wrote his short history, that the collateral death toll was probably considerable. As early as 1933, E.R. Buckell, for example, noted that several companies in British Columbia were "anxious to get into the grasshopper control business and were conducting experiments with a lead poison that would be just as deadly [as arsenic] but less harmful to animals."[54] Venables's comments nevertheless did mark an important shift in the history of insect control away from relatively weak and temporarily toxic compounds of arsenic toward more powerful and persistent synthetic chemicals such as DDT, the "atomic bomb" of pesticides.[55] The purveyors of new chemical products promised to end all insect pests. Yet, the goal of "universal destruction," as Venables called it, proved more difficult than expected. Unlike the wild horses, which were quickly reduced when the shooting started, grasshopper populations proved resilient, even when confronted with toxic chemical poisons. Grasshopper populations continued to irrupt in the post–Second World War period, and the spectre of a large-scale outbreak like that which occurred in the summer of 1944 never disappeared.

Nor did the province's regulatory problems disappear during these years. Numerous scientific studies were initiated after 1919, and countless cattle gates and drift fences were constructed. But in terms of actual changes in land use, not a lot was accomplished during the pre-1960 period. In 1919, Thomas Mackenzie argued that "prior to the passing of the Grazing Act

... grazing was carried on in an unregulated manner" and that "administration on a sound basis was urgently required."[56] Seventeen years later, in 1936, the province's chief forester, Peter Caverhill, stressed that the pioneer period in British Columbia was over, that "cattle and sheep men must look to more scientific livestock and range management for profits rather than to greater numbers under old-fashioned range practices," and that it was "plain that management must soon be instituted on Crown ranges."[57] Twenty years after that, in 1956, Chief Justice Gordon Sloan emphasized in his final report to the Royal Commission on Forest Resources that the question of overgrazing in the province posed a problem of "immediate urgency calling for the implementation of regulatory controls."[58] And nearly twenty years after that, in 1974, ecologist Alastair McLean noted in his report titled *Administration of British Columbia Ranges* that although "some ranges" had "deteriorated in recent times because of mismanagement, most of the damage was done 40 to 100 years ago." Indeed, "development over the past 30 years of the concept of controlled grazing and sound range management practices, has led us from the period of exploitation to the *beginning* of managed grazing on Western ranges."[59] Regulatory problems persisted not because of a lack of science, however, but because it was always easier to avoid regulation than it was to impose it.

Generally, range quality neither improved nor declined during the 1950s and 1960s. Yet, there is some evidence that for various economic and technological reasons ranch productivity overall went up during these years. One reason was more and better irrigation. The total area of irrigated land increased by just 8 percent between 1939 and 1960, but a shift away from relatively inefficient gravity-based flood systems to new sprinkler technologies enabled ranchers with capital to increase their yields per acre by as much as 100 percent. With better irrigation, ranchers could grow more of what their cattle consumed each year. Buttressed by higher beef prices after the war, a series of bumper crops in the prairie provinces of Alberta and Saskatchewan, and a provincial government subsidy, after 1940 many ranchers also turned to supplemental feeding of yearlings and breeding stock with grain. This too increased the productivity of ranches by reducing animal mortality rates among calves and breeding stock. Some ranchers even provided their animals with pelletized protein concentrates. The owners of the Gang Ranch, on the middle Fraser River, went so far as to distribute these pellets on privately owned winter, spring, and fall ranges by airplane.

The rise of supplemental feeding and use of protein pellets on the range heralded broader changes in the province's ranching economy. Before the early 1950s, the vast majority of cattle in British Columbia were shipped to New Westminster and Vancouver for slaughter. In 1949, for example, only 907 head were shipped to the United States, and only 277 were shipped to Alberta. By the late 1950s, less than half of all cattle in British Columbia were shipped to the coast. Most were sent to Alberta and Montana, to be fattened on grain before slaughter. People still raised cattle in order to sell them, but in many ways the very nature of the ranching business in British Columbia, and even the cattle herd itself, had radically changed. Until the early 1950s, most cattle in the province were marketed as grass-fed two- to four-year-olds. But by the early 1960s, these animals accounted for less than 8 percent of the total herd: ranchers now raised yearlings and calves for finishing (an ominous euphemism if ever there was one) on factory feedlots in Alberta and Montana. Some of the region's smaller ranchers resisted the change but found it increasingly difficult (and eventually all but impossible) to market their animals – urban butchers and chain-store operators insisted that consumers preferred the bright white fat of grain-fed cattle to the yellowish (but beta-carotene-rich) fat of grass-fed animals. Moreover, once the shift had been made, it was impossible to go back. As geographer Thomas Weir explained, "To return to selling 2-year-olds would involve the loss of a year's income which few could afford."[60] By the late 1960s, the ranches and ranges of British Columbia had been fully integrated into North America's factory feedlot system.[61] The shift to cow-calf operations after 1950 apparently increased the productivity of individual ranches in British Columbia because ranges historically set aside for fattening beef steers could now be used as breeding pastures or converted to irrigated pastures to fatten young cattle, so-called "long yearlings" that were between one and two years old. All of these changes enabled ranchers to increase (somewhat) the size of their cattle herds, even though the Crown range in many cases was still generally overgrazed. Significantly, between 1951 and 1960, the number of cattle in the drylands increased 38 percent, from 107,000 in 1951 to 148,000 in 1960.

These increases amid overgrazing did not benefit all ranches equally. The inequities of ranching had not gone away, though the Grazing Branch did at times take steps to address these inequities when it involved settlers. Writing about the Nicola Valley grazing dispute, grazing official George Copley explained in frustration that "we have tried out every scheme suggested by the smaller stockmen which did not exclude the Company stock altogether, as well as trying out many suggestions of our own, but in every case something has turned up which has broken the agreements made." Even though there had not been a bad grasshopper outbreak in the area in more than a decade, Copley wrote, there was "a festering unrest in that locality" that was "impossible to surmount."[62] Then again, the dispute between big and small ranchers ran much deeper than the insect plagues in the early twentieth century. Copley was convinced that the only way to resolve tensions was to help the small ranchers by setting aside a community field that would exclude Ward's and Guichon's cattle. "We simply told the two larger outfits they would have to keep out of the Jasper Community field altogether," he later reported, "and leave it for the smaller outfits for spring and fall use and that these smaller outfits could run with the common herd during the summer months." It never occurred to Copley that Aboriginal people needed more and better range resources. But he did believe that small-scale ranchers and farmers, people like Richard Guildford, deserved better than what they were getting.

The creation of a community field was a victory of sorts for small ranchers, and it undoubtedly helped to ease tensions. But all the old arguments about range concentration persisted into the postwar period. The economic inequities of ranching had not gone away. If anything, they became more entrenched over time. By the late 1960s, the Guichon Ranch comprised some 40,000 deeded acres plus 500,000 more in permits and leases, and the Douglas Lake Cattle Company had expanded to 170,000 acres of deeded and leased land, with perhaps another 450,000 acres of Crown land under a grazing permit. Only the Chilco Ranch, with 850,000 combined acres, and the Gang Ranch, with over a million combined acres, were larger. Grasshopper irruptions exposed these inequities but did little to resolve them.

8
Conclusion

In the late nineteenth and early twentieth centuries, a new order was imposed on the land and inhabitants of present-day Interior British Columbia. The remaking of this rather remote region of North America took place in particular ways and at a particular time, but it was neither entirely new nor, in a broad sense, unique. The Interior was distinct from other new-world settings in ecological detail and in the culture and lifeways of its indigenous inhabitants. But as Alfred Crosby and others have shown, old-world cattle and crops, along with their human custodians, had colonized numerous other forest and grassland environments in the age of European imperial expansion, and various ecological niches and many indigenous groups were profoundly altered in the process. For all their local texture, the stories of wild horses and grasshoppers were part of a larger process of "new" world resettlement and global ecological transformation.[1] As such it would be well at this point in the analysis to pull back from the grasslands in order to gain a broader perspective on the people and processes that shaped and transformed this place.

Historian Richard White describes the transition from Native to settler space in the American West in terms of two forms of bio-political organization. Before the arrival of Euro-Americans in the eighteenth century, the West was a "biological republic" where people and animals were interchangeable equals and "pity was the sentiment that animals felt toward humans."[2] By the close of the nineteenth century, however, the West had become a "biological monarchy," a place "where humans reigned, where uselessness was a crime punishable by death, and where enterprise was the reigning virtue."[3] So powerful was the instrumental logic of enterprise in the West that newcomers to this place could begin to see their individual and collective successes as being tied not just to the possession of land and resources (a commonplace of colonial historiography) but to the "destruction of entire species" as well.[4] As White observes, accommodating cattle and other favoured animal species in the West (as elsewhere) often meant attempting to annihilate others.

Much the same transition took place in the drylands of Interior British Columbia in the nineteenth and early twentieth centuries, beginning with the continental fur trade and culminating in the arrival of ranching and the rise of pest extermination as a tool of modern range improvement. In White's evocative words, "Animal persons yielded to animals of enterprise which gleaned the energy of western ecosystems – the interacting species and non-biological environments of the West – to produce hides, meat, and wool that found markets all over the world." At the same time, animals not subject to human rule – animals of inconvenience that interfered with production – effectively became enemies and pests to be exterminated. The transition from biological republic to biological monarchy in the West was neither smooth nor entirely complete. Nonetheless, it marked a major divide in environmental history. Unlike in the indigenous West, where human communities entreated animal spirits so as not to offend them, in the settler West, "human masters took tribute from subject animals and determined their fate."[5]

Ironically, this book says very little about them, but arguably it was cattle, not pests, that were the case in point. Their lives were tied to the same instrumental reasoning that determined the fates of animals identified as pests, and in many ways were the very definition of it. Even though cattle were living creatures, with irreducibly biological traits and behaviours, practically everything about a cow's life from birth to death was controlled: ranchers controlled where they grazed, when and whether they bred, and when and how they died. A wolf or pack of coyotes might claim the occasional cow, of course, and for that countless more wolves and coyotes would be exterminated. But the vast majority of cattle were destined for human dinner plates. Eventually, a rancher's cattle would be rounded up, removed from the range, sold, crowded into railcars, carried off to stockyards or feedlots for finishing; slaughtered; converted into various "modern" products such as fertilizer; and then consumed – and all of this for a profit. This was (and is) the very purpose of cattle in the world. Without this purpose, these animals would not even exist, and because of it, many others would not be allowed to exist. A partial accounting of the carnage involved would include all the bears, cougars, coyotes, wolves, bobcats, badgers, beavers, foxes, prairie dogs, pocket gophers, eagles, owls, porcupines, skunks, weasels, snakes, wild horses, and grasshoppers exterminated over the years, as well as all of the incidental deaths and collateral environmental damage – to say nothing of the social havoc – associated with state-sponsored roundups and bounty hunting and widespread use of chemical poisons, including arsenic, Compound 1080, and later even more harmful synthetics such as DDT. Although impossible to calculate, the total body count for all of western North America in the late nineteenth and twentieth centuries, including incidental deaths, must have been enormous.

None of this is to say that newcomers as a group never appreciated nature or felt sorry for animals when they were mistreated or died. Nor it is meant to be nostalgic about nature or the past, or to idealize indigenous peoples and their relations with the nonhuman world before settlers arrived. However, it is to suggest some fundamental differences between those who were in the West first and those who followed. Like all human communities, the indigenous peoples of the West sought to "order and control the natural world," but their social ordering of nature also required what amounted to a "religious negotiation" of landscape.[6] Ritualized hunting and fishing practices (first salmon and first game ceremonies, for instance) were common practice throughout the North American West, including the drylands of present-day Interior British Columbia. Some indigenous groups sweat-bathed and then sang to the spirits before hunting. Others sang to animals even as they butchered them, and all indigenous groups took special care not to offend the spirits of the animals that consented to being killed. Ultimately, as Richard White observes, the indigenous peoples of the West killed animals "as much by prayer, pleading and reverence as by the arrow or spear."[7] The Europeans who resettled the West from the late eighteenth century onward also sought to order and control the natural world, but their social ordering required nothing like a religious negotiation of landscape. Immigrant newcomers and their descendants in the West were much more instrumental in outlook. In their view (as in ours much of the time), the nonhuman world of nature was there to be used, and was useless or worse when it was not being used. Unlike in the indigenous West, oftentimes the only negotiations to be had in the settler West were narrowly instrumental ones involving land, labour, and capital – the Holy Trinity, as it were, of modern economics. Such negotiations sought not the approval of the spirits but that of the market.

Guided by the market, settlers sought not only to *use* nature but also to *improve* it.[8] As Ellen Meikens Wood reminds us, the word "improve," in its original meaning, implied more than simply making something better. It also meant "doing something for monetary profit, and especially cultivating the land for profit."[9] In John Weaver's words, "To improve the land meant to apply labour and capital, so as to boost the land's carrying capacity and hence its market value."[10] Ranching in the North American West was not cultivation in the usual sense of fenced fields and pastures – the characteristic farming landscapes of England and eastern North America by the late nineteenth century. But it was a business that relied on land, capital, and labour – including the unpaid labour of nonhumans, to say nothing at all of the dispossession of First Nations peoples – to reap profits. In Donald Worster's memorable words, it was a "modern capitalist institution."[11] This meant that pretty much anything that potentially increased the productivity of the land and thus the value and profitability of the province's ranches was potentially an improvement. Enclosure was the archetype, but improvement included less controversial concepts as well, such as irrigation, and the use of better breeds of cattle. Also part of the logic of improvement, and perfectly consistent with the idea of applying capital and labour to the land to increase its carrying capacity and market value, was pest extermination. Killing animals considered pests was simply addition by subtraction. In theory, and to put the point somewhat abstractly, extermination increased the carrying capacity and thus the quality and economic value of the land by divesting it of impediments to production. It also offered a politically expedient alternative to less popular projects for range improvement.

Whether extermination *actually* improved the range was not only another question – and for the record, there was never any evidence that it did – in retrospect, it was also the wrong question. The right question was how to help the range without harming people or the larger nonhuman environment that was both home and habitat. In fairness, some early British Columbians did ask versions of this question, even as they made plans for pest extermination. The strong tendency, however, was to frame environmental problems, which were also social problems, in ways that favoured simpler over better – which is to say easier over fairer and more "sustainable" – solutions such as range restoration and the reallocation of land and resources to the disadvantaged and the dispossessed. Early British Columbians had their reasons, of course: range degradation going back to the earliest days of resettlement; drought and deteriorating economic conditions through the 1920s, culminating in the Great Depression; the resource-draining effects of two world wars; and the very complexity and time-consuming nature of the problems they faced all mattered, as did culture, in the broad sense of generally accepted norms and values, and various other controls on social action such as popular discourse, political ideology, and the law. Economic and political considerations and simple self-interest were also important, however, and at times were determinative, even after the Grazing Act was passed in 1919 and range management fell to the state. In the final analysis, it was always easier to advocate changes in land use than it was to implement them.

And yet there was nothing inevitable about the decisions early British Columbians made: they might have restored the range rather than simply put poison in it; they might have reclaimed wild horses rather than simply annihilate them; they might have created more commonages and community pastures in the grassland rather than simply defend by doing nothing the right of individuals and capital and settlers as a group to monopolize land and resources; they might have acknowledged the inequities of Indian reserves rather than ignore them; they might have listened more to what First Nations peoples were saying rather than simply dismiss and blame them for not valuing property or knowing how to use land properly; and they might have looked more closely at their own land-use practices rather than simply demonize those of others. Even by their own standards, early British Columbians might have pursued fairer and more sustainable futures for people and nonhuman nature alike.

That they often chose not to do so is not the only ending to this story, however, for the fact remains that in many cases the people described in these pages might have done otherwise. It would be naive and contrary to some of the arguments in this book to suggest that early British Columbians were completely unconstrained in their ability to act, because they were not. Nor I am suggesting, counterfactually, that attempts to pursue a different path in this place would have been easy or successful. But I do think British Columbians could have done *better*, not just by each other but also by Aboriginal peoples, and the nonhuman world of nature. This is important, I think, because it reminds us that we could too.

Appendices

Accounting for Extermination

District 1
Wages: $122.98
Bounties: $56.00
Ammunition: $36.00
Total cost: $214.98

Animals destroyed: 56
Cost per animal: $3.83
Ammunition fired: 240 rounds
Average per animal: 4.3 rounds

District 2
Wages: $195.16
Bounties: $319.00
Ammunition: $69.45
Total cost: $583.61

Animals destroyed: 319
Cost per animal: $1.82
Ammunition fired: 631 rounds
Average per animal: 1.97 rounds

District 3
Wages: $182.26
Bounties: $258.00
Ammunition: $88.50
Total cost: $528.76

Animals destroyed: 258
Cost per animal: $2.05
Ammunition fired: 640 rounds
Average per animal: 2.5 rounds

District 4
Wages: $198.39
Bounties: $309.00
Ammunition: $93.85
Total cost: $601.24

Animals destroyed: 309
Cost per animal: $1.94
Ammunition fired: 860 rounds
Average per animal: 2.8 rounds

District 5
Wages: $183.87
Bounties: $323.00
Ammunition: $202.40
Total cost: $709.27

Animals destroyed: 323
Cost per animal: $2.19
Ammunition fired: 1,360 rounds
Average per animal: 4.2 rounds

➤

◄ APPENDIX 1

District 6

Wages: $198.39

Bounties: $383.00

Ammunition: $175.20

Total cost: $756.59

Animals destroyed: 383

Cost per animal: $1.97

Ammunition fired: 1,240 rounds

Average per animal: 3.7 rounds

District 7

Wages: $200.00

Bounties: $302.00

Ammunition: $64.55

Total cost: $566.55

Animals destroyed: 302

Cost per animal: $1.87

Ammunition fired: 620 rounds

Average per animal: 2.0 rounds

APPENDIX 2   Grazing Fees, Nicola Valley, ca. 1920

Name	Cattle	Horses	Amount due	Amount paid
J.H. Webster	4.00		1.30	1.30
Martin Olson	5.00		1.75	
Mrs. A. Patten	82.00	1.00	29.14	29.14
T. Bradshaw	20.00	3.00	9.50	9.50
R. Steffens	120.00	15.00	48.56	48.56
W. Howarth	50.00		17.50	17.50
J.W. Whiteford	560.00		193.90	193.90
W. Cameron	25.00		6.25	6.25
Guichon Ranch	**2,000.00**		**500.00**	**500.00**
Nicola Lake Farm	300.00	50.00	90.63	90.63
Thom. Anderson	38.00		2.85	2.85
F.T. Felps	90.00	12.00	23.44	23.44
J. Wilson	7.00	1.00	0.80	
G. McKay	25.00	4.00	5.75	5.75
W. Lauder	250.00		87.50	87.50
F. Wood	4.00	4.00	3.15	3.15
P. Marquart	6.00	4.00	0.70	0.70
A. Keyon	5.00	1.00	0.70	0.70
G. Allison		12.00	2.63	
J. Collett	158.00	7.00	45.86	
J. Morgan	100.00		26.95	
T. Daly	100.00		40.00	40.00
A. Oelrieh	38.00	5.00	5.00	5.00
G. Monford	27.00	3.00	7.69	7.69
J. Jameson	20.00	4.00	4.90	4.90
J. Carney	40.00	4.00	11.25	11.25
F. Hoelzel	10.00		2.44	2.44
H. Abbott	60.00		15.00	15.00

➤

◄ APPENDIX 2

Name	Cattle	Horses	Amount due	Amount paid
R. Sutherland		10.00	5.00	
F. Sutherland		3.00	1.50	1.50
R. Roberston		400.00	25.00	25.00
D. McLachlan	10.00		1.63	1.63
W. Laabs		20.00	4.08	
H. Pleticha		2.00	0.80	0.80
H. Barr	60.00	10.00	9.96	9.96
H. Cossentine			4.80	4.80
W. Hanks	12.00	6.00	6.35	6.35
Douglas Lake Cattle Co.	**2,100.00**		**525.00**	**525.00**
W.K. Evans	12.00		3.25	
O. Machlin		1.00	0.40	0.40
J. Aye	30.00	10.00	13.83	
P. Betina		3.00	0.62	0.62
W. Bardgett	3.00	7.00	0.33	0.33
R. Crow	6.00	8.00	1.30	
B. Singh	9.00		2.93	2.93
C. Pechetel		7.00	1.22	1.22
J. Desrosiere	18.00	10.00	3.17	3.17
G. Hansen	16.00	3.00	3.21	3.21
R. Cameron		6.00	1.63	1.63
Cameron Bros.	12.00	3.00	2.56	2.56
P. Woods	45.00	21.00	21.84	21.84
T.P. White	15.00	3.00	1.40	1.40
W. Manion	6.00	7.00	1.14	1.14
G. Masey	40.00	7.00	8.25	8.25
F. Thompson		1.00	0.40	
H. Kirkland		4.00	0.83	0.83
J. Fornelli	13.00	2.00	2.90	
J. Hood	50.00		16.25	16.25
A. Rault	9.00	4.00	1.00	1.00
H. Kirkland		1.00	0.40	0.40
J. Smith	40.00	2.00	12.25	
C. Campbell		5.00	2.50	2.50
Dodding and Sons	100.00		22.50	22.50
M. Lukashwich	5.00	6.00	2.38	2.38
A. Anderson	10.00		3.25	
A. Carmicheal	8.00		4.00	4.00
V. Haynes	200.00	6.00	60.00	60.00
J. Kenyon	8.00		1.95	1.95
C. Howell	2.00	3.00	0.33	0.33

➤

◄ APPENDIX 2

Name	Cattle	Horses	Amount due	Amount paid
R. Atkinson	3.00	1.00	1.30	1.30
J. Menzies	10.00	2.00	1.40	1.40
I. Richardson	10.00		4.00	4.00
W. Butler	1.00		0.50	0.50
J. Trembley	25.00		8.13	
C. Dillard	18.00	5.00	3.29	
G. Francis	5.00		1.30	1.30
A. Plath	20.00		3.25	3.25
H. Guernsey	90.00	4.00	22.00	22.00
J. Danwaters	35.00	12.00	20.00	20.00
A. Lendeck	2.00	2.00	0.35	
H. Kinghorn		5.00	2.04	
I. Lewis	87.00	6.00	33.60	33.60
J. Davis	37.00	7.00	1.40	10.40
H. Tweedle	275.00	25.00	69.37	63.37
E.S. Saunders		1.00	0.40	
M. Walker	50.00		9.00	9.00
W. Glover	30.00		4.88	4.88
H. Fremb	3.00		1.05	
Floyd Bros.	30.00		4.50	4.50
J. Budd	15.00	30.00	7.09	7.09
Auger Bros.	20.00		3.25	3.25
L. Sowerby	14.00	24.00	5.70	5.70
B. Bulkot	22.00	3.00	4.88	4.88
J. Graham	9.00	2.00	2.00	2.00
J. Neale	35.00		12.25	12.25
A. Homuth	20.00	3.00	4.75	4.75
J. Madge	40.00		3.25	3.25
S. Thompson	52.00	18.00	3.75	3.75
F. Hurry	36.00	2.00	9.10	9.10
G. Myren	110.00	5.00	9.75	9.75
L. Neimi	11.00	2.00	0.50	0.50
J. Frisken	100.00		12.50	12.50
F. Caserso	200.00	18.00	22.26	22.26
M. Brown	14.00		3.50	3.50
J. Patton	20.00		2.50	2.50
D. Hannant	11.00	10.00	4.08	4.08
J. Stephens	20.00		0.85	0.85
F. Bassett		6.00	1.50	
A. Lindgren	9.00	4.00	0.73	0.73
Total	**8,472.00**	**908.00**	**2,273.23**	**2,135.22**

Source: See note 30 on p. 180.

Notes

Foreword: Mapping the Ecology of Place

1 The "original ecology and function" quotation is from Don Gayton, *The Wheatgrass Mechanism; Science and Imagination in the Western Canadian Landscape* (Saskatoon: Fifth House, 1990), 25; elsewhere Gayton makes the forceful point that 99 percent of North America's grasslands were essentially destroyed in 150 years: Don Gayton, "Tallgrass Dream," in *Landscapes of the Interior: Re-Explorations of Nature and the Human Spirit* (Gabriola Island, BC: New Society, 1996), 96.

2 Don Gayton, Review of Chris Harris (with Ordell Steen, Kristi Iverson, and Harold Rhenisch), *Spirit in the Grass: The Cariboo-Chilcotin's Forgotten Landscape* (108 Mile Ranch, BC: Grasslands Conservation Council of BC and Country Light Publishing, 2007), available at http://www.chrisharris.com/Home/Book%20Store/Spirit%20in%20 the%20Grass.

3 The "eye of a scientist" quotation is attributed to Stuart McLean on Don Gayton's website, http://www.dongayton.ca/; Gayton, "Review."

4 Keri Cronin, *Manufacturing National Park Nature: Photography, Ecology, and the Wilderness Industry of Jasper National Park* (Vancouver: UBC Press, 2011).

5 Gayton, "Review."

6 Isaiah Berlin, *The Hedgehog and the Fox: An Essay on Tolstoy's View of History* (London: Weidenfeld & Nicolson / New York: Simon and Schuster, 1953).

7 See, for example, H.C. Darby, "On the Relations of Geography and History," *Transactions of the Institute of British Geographers* 19 (1953): 1–11; H.C. Darby, "The Problem of Geographical Description," *Transactions of the Institute of British Geographers* 30 (1962): 1–14; H.C. Darby, "Historical Geography," in *Approaches to History*, ed. H.P.R. Finberg, 127–56 (Toronto: University of Toronto Press, 1962); and Graeme Wynn, "A 'Deep History' of *The American Environment*," *Journal of Historical Geography* 43 (2014): 153–56.

8 Michèle D. Dominy, *Calling the Station Home: Place and Identity in New Zealand's High Country* (Lanham, MD: Rowman and Littlefield, 2001), 3. Arturo Escobar uses the term

"atopia" in "Culture Sits in Places: Reflections on Globalism and Subaltern Strategies of Localization," *Political Geography* 20 (2001), 139–74. For earlier reflections upon placelessness, see Edward Relph, *Place and Placelessness* (London: Pion, 1976).

9 O. Steen and K. Iverson, "Natural History," in Harris, *Spirit in the Grass,* 101.

10 The quotation is from Thomas R. Weir, "Ranch Types and Range Uses within the Interior Plateau of British Columbia," *Canadian Geographer* 1, 2 (1952): 73–79; for more recent, and quite different, academic studies of the Cariboo-Chilcotin region, see W. Turkel, *The Archive of Place: Unearthing the Pasts of the Chilcotin Plateau* (Vancouver: UBC Press, 2008), and Joanna I.E. Reid, "Grassland Debates: Conservation and Social Change in the Cariboo-Chilcotin, British Columbia," PhD diss., University of British Columbia, 2010. The latter is abstracted in Joanna Reid, "The Grassland Debates: Conservationists, Ranchers, First Nations, and the Landscape of the Middle Fraser," *BC Studies* 160 (Winter 2008/9): 93–118. See also B. Wikeem and S. Wikeem, *The Grasslands of British Columbia* (Kamloops, BC: Grasslands Conservation Council, 2004).

11 See Grasslands Conservation Council of British Columbia, http://www.bcgrasslands. org.

12 D.W. Meinig, *The Great Columbia Plain: A Historical Geography, 1805–1910* (Seattle: University of Washington Press, 1968).

13 Weir, "Ranch Types and Range Uses," and Thomas R. Weir, *Ranching on the Southern Interior Plateau* (Ottawa: Queen's Printer, 1956).

14 E.W. Tisdale, "The Grasslands of the Southern Interior of British Columbia," *Ecology* 28, 4 (1947): 346–82.

15 Grasslands Conservation Council, *BC Grasslands Mapping Project: A Conservation Risk Assessment* (Kamloops, BC: 2004), 74, cited by Reid, Grassland Debates, 96.

16 All of which has a particular resonance as I write, with the announcement of the Supreme Court of Canada's decision supporting the Tsilhqot'in Nation's claim to almost 675 square miles of forested land west of Williams Lake, British Columbia; see *Tsilhqot'in Nation v. British Columbia,* Supreme Court Judgments, 2014-06-26, Case number 34986, Neutral citation 2014 SCC 44, http://scc-csc.lexum.com/scc-csc/scc-csc/en/item/14246/index.do; also see Sean Fine, "Supreme Court Expands Land-Title Rights in Unanimous Ruling," *Globe and Mail,* 26 June 2014.

17 Peter A. Russell, *How Agriculture Made Canada: Farming in the Nineteenth Century* (Montreal and Kingston: McGill-Queen's University Press, 2012).

18 D.J. Bellegarde and S.G. Purdy, Esketemc First Nation Inquiry: IR 15, 17, and 18 Claim. Ottawa: Indian Claims Commission 2001, 134, http://publications.gc.ca/collections/ Collection/RC31-10-2001E.pdf and cited by Reid, Grassland Debates, 93; see also, for the situation in the Prairie West, Sarah Carter, *Lost Harvests: Prairie Indian Reserve Farmers and Government Policy* (Montreal and Kingston: McGill-Queen's University Press, 1990).

19 David N. Livingstone, *Putting Science in Its Place: Geographies of Scientific Knowledge* (Chicago: University of Chicago Press, 2003).

20 See, for example, Gregg Mitman, "President's Column: Revisiting the Two Cultures," in American Society for Environmental History's *Newsletter* 25, 2 (Summer 2014), which reflects on an article by Paul Voosen, "Historians of Science Seek Détente with Their Subject," *Chronicle of Higher Education,* 27 May 2014.

21 This argument draws from and rests upon the timely argument in Mitman, "President's Column," and the quotations are from this source.

22 Gayton, *Wheatgrass Mechanism,* 12.

23 Laurie Ricou, "Imprinting Landscapes," *Canadian Literature* 157 (1998): 187.

24 Dan Flores, *The Natural West: Environmental History in the Great Plains and Rocky Moun-tains* (Norman: University of Oklahoma Press, 2001), 92; for the world of words, see Benita Parry, "The Postcolonial: Conceptual Category or Chimera?" *Yearbook of English Studies* 27 (1997): 3–21, quotation on 12.

25 Susan Naramore Maher, "Deep Mapping the Biome: The Biology of Place in Don Gay-ton's *The Wheatgrass Mechanism* and John Janovy Jr.'s *Dunwoody Pond,*" *Great Plains Quarterly* 25 (2005): 7–27.

26 Randall Roorda, "Deep Maps in Eco-Literature," *Michigan Quarterly Review* 40, 1 (2001): 257–72; Susan Naramore Maher, "Deep Mapping the Great Plains: Surveying the Liter-ary Cartography of Place," *Western American Literature* 36, 1 (2001): 4–24. See also Susan Naramore Maher, *Deep Map Country: Literary Cartography of the Great Plains* (Lincoln: University of Nebraska Press, 2014). The references in the text are to William Least Heat-Moon, *PrairyErth (A Deep Map)* (New York: Houghton Mifflin, 1991); Wallace Stegner, *Wolf Willow: A History, a Story, and a Memory of the Last Plains Frontier* (New York: Viking Books, 1962); Barry Lopez, *Arctic Dreams: Imagination and Desire in a Northern Landscape* (New York: Scribner, 1986); John McPhee, *Annals of the Former World* (New York: Farrar, Straus and Giroux, 1998); H.D. Thoreau, *Walden, or Life in the Woods* (Bos-ton: Ticknor and Fields, 1854); and Aldo Leopold, *A Sand County Almanac, and Sketches Here and There* (New York: Oxford University Press, 1949).

27 Quotations in this paragraph are from Maher, "Deep Mapping the Biome," 8, 9, with reference to Gayton, *Wheatgrass Mechanism,* and John Janovy Jr., *Dunwoody Pond: Reflec-tions on the High Plains Wetlands and the Cultivation of Naturalists* (Lincoln: University of Nebraska Press, 1994).

28 William Shakespeare, *As You Like It,* act 2, scene 7.

29 Maher, "Deep Mapping the Biome," 26.

CHAPTER 1: INTRODUCTION

1 Cole Harris, "Archival Fieldwork," *Geographical Review* 91, 1/2 (2001): 328–34.

2 Cole Harris, *The Resettlement of British Columbia: Essays on Colonialism and Geographical Change* (Vancouver: UBC Press, 1996).

3 William Cronon, *Changes in the Land: Indians, Colonists and the Ecological History of New England* (New York: Hill and Wang, 1983); Arthur McEvoy, *The Fisherman's Prob-lem: Ecology and Law in the California Fisheries, 1850–1980* (Cambridge University Press, 1986); Richard White, *Land Use, Environment, and Social Change: The Shaping of Island County* (Seattle: University of Washington Press, 1980); also see J.R. McNeill, "Observa-tions on the Nature and Culture of Environmental History," *History and Theory* 42, 4 (2003): 44–59; Richard White, "American Environmental History: The Development of a New Historical Field," *Pacific Historical Review* 54, 3 (1985): 297–335; Donald Wor-ster, "Transformations of the Earth: Toward an Agroecological Perspective in History," *Journal of American History* 76, 4 (1990): 1087–1147; and Graeme Wynn, "Shall We Lin-ger along Ambitionless? Environmental Perspectives on British Columbia," *BC Studies* 142/143 (2004): 5–68.

4 See Harris, *Resettlement,* 219–49, and Cole Harris, *Making Native Space: Colonialism, Resistance, and Reserves in British Columbia* (Vancouver: UBC Press, 2002).

5 The quotation comes from Terry Jordan, *North American Cattle Ranching Frontiers: Origins, Diffusion, and Differentiation* (Albuquerque: University of New Mexico Press, 1993). The best treatment of British Columbia is also the briefest: C. Harris (with David Demeritt), "Farming and Rural Life," in *Resettlement*, especially 234–40; also see Duane Thomson, "The Response of Okanagan Indians to European Settlement," *BC Studies* 101 (Spring 1994): 96–117.

6 Thomas Weir, *Ranching in the Southern Interior Plateau of British Columbia* (Ottawa: Dominion Geographical Branch, 1955), 15.

7 See Mark Fiege, *Irrigated Eden: The Making of an Agricultural Landscape in the American West* (Seattle: University of Washington Press, 1999); Nancy Langston, *Forest Dreams, Forest Nightmares: The Paradox of Old Growth in the Inland West* (Seattle: University of Washington Press, 1996); and Joseph Taylor, *Making Salmon: An Environmental History of Northwest Fisheries Crisis* (Seattle: University of Washington Press, 1999); and Richard White, *The Organic Machine: The Remaking of the Columbia River* (New York: Hill and Wang, 1995).

8 Reviel Netz, *Barbed Wire: An Ecology of Modernity* (Middletown, CT: Wesleyan University Press, 2003), 228–29. For a short but incisive summary of this literature and the ways in which this sort of approach might inform research and storytelling in environmental history, see Linda Nash, "The Agency of Nature or the Nature of Agency," *Environmental History* 10, 1 (2005): 67–69.

9 Here I am building on recent work by Andrew Isenberg, *The Destruction of the Bison: An Environmental History, 1750–1920* (New York: Cambridge University Press, 2000); and Brett Walker, *The Lost Wolves of Japan* (Seattle: University of Washington Press, 2005); and Marsha Weisiger, *Dreaming of Sheep in Navajo Country* (Seattle: University of Washington Press, 2009).

10 The literature in this area is large but start with David Demeritt, "What Is the Social Construction of Nature: A Typology and Sympathetic Critique," *Progress in Human Geography* 26, 6 (2002): 767–90; Dena Pedynowski, "Science(s), Which, When, and Whose: Probing the Metanarrative of Scientific Knowledge in the Social Construction of Nature," *Progress in Human Geography* 27, 6 (2003): 735–52; and Graeme Wynn, "A Fine Balance? Geography at the Millennium," *Canadian Geographer* 43, 1 (1999): 220–43.

11 For an incisive response to the notion that science is "*just* another cultured way of knowing" see Edmund Russell, "Science and Environmental History," *Environmental History* 10, 1 (2005): 81 (emphasis in original). Science as "fairy tale" comes from David Demeritt, "Social Theory and the Reconstruction of Geography," *Transactions of the Institute of British Geographers* 21, 3 (1996): 484, but here too it should be said that this is simply a summary statement of the field, not necessarily Demeritt's own view of science.

12 On science as a discourse and set of culturally specific practices to be studied see Jan Golinski, *Making Natural Knowledge: Constructivism and the History of Science* (Cambridge: Cambridge University Press, 1999); for science as a "cultural formation" see David Livingstone, "Reading the Heavens, Planting the Earth: Cultures of British Science," *History Workshop Journal* 54 (2002): 56. For many brilliant examples of this particular approach to science see Mario Biagioli, ed. *The Science Studies Reader* (London: Routledge, 1999).

13 Theodore Porter, *Trust in Numbers: The Pursuit of Objectivity in Science and Public Life* (Princeton, NJ: Princeton University Press, 1995), 11. For a broader critical engagement with constructivist approaches to science see Ian Hacking, *The Social Construction of*

What? (Cambridge, MA: Harvard University Press, 1999). For a similar view also see Joseph Rouse, "Vampires: Social Constructivism, Realism, and Other Philosophical Undead," *History and Theory* 41 (2002): 60–78, and Kirstin Asdal, "The Problematic Nature of Nature: The Post-Constructivist Challenge to Environmental History," *History and Theory* 42 (2003): 60–74.

14 Notable examples would include all the entries in note 7 above, as well as Dan Flores, *The Natural West: Environmental History in the Great Plains and Rocky Mountains* (Norman: University of Oklahoma Press, 2001); Isenberg, *The Destruction of the Bison*; J.R. McNeill, *Something New Under the Sun: An Environmental History of the Twentieth Century* (New York: W.W. Norton, 2000); and many others.

15 On recent directions in environmental history see the "Anniversary Forum: What's Next for Environmental History?" *Environmental History* 10, 1 (2005): 30–109.

Chapter 2: Wrestling with Wild Horses

1 "Indians Resent Range Order: Reprisals Are Threatened," *Victoria Colonist,* 5 April 1930.

2 "Protests Against Shooting of Wild Range Horses; Indians Aroused," *Vancouver Sun,* 9 April 1930; also see "Range Death Order Stirs Indians," *Vancouver Province,* 4 April 1930.

3 See Douglas Harris, "The Nlha7kapmx Meeting at Lytton, 1879, and the Rule of Law," *BC Studies* 108 (1995–96): 5–25; more generally see J.R. Miller, "Petitioning the Great Mother: First Nations Organizations and Lobbying in London," in *Reflections on Native-Newcomer Relations* (Toronto: University of Toronto Press, 2004), 217–41.

4 Miller, *Reflections,* 227.

5 J.B. Tyrell, ed., *David Thompson's Narrative of His Explorations in Western North America, 1784–1812* (Toronto: Champlain Society, 1916), 377–78.

6 Peter O'Reilly to Superintendent General of Indian Affairs, 5 December 1888, UBC Library, RG10, Department of Indian Affairs, vol. 3704, file 17867, reel C10123.

7 Canada, *Annual Report of the Department of Indian Affairs for 1891,* Sessional Papers (Ottawa, 1892), 54.

8 Cited in British Columbia, *First Report of the Department of Agriculture, 1891* (Victoria, 1892), 847.

9 Ibid.

10 Cited in British Columbia, *Second Report of the Department of Agriculture, 1892* (Victoria, 1893), 934.

11 Ibid.

12 Ibid., 933.

13 British Columbia, *First Report of the Department of Agriculture, 1891* (Victoria, 1892), 767.

14 Cited in British Columbia, *Fourth Report of the Department of Agriculture of the Province of British Columbia, 1894* (Victoria, 1895), 884.

15 British Columbia, *Fourth Report of the Department of Agriculture, 1894* (Victoria: Queen's Printer, 1895), 851.

16 Ibid., 895.

17 This account is drawn from R. Mack, "Invaders at Home on the Range," *Natural History* 2 (1984): 40–47. For a similar analysis see Langston, *Forest Dreams*; and James Young and B. Abbott Sparkes, *Cattle in the Cold Desert* (Logan: Utah State University Press, 1985); on

the Great Plains see Geoff Cunfer, *On the Great Plains: Agriculture and Environment* (College Station: Texas A&M University Press, 2005); and Isenberg, *The Destruction of the Bison.*

18 The reasons for this were complex. According to Mack, the summer drought was probably crucial because large native ruminants like bison needed green forage after spring calving in order to produce sufficient milk for their offspring. Without this critical resource, the Intermountain West was unable to support large numbers of big, herding herbivores.

19 Cunfer, *On the Great Plains.*

20 British Columbia, *Sixth Report of the Department of Agriculture* (Victoria, 1901), 36.

21 See Stephen Pyne, *Awful Splendour: A Fire History of Canada* (Vancouver: UBC Press, 2007).

22 Fire-adapted plants include ponderosa pine, lodgepole pine, western larch, ceanothus, Saskatoon berry, and bluebunch wheatgrass.

23 Don Gayton, *Landscapes of the Interior: Re-Explorations of Nature and the Human Spirit* (Gabriola Island, BC: New Society, 1996).

24 All quotations come from Records of the Hudson's Bay Company relative to the Thompson's River Post (Kamloops, British Columbia), 1821–65, and can be accessed at http://142.36.5.21/thomp-ok/river-post/index.html. These records are also available at BC Archives (hereafter cited as BCA), Fort Kamloops Records, A/B/20/K12 and A/C/20/K12.

25 The literature on fire in the North American west effects is large. The standard reference is James Agee, *Fire Ecology of Pacific Northwest Forests* (Washington, DC: Island Press, 1993).

26 George M. Dawson, *Report on the Area of the Kamloops Map Sheet* (Ottawa, 1895), 7.

27 Ibid., 9.

28 As historian Stephen Pyne reminds us, "Dying fires can speak as trenchantly as the living one. Some of the most profound ecological measures of anthropogenic fire have come from observing the consequences of removing it, for the fire regimes aboriginal peoples laid down were as fundamental to landscapes as the rhythm of the rains and the cycle of green-up and curing."

29 Ranchers and range managers continued to wrestle with these problems well into the twentieth century. See BCA, GR1238, Kamloops Forest District Grazing Reports, 1951–55.

30 British Columbia, "An Act to Provide for the Better Protection of Cattle Ranges," *Statutes of the Province of British Columbia* (Victoria: W.H. Cullen, 1876), 55.

31 British Columbia, "An Act to Protect Winter Stock Ranges," *Statutes of the Province of British Columbia* (Victoria: W.H. Cullen, 1879), 7–8.

32 The literature on ranching is large, but I found the following especially useful: Jordan, *North American Cattle Ranching Frontiers*; Andrew Sluyter, "The Ecological Origins and Consequences of Cattle Ranching in Sixteenth Century New Spain," *Geographical Review* 86, 2 (1996): 161–77; Arnold Strickton, "The Euro-American Ranching Complex," in *Man, Culture and Animals,* ed. M. Harris and E.B. Ross (Washington, DC: Smithsonian Institution, 1965); and Weir, *Ranching.*

33 British Columbia, *Fourth Report of the Department of Agriculture, 1894* (Victoria, 1895), 895.

34 British Columbia, *Second Report of the Department of Agriculture, 1892* (Victoria, 1893), 761.

35 Ibid.

36 Cited in British Columbia, *Fourth Report of the Department of Agriculture, 1894* (Victoria, 1895), 1129.

37 Stephen Jenkins and Michael Ashley, "Wild Horse," in *The Smithsonian Book of North American Mammals,* ed. Don Wilson and Sue Ruff, 1148–63 (Washington, DC: Smithsonian Institution Scholarly Press, 1999).

38 Stephen Jenkins, personal communication.

39 British Columbia, *Seventh Report of the Department of Agriculture, 1902* (Victoria, 1903), 182.

40 See British Columbia, *First Report of the Department of Agriculture, 1891* (Victoria, 1892), 733.

41 For more on coyote hunting and the bounty system see Lillian Ford, "Coyote Goes Downriver: A Historical Geography of Coyote Migration into the Fraser Valley," MA thesis, University of British Columbia, 2000.

42 Cited in British Columbia, *Second Report of the Department of Agriculture, 1892* (Victoria, 1893), 933.

43 British Columbia, *Fourth Report of the Department of Agriculture, 1894* (Victoria: Queen's Printer, 1895), 1171.

44 Cited in British Columbia, *Second Report of the Department of Agriculture, 1892* (Victoria, 1893), 934.

45 British Columbia, *Fifth Report of the Department of Agriculture, 1895–96* (Victoria, 1897), 1171.

46 Cited in British Columbia, *Fourth Report of the Department of Agriculture of the Province of British Columbia, 1895–6* (Victoria, 1897), 1171. Emphasis added.

47 Cole Harris, "How Did Colonialism Dispossess? Comments from an Edge of Empire," *Annals of the Association of American Geographers* 94, 1 (2004): 170.

48 Gilbert Malcolm Sproat, "Report on Grazing Lands," 4 February 1878, UBC Library, RG10, vol. 3657, file 9360, reel C10115.

49 British Columbia, "An Act for the Extermination of Wild Horses," *Revised Statutes of British Columbia, 1896* (Victoria, 1897): 2193.

50 Cited in British Columbia, *Fifth Report of the Department of Agriculture, 1896* (Victoria, 1897), 1171.

51 Cited in British Columbia, *Sixth Report of the Department of Agriculture, 1900* (Victoria, 1901), 7.

52 Cited in British Columbia, *Seventh Report of the Department of Agriculture, 1902* (Victoria, 1903), 182.

53 Ibid.

54 Lieutenant Colonel H. Thomson, "Our Military Horses," lecture to the Aldershot Military Society, London, 10 December 1895.

55 "Breaking in Wild Horses," *Vancouver Sun,* 10 April 1901.

56 Untitled, *Victoria Colonist,* 8 May 1901.

57 "Mustang Hunt Planned," *Vancouver Daily Province,* 5 July 1925.

58 John Mackenzie, *The Empire of Nature: Hunting, Conservation, and British Imperialism* (Manchester: Manchester University Press, 1988), 18.

59 British Columbia, "Animals Act," *Revised Statutes of British Columbia, 1908* (Victoria, 1909).

60 This was noted in a partial letter to the deputy minister of lands dated 5 January 1911, BCA, GR1441, file 52130, reel B03541.

61 Aitken (first name illegible) to J.D. Prentice, 8 December 1910, BCA, MS2881, Western Canadian Ranching Company Records, box 503, file 1.

62 J.H. Calhoun to C.A. Holland, 27 December 1910, BCA, MS2881, Western Canadian Ranching Company Records, box 510, file 2.

CHAPTER 3: THE BIOGEOGRAPHY OF DISPOSSESSION

1 For an overview, see Richard Cannings and Sydney Cannings, *British Columbia: A Natural History* (Vancouver: Greystone Books, 2000).

2 This account draws from Richard Hebda, "Postglacial History of the Grasslands of Southern British Columbia and Adjacent Regions," in *Grassland Ecology and Classification Symposium Proceedings*, ed. A.C. Nicholson, A. McLean, and T.E. Baker (Victoria: Ministry of Forests, 1982), 157–88 and 63–91 respectively; on North American natural history more generally see E.C. Pielou, *After the Ice: The Return of Life to Glaciated North America* (Chicago: University of Chicago Press, 1991).

3 This discussion draws from Hebda, "Postglacial History." For an updated and much more technical account see Richard Hebda, "British Columbia Vegetation and Climate History with Focus on 6 KA BP," *Géographie physique et Quaternaire* 49, 1 (1995): 55–79.

4 This is an ecological conceit, of course. Human borders matter a great deal in environmental history, but if we ignore them for a moment and view the drylands the way a biogeographer might, we quickly see that they are actually part of a much larger intermountain ecosystem that extends into the present-day United States. On borders in environmental history see Joseph Taylor, "Boundary Terminology," *Environmental History* 13, 3 (2008): 454–81.

5 These reflections are based largely on Roy L. Carlson and Luke Dalla Bona, eds., *Early Human Occupation in British Columbia* (Vancouver: UBC Press, 1996); and David L. Pokotylo and Donald Mitchell, "Prehistory of the Northern Plateau," in *Handbook of North American Indians*, vol. 12, *Plateau*, ed. Deward E. Walker Jr. (Washington, DC: Smithsonian Institution Scholarly Press, 1998), 81–102. For a detailed account of one area within the drylands, see B. Hayden, *A Complex Culture of the British Columbia Plateau: Traditional Stl'atl'imx Resource Use* (Vancouver: UBC Press, 1992).

6 Bruce J. McFadden, *Fossil Horses: Systematics, Paleobiology, and Evolution of the Family Equidae* (New York: Cambridge University Press, 1992).

7 Quoted in Don Gayton, "British Columbia Grasslands: Monitoring Vegetation Change (Kamloops: Forrex – Forest Research Extension Partnership, 2003), http://www.forrex.org/publications/forrexseries/fs7_Part1.pdf, 11, 12.

8 David Wyatt, "Nicola," in Walker, *Handbook of North American Indians*, vol. 12, *Plateau*, 220–22.

9 These reflections are based on Iain Gordon and Herbert Prins, eds., *The Ecology of Grazing and Browsing* (Berlin: Springer, 2008).

10 Elizabeth Vibert, *Traders' Tales: Narratives of Cultural Encounters in the Columbia Plateau, 1807–1846* (Norman and London: University of Oklahoma Press, 1997), 223.

11 Deward Walker and Roderick Sprague, "History until 1846," in Walker, *Handbook of North American Indians*, vol. 12, *Plateau*, 142.

12 James Teit, "The Salishan Tribes of the Western Plateau," in *Forty-Fifth Annual Report of the Bureau of American Ethnology to the Secretary of the Smithsonian Institution, 1927–1929* (Washington, DC: Government Printing Office, 1930), 277; anthropologist Paul Nadasdy warns that words like "property" often have no analogue in Aboriginal languages; see his essay "'Property' and Aboriginal Land Claims in the Canadian Subarctic: Some Theoretical Considerations," *American Anthropologist* 104, 1 (2002): 247–61.

13 Paige Raibmon, *Authentic Indians: Episodes of Encounter from the Late-Nineteenth-Century Northwest Coast* (Durham, NC: Duke University Press, 2005).

14 See, for example, Jesse Morin et al., "Late Prehistoric Settlement Patterns and Population Dynamics along the Mid-Fraser," *BC Studies* 160 (2008/09): 9–34.

15 Scholars debate how the fur trade affected Native society, but the fact of change is not in doubt. See Harris, *Resettlement,* 31–67; for an alternative perspective, see Duane Thomson and Marianne Ignace, "They Made Themselves Our Guests": Power Relationships in the Interior Plateau Region of the Cordillera in the Fur Trade Era," *BC Studies* 146 (2005): 3–35; the classic account of the continental fur trade is Harold Innis, *The Fur Trade in Canada: An Introduction to Economic History* (Toronto: University of Toronto Press, 1962); also see Arthur Ray, *Indians in the Fur Trade: Their Role as Trappers, Hunters and Middlemen in the Lands Southwest of Hudson Bay, 1660–1870* (Toronto: University of Toronto Press, 1974).

16 R.M. Galois, "Measles, 1847–1850: The First Modern Epidemic in British Columbia," *BC Studies* 109 (1996): 31–43. On disease more generally see Robert Boyd, *The Coming of the Spirit of Pestilence: Introduced Infectious Diseases and Population Decline among Northwest Coast Indians* (Seattle: University of Washington Press, 1999), and Harris, *Resettlement,* 3–30.

17 Daniel Clayton, *Islands of Truth: The Imperial Fashioning of Vancouver Island* (Vancouver: UBC Press, 2000), 236.

18 W. Cox to W.A.G. Young, 16 February 1861, University of British Columbia Archives (hereafter cited as UBCA), Colonial Office, British Columbia Correspondence (hereafter cited as CO 60), file 367, reel B1320. The quotation comes from C. Harris, *Resettlement,* 111.

19 Walker and Sprague, "History until 1846," 142. On the role of missionaries in British Columbia see Brett Christophers, *Positioning the Missionary: John Booth Good and the Confluence of Cultures in Nineteenth-Century British Columbia* (Vancouver: UBC Press, 1998).

20 G.M. Grant, *Ocean to Ocean: Sanford Fleming's Expedition through Canada in 1872 ...* (Toronto, 1873), 288, http://eco.canadiana.org.

21 Ibid.

22 A. Birch to Chief Commissioner of Lands and Works, 22 November 1867, UBCA, Colonial Correspondence CO 60/29, reel 21.

23 British Columbia, *Report of the Commission of Lands and Works for 1873* (Victoria, 1874).

24 This phrase comes from James Belich, *Replenishing the Earth: The Settler Revolution and the Rise of the Anglo-World, 1783–1939* (New York: Oxford University Press (2009), 261.

25 On Australia see Robert Foster, "Coexistence and Colonization on Pastoral Leases in South Australia, 1851–99," in *Despotic Dominion,* ed. John McLaren, A.R. Buck, and Nancy Wright, 248–65 (Vancouver: UBC Press, 2005); on New Zealand see Vaughan Wood, Tom Brooking, and Peter Perry, "Pastoralism and Politics: Reinterpreting Contests for Territory in Auckland Province, New Zealand, 1853–1864," *Journal of Historical Geography* 34 (2008): 220–41.

26 For a similar observation in the New Zealand context see Wood, Brooking, and Perry, "Pastoralism and Politics," 220–41.

27 Edwin Tisdale, "The Grasslands of the Southern Interior of British Columbia," *Ecology* 28, 4 (1947): 346–82. Lower grasslands were separate and distinct from what Tisdale called "middle" and "upper" grasslands, which, at the time he wrote, were generally used for spring and fall range (cattle spent the dry summer months foraging for pine grass in forested uplands).

28 Don Gayton, *British Columbia Grasslands: Monitoring Vegetation Change* (Kamloops: Forrex–Forest Research Extension Partnership, 2003), http://www.forrex.org/publications/forrexseries/fs7_Part1.pdf.

29 These numbers come from BCA, MS2881, Western Canadian Ranching Company Records, box 256, file 1, and Weir, *Ranching*, 145.

30 Cited in C. Harris, *Making Native Space*, 39.

31 William Cox to Colonial Secretary, 25 October 1862, B1320, file 377/22.

32 Ibid., 42.

33 C. Harris, *Making Native Space*.

34 All quotations come from I.W. Powell, Report, 27 July 1874, UBC Library, RG10, vol. 11028, file SRR-1, reel T-3967. Also see C. Harris, *Making Native Space*, 82–84.

35 Petitions from the Thompson River District, 25 March 1875, UBC Library, RG10, vol. 3617, file 4590b, reel C10107.

36 C.J. Grandidier to Lieutenant Colonel Powell, Commissioner of Indian Affairs, UBC Library, RG10, vol. 3612, file 3763, reel C10106.

37 C.J. Grandidier to Editor of *Victoria Standard*, Okanagan Mission, 28 August 1874, Journals of the Legislative Assembly of the Province of British Columbia, 4th Session, 1st Parliament, 1875.

38 C. Harris, *Making Native Space*, 120.

39 G.M. Sproat to Superintendent General of Indian Affairs, 30 June 1877, UBC Library, RG10, vol. 3650, file 8497, reel C10114.

40 Gilbert Sproat, "Grazing Lands" (extract from a general report to the provincial government), 4 February 1878, UBC Library, RG10, Department of Indian Affairs, vol. 3657, file 9360, reel C10115.

41 Gilbert M. Sproat, Minutes of Decision, vol. 4, book 11, Field Notes Nicola Valley, 28 September 1878 (copy held by Natural Resources Canada, Vancouver Regional Office).

42 G.M. Sproat, Report on Stock Raising, 9 August 1877, UBC Library, RG10, vol. 3612, file 3756–16, reel C10106.

43 Ibid.

44 Ibid.

45 Ibid.

46 C. Harris, *Making Native Space*, 131.

47 G.M. Sproat to E.A. Meredith, Ottawa, 27 October 1877, UBC Library, RG10, vol. 3656, file 9063, reel 10115.

48 See C. Harris, *Making Native Space*, especially 265–323.

49 See "Correspondence regarding Commonages, 1880–1888," UBC Library, RG10, vol. 3701, file 17514–11, reel C10123.

50 These quotations come from G.M. Sproat to Superintendent General of Indian Affairs, 16 November 1879, UBC Library, RG10, vol. 3703, file 17626, reel C10123.

51 Indian Agent McKay to Superintendent General of Indian Affairs, 22 January 1885, UBC Library, RG10, vol. 3704, file 17867.

52 Peter O'Reilly to Superintendent General of Indian Affairs, 23 November 1889, UBC Library, RG10, vol. 3704, file 17867, reel C10123.

53 Forbes Vernon to Isaiah Powell, 28 January 1888, UBC Library, RG10, Department of Indian Affairs, vol. 3701, file 17514–1, reel C10123.

54 Johnny Chilliheetza, Francois Chilliheetza, Alexander Chilliheetza, and Jimmy Illichullet to Hon. Mr. Dewdney, Department of Indian Affairs, 25 October 1889, UBC Library, RG10, vol. 3704, file 17867, reel C10123.

55 For a full summary of the land purchases associated with the amendment see British Columbia *Sessional Papers*, 4th Parliament, 3rd Session, Victoria, 1885. Many of these ranches still exist.

56 The northern portion of the dry Interior is poorly drained in many places, resulting in numerous swamps and marshes in depressions caused by the uneven deposition of moraines from the last ice age. It was in these many glacial depressions that water accumulated, and created conditions conducive to meadow growth. See Weir, *Ranching*.

57 Nancy Langston noted a similar relationship in her book *Where Land and Water Meet: A Western Landscape Transformed* (Seattle: University of Washington Press, 2003), 18–19 and 101–6.

58 See, for example, BCA, MS1633, Kenworthy Family Fonds (Empire Valley Ranch, Chilcotin), reel 1.

59 "Brief from Cariboo Cattleman's Association, October 1944," BCA, GR0520, Royal Commission on Forestry, box 16, file 4.

60 "Grazing Report for 1954, H.K. Debeck," BCA, GR1238, box 1, file 2.

61 See, for example, "Range Burning (Hargreaves), Correspondence and Reports, April 1916–April 1917," BCA, GR1441, file 7679, reel 93.

62 For early-twentieth-century accounts of meadow use by ranchers see "Grazing Reconnaissance Chilcotin Division, 1914," BCA, GR1441, file 2822, reel 44, and "Grazing Report, 1914–1915," file 2824. On meadow use in the mid-twentieth century see Weir, *Ranching*.

63 Ken Brealey, "Travels from Point Ellice: Peter O'Reilly and the Indian Reserve System in British Columbia," *BC Studies* 115/116 (Autumn/Winter 1997/98): 181–236.

64 Peter O'Reilly, Minutes of Decision, Correspondence and Sketches, June 1885–March 1889, O'Reilly to Superintendent General of Indian Affairs, 16 August 1887 (copies held by Natural Resources Canada, Vancouver Regional Office).

65 Ibid.

66 Ibid.

67 Extract of Letter from Fletcher, 8 July 1891, Minutes of Decision, Correspondence and Sketches, June 1885–March 1889 (copy held by Natural Resources Canada, Vancouver Regional Office).

68 This account is drawn variously from BCA, MS2811, Western Canadian Ranching Company Records; BCA, MS1286, J.D. Prentice Papers; BCA, MS1648, J.D. Prentice Papers about Ranching; BCA, MS1692, Bayiff Family Papers, 1845–1968; the best secondary source on ranching the Cariboo-Chilcotin region is still Weir, *Ranching*.

69 This account is drawn variously from BCA, MS1083, Douglas Lake Cattle Company Records, 1880–1979.

70 For more on this see C. Harris, *Making Native Space*, 45–166.

71 British Columbia, *Transcripts of the Royal Commission on Indian Affairs for the Province of British Columbia*, Meeting with the Canoe Creek Band or Tribe of Indians at Canoe Creek Indian Reserve, 17 July 1914.

72 British Columbia, *Transcripts*, Meeting with the Stone Band or Tribe of Indians on Anaham Indian Reserve, 22 July 1914.

73 British Columbia, *Transcripts*, Meeting with the Indians of the Alkali Lake Tribe on the Alkali Lake Reserve, 10 July 1914.

74 British Columbia, *Transcripts*, Meeting with the Indians of the Bonaparte Tribe on the Bonaparte Reserve, 31 October 1913.

75 British Columbia, *Transcripts*, Meeting with the Ashnola Band or Tribe of Indians on the Ashnola Reserve, 13 October, 1913.

76 British Columbia, *Transcripts*, Meeting with the Kamloops Band or Tribe of Indians on the Kamloops Indian Reserve, 28 October 1913

77 British Columbia, *Transcripts*, Meeting with the Shuswap Band or Tribe (Dog Creek Band) of Indians on Dog Creek Indian Reserve, 18 July 1914.

78 British Columbia, *Transcripts*, Meeting with the Shuswap Band or Tribe of Indians at the Alkali Lake Reserve, 10 July 1914. "Cayuse" was a common word used to describe "Indian horses."

79 British Columbia, *Transcripts*, Meeting with the Canoe Creek Band or Tribe of Indians at Canoe Creek Indian Reserve, 17 July 1914.

80 British Columbia, *Transcripts*, Meeting with the Stone Band or Tribe of Indians on Anaham Indian Reserve, 22 July 1914.

81 Indian Agent John Smith to Secretary, Royal Commission on Indian Affairs, 12 June 1915, UBCA, RG10, Department of Indian Affairs, vol. 11021, file 538, reel T3958.

82 Owen Sanger, "Report on Grazing Reconnaissance, Chilcotin District," 21 December 1914, BCA, GR1441, file 2822, reel 44.

83 Ashdown Green to Secretary, Royal Commission on Indian Affairs, 29 April 1914, UBC Library, RG10, Department of Indian Affairs, vol. 11021, file 538, reel T3958.

84 William Ditchburn to Duncan Scott, 7 July 1914, UBC Library, RG10, vol. 11009, file 510, reel T3956.

85 The literature on conservation is large. The classic account in the American context is Samuel P. Hays, *Conservation and the Gospel of Efficiency: The Progressive Conservation Movement* (Pittsburgh: University of Pittsburgh Press, 1999); for a critique and recent overview of the literature see Richard Judd, *Common Lands, Common Peoples: The Origins of Conservation in Northern New England* (Cambridge: Cambridge University Press, 1997). On early fisheries conservation in British Columbia see Matthew Evenden, "Locating Science, Locating Salmon: Institutions, Linkages, and Spatial Practices in Early British Columbia Fisheries Science," *Environment and Planning D: Society and Space* 22, 3 (2004): 355–72; and on forestry see T.R. Roach, "Stewards of the People's Wealth: The Founding of British Columbia's Forest Branch," *Journal of Forest History* 28, 1 (1984): 14–23; there are no comprehensive studies of range conservation in British Columbia but see Edwin Tisdale, A. McLean, and S.E. Clarke, "Range Resources and Their Management in British Columbia," *Journal of Range Management* 7, 1 (1954): 3–9; Edwin Tisdale, "Grazing of Forest Land in Interior British Columbia," *Journal of Forestry* 12, 1 (December 1950): 856–60; on very recent developments see Joanna Reid, "The Grassland Debates: Conservationists, Ranchers, First Nations, and the Landscape of the Middle Fraser," *BC Studies* 160 (2008/09): 93–118.

86 The American forester Gifford Pinchot, for example, argued that conservation was "the greatest good to the greatest number for longest time." See Char Miller, *Gifford Pinchot and the Making of Modern Environmentalism* (Washington, DC: Island Press, 2004); on utilitarianism in general see Richard T. Garner and Andrew Oldenquist, eds., *Society and the Individual: Readings in Political and Social Philosophy* (Belmont, CA: Wadsworth, 1990), 194–203.

87 Barry Ferguson, *Remaking Liberalism: The Intellectual Legacy of Adam Shortt, O.D. Skelton, W.C. Clark and W.A. Mackintosh, 1890–1925* (Montreal and Kingston: McGill-Queen's University Press, 1993).

88 James Murton, *Creating a Modern Countryside: Liberalism and Land Resettlement in British Columbia* (Vancouver: UBC Press, 2007), 16.

89 On similar problems elsewhere in Canada see John Sandlos, *Hunters at the Margin: Native People and Wildlife Conservation in the Northwest Territories* (Vancouver: UBC Press, 2007).

90 This notion of a state commons borrows from Louis Warren, *The Hunter's Game: Poachers and Conservationists in Twentieth Century America* (New Haven, CT: Yale University Press, 1997); also see Patricia Marchak, "What Happens When Common Property Becomes Uncommon?" *BC Studies* 80 (1989): 3–23.

CHAPTER 4: ERADICATING WILD HORSES

1 Thomas Mackenzie to the Minister of Lands, 12 August 1918, BCA, GR1441, file 2733–2, reel 44.

2 See Arthur Sampson, "Succession as a Factor in Range Management," *Journal of Forestry* 15, 5 (1917): 593–96; Arthur Sampson, "Natural Re-Vegetation of Rangelands Based upon Growth Requirements and Life History of the Vegetation," *Journal of Agricultural Research* 3, 2 (1914): 93–147; Arthur Sampson, *Pasture and Range Management* (New York: John Wiley and Sons, 1923), summarizes and expands on these ideas; on Clements's influence in plant ecology, see Donald Worster, *Nature's Economy: A History of Ecological Ideas* (Cambridge: Cambridge University Press, 1985).

3 Sampson, "Succession as a Factor," 593.

4 Mark Westoby, Brian Walker, and Imanuel Noy-Meir, "Opportunistic Management for Rangelands Not at Equilibrium," *Journal of Range Management* 42, 4 (1989): 266–74; Worster, *Nature's Economy*.

5 D.D. Briske, S.D. Fuhlendorf, and F.E. Smeins, "State and Transition Models, Thresholds, and Rangeland Health: A Synthesis of Ecological Concepts and Perspectives," *Rangeland Ecology and Management* 58 (2005): 1–10.

6 Reed F. Noss and Allen Y. Cooperrider, *Saving Nature's Legacy: Protecting and Restoring Biodiversity* (Washington, DC: Island Press, 1994); on the state and transition model see Westoby, Walker, and Noy-Meir, "Opportunistic Management for Rangelands"; also see M.H. Friedel, "Range Condition Assessment and the Concept of Thresholds," *Journal of Range Management* 44, 5 (1991): 422–26, and W.A. Laycock, "Stable States and Thresholds of Range Condition on North American Rangelands: A Viewpoint," *Journal of Range Management* 44, 5 (1991): 427–33.

7 Worster, *Nature's Economy*.

8 The notion of panoptic vision comes from Michel Foucault, *Discipline and Punish: The Birth of the Prison* (London: Vintage Books, 1979).

9 This discussion of numbers and management builds on Bruno Latour, *Science in Action: How to Follow Scientists and Engineers through Society* (Cambridge, MA: Harvard University Press, 1987), which uses the concept of centres of calculation; and also Porter, *Trust in Numbers*, which treats numbers as "technologies of distance," ix.

10 The concept of legibility comes from James Scott, *Seeing Like a State: How Certain Schemes to Improve the Human Condition Have Failed* (New Haven, CT: Yale University Press, 1998).

11 Thomas Mackenzie to William Ditchburn, 4 February 1924, UBC Library, RG10, Department of Indian Affairs, vol. 11001, file 901/36–11, reel T3951.

12 Ibid.

13 Thomas Mackenzie, "Report on Wild and Stray Horse Control," 1 January 1924, BCA, GR1441, file 52130, part 1, reel 1281.

14 Johnny Chilliheetza to George Pragnell, 13 March 1924, UBC Library, RG10, Department of Indian Affairs, vol. 11001, file 901/36–11, reel T3951.

15 On western property law and colonial dispossession see Nicholas Blomley, "Law, Property, and the Geography of Violence: The Frontier, the Survey and the Grid," *Annals of the Association of American Geographers* 93, 1 (2003): 121–41; more generally see McLaren, Buck, and Wright, *Despotic Dominion,* and John Weaver, *The Great Land Rush and the Making of the Modern World, 1650–1900* (Montreal and Kingston: McGill-Queen's University Press, 2003).

16 Joseph Raz, "The Rule of Law and Its Virtue," in *The Authority of Law: Essays on Law and Morality* (Oxford: Clarendon Press, 1979), 213.

17 D. Harris, "The Nlha7kapmx Meeting at Lytton," 17.

18 Thomas Mackenzie to William Ditchburn, 15 April 1924, UBC Library, RG10, Department of Indian Affairs, vol. 11001, file 901/36–11, part B, reel T3951.

19 William Ditchburn to Thomas Mackenzie, 2 May 1924, UBC Library, RG10, vol. 11001, file 901/36–11, part B, reel T3951. For an analysis of federal-provincial problems in the context of reserve creation in British Columbia see C. Harris, *Making Native Space,* 70–166.

20 William Ditchburn to George Pragnell, 28 March 1924, UBC Library, RG10, vol. 11001, file 901–36–11.

21 "Conference of Dr. Duncan Scott, Deputy Superintendent General of Indian Affairs of the Dominion of Canada, W.E. Ditchburn, Chief Inspector of Indian Agencies of British Columbia, with the Executive Committee of the Allied Tribes of British Columbia," 7 August 1923 (copies held by Department of Indian Affairs and Northern Development, Vancouver Regional Office).

22 On similar problems in the United States see Marsha Weisiger, *Dreaming of Sheep in Navajo Country.*

23 George Pragnell to William Ditchburn, 9 April 1924, UBC Library, RG10, Department of Indian Affairs, vol. 11001, file 901/36–11, part B, reel T3951.

24 Ibid.

25 George Pragnell to William Ditchburn, 31 March 1924, UBC Library, RG10, Department of Indian Affairs, vol. 11001, file 901/36–11, part B, reel T3951.

26 The reasons are unclear, but perhaps they were uneasy about having their horses near military men with guns.

27 This summary is drawn variously from reports and correspondence in UBC Library, RG10, vol. 11001, file 901/36–11, parts A and B, reel T3951.

28 Pragnell to Ditchburn, 11 April 1924, UBC Library, RG10, vol. 11001, file 901/36–11, part B, reel T3951.

29 George Pragnell to William Ditchburn, 19 April 1924, UBC Library, RG10, vol. 11001, file 901/36–11, parts A and B.

30 Thomas Mackenzie, "Report in Connection with Wild and Stray Horse Control on the Crown Ranges of British Columbia since January 1 1924" (unpublished), BCA, GR1441, file 52130, reel 1281.

31 William Ditchburn to Thomas Mackenzie, 9 April 1926, BCA, GR1441, file 52130, reel B03541.

32 A.E. MacLeod to William Ditchburn, 22 April 1924 , BCA, GR1441, file 52130, reel B03541.

33 Thomas Mackenzie to A.E. MacLeod, 6 September 1924, BCA, GR1441, file 52130, part 2, reel 1281.

34 George C. Hay to J.H. Grisdale, 26 December 1926, UBC Library, RG10, Department of Indian Affairs, vol. 11001, file 901/36–11, reel T3951.

35 William Ditchburn to George Pragnell, 28 February, 1927, UBC Library, RG10, Department of Indian Affairs, vol. 11001, file 901/36–11, part B, T3951.

36 The quotations in the paragraph are from George Pragnell to William Ditchburn, 2 March 1927, UBC Library, RG10, Department of Indian Affairs, vol. 11001, file 901/36–11, part B, reel T3951.

37 Chief Chilliheetza, Jack Quattelle, Jim Alexander, Johnnie Tezestky, and William Jack to Indian Agent Barber, 5 December 1929, BCA, GR1441, file 52130a, reel 03542.

38 W.H. Brown to Thomas Mackenzie, 6 December 1929, BCA, GR1441, file 52131a, reel 03542.

39 Thomas Mackenzie to Peter Caverhill (n.d., likely January 1930), BCA, GR1441, file 52131a, reel 03542.

40 Grazing Commission transcripts, May–June 1930 (unpublished copies held by Ministry of Range and Forestry Library, Victoria), 162.

41 Ibid., 671.

42 Ibid.

43 Ibid., 679.

44 Ibid., 338.

45 Ibid., 95.

46 Ibid., 800.

47 Thomas Mackenzie to Harry Tweedle, 4, January 1930, BCA, GR1441, file 52131a, reel 03542.

48 Thomas Mackenzie to W.H. Brown, 22 December 1930, BCA, GR1441, file 52131a, reel 03542. Emphasis added.

49 J.J. Gillis to Hon. F.P. Burden, Minister of Lands, 5 April 1930, BCA, GR1441, file 52130, part 1, reel 1281.

50 "Indians Drop Old Wealth Tradition," *Merritt Herald*, 24 April 1930.

51 St. Clair to the District Forester, 3 February 1947, BCA, GR1441, file 5213, reel 03541, is one example.

52 McKay to George Melrose, 8 February 1946, BCA, GR1441, file 52131, reel 03541.

53 Chief Sam Mitchell to Mr. E. Kenney, Minister of Lands and Forests, 10 January 1947, BCA, GR1441, file 52131, reel 03541.

54 This account is drawn from Robert Cameron to the District Forester, 13 December 1938, and other files in BCA, GR1441, file 11064, reel 144.

55 M.T. Wallace, "Grazing Report for 1951," BCA, GR1238, Kamloops Forest District, Grazing Reports, 1951–55.

56 This account is drawn from BCA, GR1441, file 52130, part 1, reel 1281.

57 Ibid.

58 Dan Weir to Louis LeBourdais, 2 January 1946, BCA, MS0676, Louis LeBourdais Papers, box 6, file 25.

59 BCA, MS0676, Louis LeBourdais Papers, box 6, file 25, "Plan for the Reclamation of British Columbia's Wild Horses" (n.d. but probably 1940).

60 R.G. McKee to Louis LeBourdais, 1 June 1940, BCA, MS0676, Louis LeBourdais Papers, box 6, file 25.

61 "Brutality Claimed in Horse Kills," *Victoria Daily Times*, 28 February 1951.

62 "Horses Suffocate in Sealed Boxcar," *Vancouver Daily Province*, 7 August 1951.

63 "SPCA Charges Wild Horses Mistreated," *Victoria Daily Times*, 12 November 1958.

64 There is a large literature on the rise of animal rights in Europe and the United States, but to my knowledge only scattered and general coverage of Canada. In the American context

see Dianne L. Beers, *For the Prevention of Cruelty: The History and Legacy of Animal Rights Activism in the United States* (Athens: Ohio University Press, 2006); for a broader and deeper perspective on these matters see Rod Preece, *Brute Souls, Happy Beasts, and Evolution: The Historical Status of Animals* (Vancouver: UBC Press, 2006).

65 Vancouver Public Library, Canadian Wild Horse Society Scrapbook, article by Tom Hazlitt, "The Best Friend a Wild Horse Ever Had."

66 H.K. Debeck, "Eliminating Excess Horses in British Columbia," *Journal of Range Management* 6, 2 (March 1953): 132–36.

67 Louise McFadden, "Let's Stop Killing Our Wild Horses," *British Columbia Journal* (December 1965): 12.

68 Henry Parham, *Nature Lover in British Columbia* (London: H.F. & G. Witherby, 1937).

69 William Turkel, *The Archive of Place: Unearthing the Pasts of the Chilcotin Plateau* (Vancouver: UBC Press, 2007). Although this book places considerable emphasis on the role of material artifacts in the land in constructing local histories of place, it also observes that "the different ways a place is imagined do as much to shape the understanding of what happened there as any physical trace ever could," 227.

70 "Special Report: The Killing of Wild Horses," *Vancouver Sun,* 18 March 1988.

71 Ibid.

72 See British Columbia, *Reports of the Forest Branch*, 1924–60 (Victoria: Government Printing Office).

73 M.I. Aiche to Deputy Minister of Agriculture, 12 November 1925, BCA, GR1441, file 52130, part 2, reel 1281.

74 George Poolman to Thomas Mackenzie, 26 October 1925, BCA, GR1441, file 52130, part 2, reel 1281.

75 Thomas Mackenzie to the Chief Forester, 18 September 1929, BCA, GR1441, file 52130, part 1, reel 1281.

76 John S. Chapman to W.H. Brown, 29 November 1929, BCA, GR1441, file 52130, part 1, reel 1281.

77 Chas. Anders to Henry Young, 12 April 1930, BCA, GR1441, file 52130, part 1, reel 1281.

78 Thomas Mackenzie to George Ball, 14 May 1927, BCA, GR1441, file 52130, reel 1281. For more on Russian contracts see "Breaking in Wild Horses," *Vancouver Province,* 10 April 1902.

79 For a recent example see Elwyn Hartley Edwards, *Wild Horses: A Spirit Unbroken* (Stillwater, MN: Voyageur Press, 1995).

CHAPTER 5: GRAPPLING WITH GRASSHOPPERS

1 Harris (with David Demeritt), "Farming and Rural Life," in *Resettlement*, 236.

2 The scientific literature on grasshoppers is large, but I found the following useful: Dennis Fielding and Merlyn Brusven, "Livestock Grazing and Grasshoppers: An Interregional Perspective," *University of Idaho College of Agriculture Bulletin* 786 (1996): 1–12, and Robert E. Pfadt, *Field Guide to Common Western Grasshoppers* (Laramie, WY: Agricultural Experiment Station, 2002).

3 British Columbia, *First Report of the Department of Agriculture for 1890* (Victoria, 1891), 827. On the Rocky Mountain locust see Annette Atkins, *Harvest of Grief: Grasshopper Plagues and Public Assistance in Minnesota, 1873–1878* (St. Paul: Minnesota Historical Society Press, 1984), and Jeffery A. Lockwood, *Locust: The Devastating Rise and Mysterious Disappearance of an Insect That Shaped the American Frontier* (New York: Basic Books, 2004).

4 On the role of birds in the history of insect control see Matthew Evenden, "The Laborers of Nature: Economic Ornithology and the Role of Birds as Agents of Biological Pest Control in North American Agriculture, 1880–1930," *Forest and Conservation History* 39, 4 (1995): 172–83.

5 Reprinted in British Columbia, *First Report of the Department of Agriculture, 1891* (Victoria, 1892), 827.

6 Ibid., 742.

7 British Columbia, *Second Report of the Department of Agriculture of the Province of British Columbia, 1892* (Victoria, 1893), 722.

8 "Locust Control," *British Columbia Department of Agriculture Circular* (Victoria, 1921), 4.

9 Historian James Whorton notes that they had been used "since at least the beginning of the Christian era, and were still being recommended, on a small scale, in the mid-1800s." See James Whorton, *Before Silent Spring: Pesticides and Public Health in Pre-DDT America* (Princeton, NJ: Princeton University Press, 1974), 17.

10 Jackson to Thomas Ellis, 6 April 1900, BCA, BC Cattle Company Records, MS2882, box 254, file 14.

11 Cited in E.R. Buckell, "The Locusts of British Columbia," in *Proceedings of the Entomological Society of British Columbia* (Victoria: King's Printer, 1921), 114. Presented to the British Columbia Entomological Society, March 1919.

12 Ibid.

13 Lockwood, *Locust,* xix.

14 British Columbia, *First Report of the Department of Agriculture, 1891* (Victoria, 1892), 827.

15 Canada, *Annual Report of the Dominion Entomologist for 1903* (Ottawa: King's Printer, 1904), 176.

16 On American entomology see W. Conner Sorenson, *Brethren of the Net: American Entomology, 1840–1880* (Tuscaloosa: University of Alabama Press, 1995); on Canadian entomology see Stéphane Castonguay, "Naturalizing Federalism: Insect Outbreaks and the Centralization of Entomological Research in Canada, 1884–1914," *Canadian Historical Review* 85, 1 (2004): 1–34.

17 Canada, *Annual Report of the Dominion Entomologist for 1900* (Ottawa: King's Printer, 1901). For more on James Fletcher's career see Paul Riegart, *From Arsenic to DDT: A History of Entomology in Western Canada* (Toronto: University of Toronto Press, 1980), 59–80.

18 British Columbia, *Proceedings of the Entomological Society of British Columbia* (Victoria: King's Printer, 1921), 116.

19 Tom Wilson, "The Outbreak of Locusts of 1914," in *Proceedings of the Entomological Society of British Columbia* (Victoria: King's Printer, 1915), 41–42; on the history of mobile nature in the American West see Fiege, *Irrigated Eden,* and Mark Fiege, "The Weedy West: Mobile Nature, Boundaries, and Common Space in the Montana Landscape," *Western Historical Quarterly* 36, 1 (2005): 22–48.

20 Cited in Buckell, "The Locusts of British Columbia," 114.

21 Wilson, "The Outbreak of Locusts."

22 Owen Sanger, "Grazing Reconnaissance, Chilcotin District," 21 December 1914, BCA, GR1441, file 2822, reel 44.

23 On ecological patchiness, including discussions of grasshoppers, see Monica Turner, Robert Gardener, and Robert O'Neill, *Landscape Ecology in Theory and Practice: Pattern and Process* (Madison: University of Wisconsin Press, 2001); on the historical ecology of patchy landscape in the American Intermountain West see Langston, *Forest Dreams.*

24 Canada, *Annual Report of the Department of Indian Affairs for 1890* (Ottawa: King's Printer, 1891), 54.

25 Canada, *Annual Report of the Department of Indian Affairs for 1914* (Ottawa: King's Printer, 1915).

26 On colonial science and its connections in British Columbia see Evenden, "Locating Science, Locating Salmon"; on colonial science more generally see Roy McLeod, ed., *Nature and Empire: Science and the Colonial Enterprise* (Chicago: University of Chicago Press, 2011).

27 Thomas Mackenzie to Ernest Simms, 19 April 1921, BCA, GR1441, file 8657, reel 108.

28 Thomas Mackenzie to the Department of Militia and Defense, 6 August 1919, BCA, GR1441, file 8657, reel 108.

29 Lt. Colonel (name illegible) to Thomas Mackenzie, 12 August 1919, BCA, GR1441, Lands and Works, file 8657, reel 108.

30 On war and pest control see Edmund Russell, *War and Nature: Fighting Humans and Insects with Chemicals from World War I to Silent Spring* (New York: Cambridge University Press, 2001); Joshua Blu Buhs, *The Fire Ant Wars: Nature, Science, and Public Policy in Twentieth-Century America* (Chicago: University of Chicago Press, 2004); and Clinton Evans, *The War on Weeds in the Prairie West: An Environmental History* (Calgary: University of Calgary Press, 2002).

31 See, for example, "Farmers Prepare to Halt Armies," *Victoria Daily Times*, 13 May 1927; "Ready for War on BC Grasshoppers," *Vancouver Province*, 20 May 1927; and "War with Grasshoppers," *Victoria Colonist*, 22 May 1927.

32 See Castonguay, "Naturalizing Federalism."

33 E.R. Buckell, "The Grasshopper Problem in Canada," in *Proceedings of the Fourth International Locust Conference, Cairo, Egypt, April 22, 1936*, Appendix 42 (Cairo: Government Press, 1937).

34 Edmund Russell, "Speaking of Annihilation: Mobilizing for War against Human and Insect Enemies, 1914–1945," *Journal of American History* 82, 4 (1996): 1509.

35 Thomas Mackenzie, "Report of the Grazing Commissioner," in *Report of the Forest Branch for 1921* (Victoria: Government Printer, 1922), 54.

36 R.C. Treherne, "The Grasshopper and the Range" (n.d. but probably 1919), BCA, GR1441, file 8657, reel 108.

37 Castonguay, "Naturalizing Federalism," 19. On inventory sciences in Canada more generally see Suzanne Zeller, *Inventing Canada: Early Victorian Science and the Idea of a Transcontinental Nation* (Toronto: University of Toronto Press, 1987).

38 For an account of the spread of Darwinian thinking in the life and environmental sciences, see Peter J. Bowler, *The Norton History of the Environmental Sciences* (New York: W.W. Norton, 1992), especially 428–502.

39 R.C. Treherne, "The Grasshopper and the Range" (n.d. but probably 1919), BCA, GR1441, file 8657, reel 108.

40 This analysis draws from recent scholarly emphasis on situating science in its spatial as well as historical contexts. See Matthew Evenden, "Locating Science, Locating Salmon," 355–72; Arn M. Keeling, "Charting Marine Pollution Science: Oceanography on Canada's West Coast, 1938–1970," *Journal of Historical Geography* 33 (2007): 403–28; Robert Kohler, "Place and Practice in Field Biology," *History of Science* 11 (2002): 189–210; David Livingstone, *Putting Science in Its Place: Geographies of Scientific Knowledge* (Chicago: University of Chicago Press, 2003); David Livingstone, "The Spaces of Knowledge: Contributions Toward an Historical Geography of Science," *Environment and Planning D: Society and*

Space 13 (1995): 5–34; Simon Naylor, "Historical Geographies of Science; Places, Contexts, Cartographies," *British Journal for the History of Science* 38 (2005): 1–12; and Steven Shapin, "Placing the View from Nowhere: Historical and Sociological Problems in the Location of Science," *Transactions of the Institute of British Geographers,* n.s., 23, 1 (1998): 5–12.

41 This is suggested by Boyd, *The Coming of the Spirit of Pestilence*; Cole Harris, "Voices of Smallpox around the Strait of Georgia," in *Resettlement,* 3–30.

42 Historians and geographers have done much to deconstruct Western (particularly North American) notions of wilderness. There are numerous entries in this literature but the classic recent account is William Cronon, "The Trouble with Wilderness, or Getting Back to the Wrong Nature," in *Uncommon Ground: Rethinking the Human Place in Nature,* ed. William Cronon, 69–90 (New York: W.W. Norton, 1995).

43 Virginia DeJohn Anderson, *Creatures of Empire: How Domestic Animals Transformed Early America* (New York: Oxford University Press, 2004); the phrase "animals of enterprise" comes from Richard White, "Animals and Enterprise," in *The Oxford History of the American West,* ed. Clyde Milner, 237–73 (New York: Oxford University Press, 1994).

44 These details are drawn from various files in BCA, MS2881, Western Canadian Ranching Company Papers, 1884–1952.

45 E.R. Buckell, "The Influence of Locusts on the Ranges of British Columbia," in *Fifty-First Report of the Entomological Society of Ontario, 1920* (Toronto: printed by Clarkson James, 1921), 24–25.

46 Cronon, *Changes in the Land,* especially 127–56.

47 Buckell, "Influence of Locusts," 26.

48 Ontario, *Proceedings of the Ontario Entomological Society, 1921* (Toronto: printed by Clarkson James, 1922).

49 Sharon Kingsland, *Modeling Nature: Episodes in the History of Population Ecology* (Chicago: University of Chicago Press, 1995); also see Bowler, *Norton History* and Worster, *Nature's Economy.*

50 Quoted in Bowler, *Norton History,* 530.

51 On oceanographic approaches to fisheries science see Tim Smith, *Scaling Fisheries: The Science of Measuring the Effects of Fishing, 1855–1955* (New York: Cambridge University Press, 1994).

52 R.C. Treherne and E.R. Buckell, *The Grasshoppers of British Columbia with Particular Reference to the Influence of Injurious Species on the Range Lands of the Province,* Entomological Branch Circular No. 25 (Ottawa: King's Printer 1924), 2–3.

53 Their differences were probably more a matter of emphasis, since Elton understood that hunting affected the animal populations he studied. On the other hand, Elton's research interest was clearly directed toward natural determinants of fluctuations. See C.S. Elton, "Periodic Fluctuations in the Numbers of Animals: Their Causes and Effects," *Journal of Experimental Biology* 2 (1924): 119–63.

54 For an examination of this problem in environmental history see John Sandlos and Yolanda Wiersma, "Once There Were So Many: Animals as Ecological Baselines," *Environmental History* 16, 3 (July 2011): 400–7.

55 For new entomological understandings see Fielding and Brusven, "Livestock Grazing and Grasshoppers."

56 Robert E. Pfadt, *Field Guide.*

57 Cited in Ontario, *Proceedings of the Ontario Entomological Society,* 28.

58 R.C. Treherne to Thomas Mackenzie, 6 August 1919, BCA, GR1441, file 8657a, reel 3279.

59 For an analysis of similar influences in the history of fishery science see Joseph Taylor III, "The Political Economy of Fishery Science and the Road Not Taken," *Journal of the History of Biology* 31, 1 (1998): 33–59.

60 Thomas Mackenzie to E.R. Buckell, 22 December 1922, BCA, GR1441, file 8657, reel 108.

61 On early twentieth-century range conservation practices see Arthur Sampson, *Range and Pasture Management* (New York: John Wiley and Sons, 1923). On the history of range science and management in the American context see Thomas G. Alexander, "From Rule of Thumb to Scientific Range Management: The Case of the Intermountain Region of the Forest Service," *Western Historical Quarterly* 18, 4 (1987): 409–28; William D. Rowley, *U.S. Forest Service Grazing and Rangelands: A History* (College Station: Texas A&M University Press, 1985); Nathan Sayre, "The Genesis, History and Limits of Carrying Capacity," *Annals of the Association of American Geographers* 98, 1 (2008): 120–34; and Christian C. Young, "Defining the Range: The Development of Carrying Capacity in Management Practice," *Journal of the History of Biology* 31, 1 (1998): 61–83.

62 On similar problems in the Alberta range cattle industry see Max Foran, *Trails and Trials: Markets and Land Use in the Alberta Cattle Industry* (Calgary: University of Calgary Press, 2003).

63 These reflections are drawn from BCA, MS1083, Douglas Lake Cattle Company Records, 1880–1979; also see Nina Wooliams, *Cattle Ranch: The Story of the Douglas Lake Cattle Company* (Vancouver: Douglas and McIntyre, 1979).

64 David Igler, *Industrial Cowboys: Miller and Lux and the Transformation of the Far West, 1850–1920* (Berkeley: University of California Press, 2001), 5.

65 Frank Ward, "Report to the Shareholders for the Year Ending April 30, 1925," BCA, MS1082, box 3, file 1.

66 Nicola Stock Breeders' Association to T.D. Pattullo, Minister of Lands, 5 March 1925, BCA, GR1441, file 8657, reel 108. Emphasis added.

67 Buckell's account comes from Treherne and Buckell, "Grasshoppers of British Columbia," 20.

68 "Turkeys Will Halt Hopper Pest," *Vancouver Daily Province*, 27 May 1926.

69 Treherne and Buckell, "Grasshoppers of British Columbia," 19.

70 E.R. Buckell, "The Grasshopper Problem in Canada," 4.

71 W.H. Brown to Thomas Mackenzie, 11 September 1924, BCA, GR1441, file 8567, reel 108.

72 "Farmers Prepare to Halt Insect Armies," *Victoria Daily Times*, 13 May 1924.

73 W.H. Brown to Thomas Mackenzie, 11 September 1924, BCA, GR1441, file 8675a, reel 108.

74 Thomas Mackenzie, "Memorandum for the Honorable Minister of Lands," 6 August 1924, BCA, GR1441, file 8657, reel 108.

Chapter 6: Resisting Range Monopoly

1 Wooliams, *Cattle Ranch*.

2 Ibid., 87.

3 Harris (with Demeritt), *Resettlement*, 237.

4 The archival record appears to be incomplete.

5 "British Columbia and the Livestock Industry," 9 September 1913, BCA, GR1441, file 2733.

6 On the importance of staples production in British Columbia, see Cole Harris, "Industry and the Good Life around Idaho Peak," *Canadian Historical Review* 66, 3 (1985): 325–43;

Roger Hayter, *Flexible Crossroads: The Restructuring of British Columbia's Forest Economy* (Vancouver: UBC Press, 2000); and Dianne Newell, "Dispersal and Concentration: The Slowly Changing Spatial Pattern of the British Columbia Salmon Canning Industry," *Journal of Historical Geography* 14, 1 (1988): 22–36. On the staples production more generally see Harold Innis, *Staples, Markets, and Cultural Change: Selected Essays*, ed. Daniel Drache (Montreal and Kingston: McGill-Queen's University Press, 1995).

7 Peter Hulme, "The Spontaneous Hand of Nature: Nature, Savagery, Colonialism and the Enlightenment," in *The Enlightenment and Its Shadows*, ed. Peter Hulme and L.J. Jordanova, 16–34 (London: Routledge, 1990).

8 At least not agriculture they recognized. On forms of Aboriginal cultivation see Nancy J. Turner, "Burning Mountainsides for Better Crops: Aboriginal Burning Practices in British Columbia," *Archaeology in Montana* 32, 2 (1991): 57–73.

9 Dispossession could be justified on numerous other grounds. See C. Harris, "How Did Colonialism Dispossess?"

10 Harris (with Demeritt), *Resettlement*, 220; also see David Demeritt, "Visions of Agriculture in British Columbia," *BC Studies* 108 (1995–96): 29–59.

11 James Douglas to the Duke of Newcastle, 25 October 1860, UBCA, Colonial Correspondence CO 60, reel 1.

12 George M. Grant, *Ocean to Ocean: Sanford Fleming's Expedition through Canada in 1872 ...*, http://eco.canadiana.ca/view/oocihm.30275/3?r=0&s=1.

13 Simon Ryan, *The Cartographic Eye: How Explorers Saw Australia* (New York: Cambridge University Press, 1996), 75.

14 M. Begbie, Report on Captain Clarke's Land Scheme (n.d. but probably August 1860), UBCA, Colonial Correspondence CO 60/8, reel 10.

15 Landscape as both "visual ideology" and "a way of seeing" comes from Denis Cosgrove, "Prospect, Perspective and the Evolution of the Landscape Idea," *Transactions of the Institute of British Geographers* 10, 1 (1985): 45–62; the notion of landscape as an act of "colonial erasure" is suggested by Mary Louise Pratt, *Imperial Eyes: Travel Writing and Transculturation* (London: Routledge, 1992).

16 Landscape as "text" comes from Trevor J. Barnes and James Duncan, *Writing Worlds: Discourse, Text and Metaphor in the Representation of Landscape* (London: Routledge, 1991).

17 Turner, "Burning Mountainsides"; Pyne, *Awful Splendour*.

18 This analysis draws inspiration from White, *The Organic Machine*, and Fiege, *Irrigated Eden*.

19 Alan Seager, "The Resource Economy," in *The Pacific Province: A History of British Columbia*, ed. Hugh Johnson, 231–32 (Vancouver: Douglas and McIntyre, 1996).

20 Ian MacLachlan, *Kill and Chill: Reconstructing Canada's Beef Commodity Chain* (Toronto: University of Toronto Press, 2001), 96.

21 On "time-space compression" see Harris, *Resettlement*, and more generally, David Harvey, *The Condition of Postmodernity: An Enquiry into the Origins of Cultural Change* (Cambridge, MA: Blackwell, 1990), especially 201–323.

22 G.M. Dawson, "Note on agriculture and stock raising and extent of cultivable land in British Columbia," *Report on Surveys and Preliminary Operations on the Canadian Pacific Railway up to January 1877* (Ottawa, 1878), 252.

23 These figures come from Gregory Thomas, *The British Columbia Ranching Frontier, 1858–1896*, MA thesis, University of British Columbia, 1976.

24 Jordan, *North American Cattle Ranching Frontiers*, 260n24; White, "Animals and Enterprise," in Milner, *Oxford History of the American West*, 254.

25 BCA, MS2881, Western Canadian Ranching Company Records, box 506, files 1–3.

26 BCA, MS1648, J.D. Prentice Papers about Ranching, 193–46, microfilm, reel 98102–4.

27 C.A. Holland to W. Brayne, 10 August 1910, BCA, MS2881, Western Canadian Ranching Company Records, box 503, file 1.

28 On urbanization in British Columbia see Graeme Wynn, "The Rise of Vancouver," in *Vancouver and Its Region,* ed. Graeme Wynn and Timothy Oke, 69–148 (Vancouver: UBC Press, 1992).

29 R.R. Benedict, *Report on Grazing of Livestock on Crown Lands* (n.d. but probably 1911–12), BCA, GR0948, BC Forest Branch, box 1, file 10.

30 This analysis is based on the Douglas Lake Cattle Company Papers, BCA, MS1082, boxes 3 and 4, numerous files; also see Wooliams, *Cattle Ranch,* and Weir, *Ranching,* 121–56.

31 Benedict, *Report on Grazing of Livestock on Crown Lands* (n.d. but probably 1911–12), BCA, GR0948, BC Forest Branch, box 1, file 10.

32 British Columbia, *Report of Forest Branch of the Department of Lands for the Year Ending December 31st, 1912* (Victoria, 1913), 23.

33 H.H. Christie, *British Columbia and the Livestock Industry,* BCA, GR1441, Department of Lands and Works, file 2733, reel 121.

34 Owen Sanger to Deputy Minister of Agriculture, n.d., BCA, GR1441, file 2823, reel 44.

35 Sanger's views are also evident in Owen Sanger, *Grazing Reconnaissance, Chilcotin District,* 21 December 1914, BCA, GR1441, file 2822, reel 44.

36 Percy LeMare (District Forester), "Report on Grazing, Lillooet District," ca. 10 July 1914, BCA, GR1441, reel 44, file 2824.

37 "Petition from the Ranchers and Cattlemen of Aspen Grove," February 1914, BCA, GR1441, file 2733, reel 44.

38 H. Cleasby to R.E. Benedict (Forestry Department), 16 February 1917, BCA, GR1441, file 2733, reel 44.

39 H.E. Foster (or Forster, a rancher, I believe) to W.R. Ross, 12 February 1914, BCA, GR1441, file 2733, reel 44.

40 Thomas Mackenzie to the Deputy Minister of Lands (n.d. but most likely summer 1918), BCA, GR1441, file 8550, reel B3279.

41 Thomas Mackenzie to the Minister of Lands, 24 August 1920, BCA, GR1441, file 7682, reel 93.

42 Thomas Mackenzie, "Memorandum for the Honorable Minister of Lands," 24 August 1920, BCA, GR1441, file 7682, reel 93.

43 E.R. Buckell to Thomas Mackenzie, telegram, 9 July 1926, BCA, GR1441, file 8567b, reel 3279.

44 Andrew Hutchinson to Thomas Mackenzie, UBCA, box 18, file 12.

45 Richard Guilford to Thomas Mackenzie, 20 August 1920, BCA, GR1441, file 7682, reel 93.

46 E.R. Buckell to Thomas Mackenzie, 14 July 1925, BCA, GR1441, file 8567a, reel 108.

47 Thomas Mackenzie to the Deputy Minister of Agriculture, 14 November 1925, BCA, GR1441, file 8567, reel 108.

48 Thomas Mackenzie to E.R. Buckell, 15 September 1925, BCA, GR1441, file 8657a, reel 108.

49 On South African approaches to insect control see Lize-Marié van der Watt, "'To Kill the Locusts, but Not Destroy Farmers': Officials, Farmers, and the Plagues of Pharaoh, 1920–1935," *South African Historical Journal* 62, 2 (2010): 356–83; more generally see William Beinart, *The Rise of Conservation in South Africa: Settlers, Livestock and the Environment, 1770–1950* (Oxford: Oxford University Press, 2003).

50 Thomas McKenzie to E.R. Buckell, 12 January 1923, BCA, GR1441, file 8657, reel 108.
51 Ibid.
52 Thomas Mackenzie to the District Forester (at Vernon), 27 January 1925, BCA, GR1441, file 8567a, reel 108.
53 W.H. Brown to Thomas Mackenzie, 25 July 1925, BCA, GR1441, file 8567a, reel 108.
54 L.P. Guichon to Thomas Mackenzie, 22 August 1927, BCA, GR1441, file 8567a, reel 108.
55 On a similar spatial approach to weed control in the American west, see Fiege, "Weedy West."
56 Thomas Mackenzie, Minutes of the Grasshopper Control Committee, 16 January 1930, BCA, GR1441, file 8567, reel 108.
57 White, *The Organic Machine*, 15.
58 On the intersection of power, law, and space more generally see Nicholas Blomley, *Law, Space and the Geographies of Power* (New York: Guilford Press, 1994).
59 Ibid.
60 "Grasshopper Control Act, 1930," BCA, GR1441, file 8567, reel 108.
61 Ibid.
62 Ibid.

Chapter 7: New Enemies, Enduring Difficulties

1 E.R. Buckell to P.Z. Caverhill, 7 February 1935, BCA, GR1441, file 8567, reel 108.
2 George Melrose to Supervisors and Rangers, 21 April 1932, BCA, GR1453, Kamloops Forest District, box 4, file 47.
3 British Columbia, *Grazing Manual for the General Information and Guidance of Forest Officers* (Victoria: Forest Service, 1935), 19 (copy held by Ministry of Forests Library, Victoria).
4 George Melrose to Supervisors and Rangers, 17 November 1932, BCA, GR1453, Kamloops Forest District, box 4, file 42.
5 L.B. Thomson, "A Survey of the Problems of the Range Livestock Industry in British Columbia in 1931." Unpublished report, LAC, RG 17, Dept. of Agriculture, vol. 3233, file 169-1, 5.
6 Ibid., 6.
7 Ibid., 9.
8 L.B. Thomson, E.W. Tisdale, and L.P. Guichon, *Report of the Committee to Investigate Range Matters in the Riske Creek Area, August 1938* (copy of unpublished report held by Ministry of Forests Library, Victoria).
9 George Copley to the District Forester, 19 July 1932, BCA, MS1082, Douglas Lake Cattle Company Records, box 5, file 7.
10 George Melrose to the Chief Forester, 8 September 1933, BCA, GR1191, box 15, file 482.
11 H.N. Whitford and R.D. Craig, *The Forests of British Columbia* (Ottawa: Commission of Conservation, 1918), 64.
12 This account comes from Owen Sanger (Forest Assistant) to Percy LeMare (District Forester), "Report on Grazing" (n.d.), BCA, GR1441, file 2822, reel 44.
13 Percy Lemare to Owen Sanger (n.d. but almost certainly 1917), BCA, GR1441, file 2822, reel 44.
14 See Langston, *Forest Dreams*; Stephen Pyne, *Fire in America: A Cultural History of Wildland and Rural Fire* (Princeton, NJ: Princeton University Press, 1982).

15 Quoted in British Columbia, *Report of the British Columbia Forest Branch for 1913* (Victoria, 1914), 23.
16 Langston, *Forest Dreams*.
17 Stephen Pyne, *Awful Splendour*, 315.
18 John Parminter, *Protection as Conservation: Safeguarding British Columbia's Forests from Fire* (Victoria: Ministry of Forests, 1982).
19 This episode is based correspondence and reports in "Range Burning," BCA, GR1441, file 7679, reel 93.
20 Don Gayton, *British Columbia Grasslands: Monitoring Vegetation Change* (Kamloops: Forrex – Forest Research Extension Partnership, 2003), 8.
21 Ibid. There is some debate about the dramatic increase in woody shrub density in the late nineteenth and early twentieth centuries; see K.B. Cawker, "Fire History and Grassland Vegetation Change: Three Pollen Diagrams from Southern British Columbia," *Canadian Journal of Botany* 61, 4 (1983): 1126–39.
22 By the 1950s, forest encroachment had become a focus for research. See "Report to the Royal Commission on Forests and Forestry, British Columbia by W.C. Pendray, Forest Agrologist," BCA, GR1379, British Columbia Forest Service, Forest Briefs to the Commission on Forest Resources, box 1, file 4.
23 Ralph Hopping, "Depreciation by Forest Insects," paper presented at the British Columbia Forest Convention, Victoria, 1921 (copy held by Ministry of Forests Library); also see R. Hopping and M. Prebble, "The Principal Forest Insects," BCA, GR0520, Commission on Forests Resources, box 10, file 15; and C.S. Wood and L. Unger, *Mountain Pine Beetle: A History of Outbreaks in Pine Forests in British Columbia, 1910–1995* (Victoria: Canadian Forest Service, 1996).
24 Hopping, "Depreciation by Forest Insects."
25 Frank Ward, "Report to Nicola Stockbreeders Association, November 1936," BCA, MS1082, box 1, file 6.
26 "Egypt Adopts Nicola Valley Plan to Rid Land of Age-Old Scourge of Grasshoppers," *Vancouver Province*, 13 June 1936.
27 E.R. Buckell, "Regional Problems: The Problem of Non-Gregarious Grasshoppers, Draft Resolution," in *Proceedings of the Fourth International Locust Conference, Cairo, Egypt, April 22, 1936*, Appendix 43 (Cairo: Government Press, 1937).
28 "Scourge of the Range: BC Grasshopper Plague Beaten," *Vancouver Province*, 13 October 1938.
29 "Worst Grasshopper Plague Hits the Interior," *Vancouver Province*, 3 October 1943.
30 Canada, Department of Mines and Resources, *Report of Indian Affairs Branch for 1944* (Ottawa: Kings Printer, 1945), 198.
31 "Joe Coutlee, Who Has Ridden Ranges for Sixty Years, Has Never Seen Red-Legged Grasshoppers As Bad," *Merritt Herald*, 13 August 1944.
32 "Douglas Lake Cattle Company Annual Report, 1943–44," BCA, MS1082, Douglas Lake Cattle Company Records, box 1, file 1.
33 "Douglas Lake Ranch Annual Report for 1944–45," BCA, MS1082, Douglas Lake Cattle Company Records, box 1, file 1.
34 E.R. Buckell, "The Grasshopper Outbreak of 1944 in British Columbia," *Canadian Entomologist* 67 (1944): 115–16.
35 Lockwood, *Locust*; W. Conner Sorrenson, *Brethren of the Net: American Entomology, 1840–1880* (Tuscaloosa: University of Alabama Press, 1995), 127–49.

36 Jacobus Faure, "The Phases of the Rocky Mountain Locust *Melanoplus mexicanus*," *Journal of Economic Entomology* 26 (1933): 706–18.

37 See Boris B.P. Uvarov, *Locusts and Grasshoppers: A Handbook for Their Study and Control* (London: Imperial Bureau of Entomology, 1928). For a general overview of phase theory see Lockwood, *Locust*, 125–58.

38 For contemporary understandings of locust and grasshopper biology (and control) see S.K. Gangwere, M.C. Muralirangan, and M. Muralirangan, eds., *Bionomics of Grasshoppers, Katydids, and Their Kin* (Oxford: CAB International, 1997).

39 Lockwood, *Locust*, 154.

40 Ibid.

41 Jeffrey Lockwood, "Taxonomic Status of the Rocky Mountain Locust: Morphometric Comparisons of *Melanoplus spretus* (Walsh) with Solitary and Migratory *Melanoplus sanguinipes* (F.)," *Canadian Entomologist* 121, 12 (1989): 1103–09; Lockwood, *Locust*, 180–224.

42 Lockwood, *Locust*, 225–54.

43 "Control Areas Should Not Be Discouraged Because of 1944 Grasshopper Outbreak," *Kamloops Sentinel*, 22 November 1944; "Red Leg Grasshopper Pest in 1944 Expected Back in 1945," *Merritt Herald*, 17 November 1944.

44 Ibid. Interestingly, Buckell noticed the increase in gophers and the way it expanded *mexicanus* breeding areas but apparently did not sound any alarm at the time. See E.R. Buckell, "The Use of Oil Sprays in Grasshopper Control in British Columbia," *Canadian Entomologist* 72, 8 (1940): 149–50.

45 David W. Nagorsen, *Rodents and Lagomorphs of British Columbia* (Victoria: Royal BC Museum, 2005), 220.

46 On pocket gopher ecology see "Northern Pocket Gopher," in *The Smithsonian Book of North American Mammals*, ed. Don Wilson and Sue Ruff, 474–77 (Washington, DC: Smithsonian Institution Scholarly Press, 1999); Robert Baker, Robert D. Bradley, and Lee R. McAlily Jr., "Pocket Gophers," in *Wild Mammals of North America: Biology, Management, and Conservation*, ed. George Feldhamer, Bruce Thompson, and Joseph Chapman, 276–87 (Baltimore: Johns Hopkins University Press, 2003).

47 There are no specific scientific studies of gopher-badger interactions in British Columbia that could be used to give the analysis greater rigour. However, see C. Hoodicoff, *Badger Prey Ecology: The Ecology of Six Small Mammals found in British Columbia* (Victoria: Ministry of Environment, 2006).

48 On the tick paralysis problem see Eric Hearle, "Notes on a Serious Outbreak of Tick Paralysis in Cattle," *Proceedings of the BC Entomological Society, March 1933* (Victoria, 1933), 11–16.

49 E.R. Buckell to George Spencer, 23 November 1944, UBCA, George J. Spencer Papers, box 2, file 17.

50 George Spencer to E.R. Buckell, 2 December 1944, UBCA, George J. Spencer Papers, box 2, file 18.

51 George Spencer to Lawrence Guichon, 15 April 1947, UBCA, George J. Spencer Papers, box 2, file 17.

52 E.P. Venables, "Fifty Years of Entomology in the Interior of British Columbia," in *Proceedings of the Entomological Society of British Columbia* 48 (1953): 19.

53 "Grasshopper War Blamed," *Victoria Daily Times*, 26 June 1936; phrase from Rachel Carson, *Silent Spring* (Greenwich: Fawcett Publications, 1962).

54 E.R. Buckell, "Grasshopper Control," *Merritt Herald*, 24 November 1933. There are no data on arsenic poisoning of other animals that could be used to give this statement greater substance.

55 Thomas Dunlop, *DDT: Scientists, Citizens and Public Policy* (Princeton, NJ: Princeton University Press, 1981). Buckell and Spencer experimented with DDT in 1947; see George Spencer to E.R. Buckell, 24 July 1947, UBCA, George J. Spencer Papers, box 2, file 17.

56 Thomas P. Mackenzie, "Report of the Commissioner of Grazing," in *Report of the Forest Branch for 1919* (Victoria: King's Printer, 1920), 27.

57 Peter Z. Caverhill, *Report of the Forest Branch for 1936* (Victoria: King's Printer, 1937), 43.

58 Gordon Sloan, *Report of the Commissioner Relating to the Forest Resources of British Columbia*, vol. 1 (Victoria: Queen's Printer, 1957), 705–6.

59 Alastair McLean, "Administration of British Columbia Ranges," unpublished report, December 1974, Crown Land Registry, Range Management, file 325, 148. Emphasis added.

60 Weir, *Ranching*, 117.

61 MacLachlan, *Kill and Chill*.

62 George Copley to the Chief Forester, 10 July 1939, BCA, GR1191, Kamloops Forest District, box 7, file 206.

Chapter 8: Conclusion

1 Alfred Crosby, *Ecological Imperialism: The Biological Expansion of Europe, 900–1900* (New York: Cambridge University Press, 1986); William Beinart, *Environment and Empire* (Oxford: Oxford University Press, 2007); Tom Griffiths and Libby Robin, eds., *Ecology and Empire: Environmental History of Settler Societies* (Edinburgh: Keele University Press, 1997); Eleanor Melville, *A Plague of Sheep: Environmental Consequences of the Conquest of Mexico* (New York: Cambridge University Press, 1994).

2 White, "Animals and Enterprise," in Milner, *Oxford History of the American West*, 237.

3 Ibid., 257.

4 Ibid., 238.

5 Ibid., 257.

6 Ibid., 237.

7 Ibid., 238.

8 On the concept of improvement in agriculture see Weaver, *The Great Land Rush*, and Ellen Meikens Wood, *The Origins of Capitalism: A Longer View* (New York: Verso, 2002); for a useful summary see Ellen Meikens Wood, "The Agrarian Origins of the Capitalism," *Monthly Review* 50, 3 (1998), http://monthlyreview.org/1998/07/01/the-agrarian-origins-of-capitalism.

9 Wood, *Origins*, 106.

10 Weaver, *The Great Land Rush*, 81.

11 See Donald Worster, *Under Western Skies: Nature and History in the American West* (New York: Oxford University Press, 1992), 40.

Selected Bibliography

ARCHIVAL SOURCES

BC Archives
Fort Kamloops Records, A/B/20/K12; A/C/20/K12.
GR0324. British Columbia, Royal Commission on Agriculture, 1912.
GR0520. British Columbia, Royal Commission on Forest Resources, 1944–45.
GR0948. BC Forest Branch Chief Foresters Correspondence, 1915–20.
GR1191. British Columbia, Kamloops Forest District, 1917–81.
GR1238. British Columbia, Kamloops Forest District Grazing Reports, 1951–55.
GR1379. British Columbia Forest Service, Forest Service Briefs to the Commission on Forest Resources, 1955–57.
GR1440. Correspondence files with regard to Crown Lands, 1872–1918.
GR1441. British Columbia, Lands and Works, 1918–85.
GR1453. British Columbia, Kamloops Forest District, Operational Records, 1896–1980.
MS0676. Louis LeBourdais Papers.
MS1083. Douglas Lake Cattle Company Fonds, 1880–1979.
MS1633. Kenworthy Family Fonds.
MS2881. Western Canadian Ranching Company Records, 1884–1952.

Library and Archives Canada
RG 17, Agriculture.

University of British Columbia Archives
British Columbia. 1930 Grazing Commission Transcripts. (Originals held by Ministry of Forests and Range Library, Victoria.)
British Columbia. Transcripts of the Royal Commission on Indian Affairs for the Province of British Columbia. (Copies held by University of British Columbia Library.)

Colonial Office, British Columbia Correspondence (hereafter CO 60).

Department of Indian Affairs, Minutes of Decision, Indian Reserve Commission, 1874–90. (Copies held by Natural Resources Canada, Vancouver Regional Office.)

Andrew Hutchinson Records, 1888–1975.

RG10. Department of Indian Affairs, Black Series Collection, University of British Columbia Library/Library and Archives Canada.

Royal Commission on Indian Affairs for the Province of British Columbia, microfilmed, original transcripts, University of British Columbia Library.

George J. Spencer Fonds, 1914–65.

GOVERNMENT REPORTS AND PUBLICATIONS

British Columbia. *Annual Report of the Forest Branch.* Victoria, 1912–60.

–. *Grazing Manual for the General Information and Guidance of Forest Officers.* Victoria, Forest Service, 1935, 19. (Copy held by Ministry of Forests Library, Victoria.)

–. *Report of the Commission of Lands and Works for 1873.* Victoria, 1874.

–. *Report of the Department of Agriculture.* Victoria, 1891–1906.

–. *Report of the Provincial Game Warden.* Victoria: King's Printer, 1909–16.

–. *Report of the Royal Commission on Indian Affairs for the Province of British Columbia.* Victoria, 1916.

–. *Sessional Papers.* Journals of the British Columbia Legislative Assembly. Victoria, 1872–.

Buckell, E.R. "The Grasshopper Problem in Canada." In *Proceedings of the Fourth International Locust Conference, Cairo, Egypt, April 22, 1936,* Appendix 42. Cairo: Government Press, 1937.

–. "The Influence of Locusts on the Ranges of British Columbia." In *Fifty-First Report of the Entomological Society of Ontario, 1920.* Toronto: printed by Clarkson James, 1921, 24–25.

–. "The Locusts of British Columbia." In *Proceedings of the Entomological Society of British Columbia.* Victoria: King's Printer, 1921, 114.

–. "Regional Problems: The Problem of Non-Gregarious Grasshoppers, Draft Resolution." In *Proceedings of the Fourth International Locust Conference, Cairo, Egypt, April 22, 1936,* Appendix 43. Cairo: Government Press, 1937.

Canada. *Annual Report of the Dominion Entomologist for 1903.* Ottawa: King's Printer, 1904.

–. *Annual Report of the Department of Indian Affairs for 1891.* Canada. Sessional Papers.

–. "Conference of Dr. Duncan Scott, Deputy Superintendent General of Indian Affairs of the Dominion of Canada, W.E. Ditchburn, Chief Inspector of Indian Agencies of British Columbia, with the Executive Committee of the Allied Tribes of British Columbia, 7 August 1923." (Copy held by Department of Indian Affairs and Northern Development, Vancouver Regional Office.)

–. *Report of the Dominion Entomologist for 1900.* Ottawa: King's Printer, 1901.

Daigle, Patrick. *Fire in the Dry Forests of Interior British Columbia,* Extension Note 08. Victoria: BC Ministry of Forests Research Branch, 1996.

Dawson, G.M. "Note on Agriculture and Stock Raising and Extent of Cultivable Land in British Columbia." In *Report on Surveys and Preliminary Operations on the Canadian Pacific Railway up to January 1877.* Ottawa, 1878, 252.

Hodgins, H.J. "Hat Creek Forest Survey and Preliminary Management Recommendations, 1932." Unpublished report, Ministry of Forests Library.

Hopping, Ralph. "Depreciation by Forest Insects." Paper presented at the British Colum-
bia Forest Convention, Victoria, 1931. (Copy held by Ministry of Forests Library.)
Meidinger, Dellis, and Jim Pojar. *Ecosystems of British Columbia*. Victoria: Ministry of
Forests, 1991.
Thomson, L.B., E.W. Tisdale, and L.P. Guichon. *Report of the Committee to Investigate
Range Matters in the Riske Creek Area, August 1938*. (Copy of unpublished report held
by Ministry of Forests Library, Victoria.)
Tisdale, E.W. *Dominion Range Experiment Substation Summary Report 1935–1939*. Kamloops
Substation, 1939.
Treherne, R.C., and E.R. Buckell. *The Grasshoppers of British Columbia with Particular
Reference to the Influence of Injurious Species on the Rangelands of the Province*. Entomo-
logical Branch Circular no. 25. Ottawa: King's Printer, 1924.
Whitford, H.N., and R.D. Craig. *The Forests of British Columbia*. Ottawa: Commission
on Conservation, 1918, 64.
Wilson, Tom. "The Outbreak of Locusts of 1914." In *Proceedings of the Entomological
Society of British Columbia*. Victoria: King's Printer, 1915, 41–42.
Wood, C.S., and L. Unger. *Mountain Pine Beetle: A History of Outbreaks in Pine Forests in
British Columbia, 1910–95*. Victoria: Canadian Forest Service, 1996.

LEGAL STATUTES

British Columbia, Land Ordinance, Statutes of British Columbia (Victoria, 1860).
British Columbia, Act for the Better Protection of Winter Ranges, Statutes of British
Columbia (Victoria, 1879).
British Columbia, Stock Ranges Act, Statutes of British Columbia (Victoria, 1876).
British Columbia, An Act for the Extermination of Wild Horses, Revised Statutes of Brit-
ish Columbia, 1897 (Victoria 1897): 2193.
British Columbia, Grazing Act, Statutes of British Columbia (Victoria, 1919).
British Columbia, Grasshopper Control Act, Revised Statutes of British Columbia (Victoria,
1930).

NEWSPAPERS

Kamloops Standard Sentinel
Merritt Herald
Vancouver Province
Vancouver Sun
Victoria Daily Colonist
Victoria Daily Times

SECONDARY SOURCES

Alexander, Thomas G. "From Rule of Thumb to Scientific Range Management: The Case
of the Intermountain Region of the Forest Service." *Western Historical Quarterly* 18,
4 (1987): 409–28. http://dx.doi.org/10.2307/969365.
Anderson, Kay. "'The Beast Within': Race, Humanity and Animality." *Environment and
Planning D: Society and Space* 18, 3 (2000): 301–20. http://dx.doi.org/10.1068/d229.

Anderson, Virginia DeJohn. *Creatures of Empire: How Domestic Animals Transformed Early America*. New York: Oxford University Press, 2004. http://dx.doi.org/10.1093/acprof:oso/9780195158601.001.0001.

Atkins, Annette. *Harvest of Grief: Grasshopper Plagues and Public Assistance in Minnesota, 1873–1878*. St. Paul: Minnesota Historical Society Press, 1984.

Baker, Robert, Robert D. Bradley, and Lee R. McAlily Jr. "Pocket Gophers." In *Wild Mammals of North America: Biology, Management, and Conservation*, ed. George Feldhamer, Bruce Thompson, and Joseph Chapman, 276–87. Baltimore: Johns Hopkins University Press, 2003.

Barnes, Trevor J., and James Duncan. *Writing Worlds: Discourse, Text and Metaphor in the Representation of Landscape*. London: Routledge, 1991.

Barnes, Trevor, and Derek Gregory, eds. *Reading Human Geography: The Poetics and Politics of Inquiry*. New York: Arnold, 1997.

Bearcroft, Norma. *The Wild Horses of Canada*. Richmond, BC: Canadian Wild Horse Society, 1972.

Beers, Dianne L. *For the Prevention of Cruelty: The History and Legacy of Animal Rights Activism in the United States*. Athens: Ohio University Press, 2006.

Beinart, William. *Environment and Empire*. Oxford: Oxford University Press, 2007.

Belsky, Joy, and Dana Blumenthal. "Effect of Livestock Grazing on Stand Dynamics and Soils in Upland Forests of the Interior West." *Conservation Biology* 11, 2 (1997): 315–27. http://dx.doi.org/10.1046/j.1523-1739.1997.95405.x.

Berger, Joel. *Wild Horses of the Great Basin: Social Competition and Population Size*. Chicago: University of Chicago Press, 1986.

Biagioli, Mario. *The Science Studies Reader*. London: Routledge, 1999.

Blomley, Nicholas. "Law, Property, and the Geography of Violence: The Frontier, the Survey and the Grid." *Annals of the Association of American Geographers* 93, 1 (2003): 121–41. http://dx.doi.org/10.1111/1467-8306.93109.

–. *Law, Space and the Geographies of Power*. New York: Guilford Press, 1994.

Botkin, Daniel. *Discordant Harmonies: A New Ecology for the Twenty-First Century*. Oxford: Oxford University Press, 1990.

Bowler, Peter J. *The Norton History of the Environmental Sciences*. New York: W.W. Norton, 1992.

Boyd, Robert. *The Coming of the Spirit of Pestilence: Introduced Infectious Diseases and Population Decline among Northwest Coast Indians, 1774–1874*. Seattle: University of Washington Press, 1999.

–. *Indians, Fire and the Land in Pacific Northwest*. Corvallis: Oregon State University Press, 1999.

Brealey, Ken. "Travels from Point Ellice: Peter O'Reilly and the Indian Reserve System in British Columbia." *BC Studies* 115/116 (Autumn/Winter 1997/98): 181–236.

Breen, David. *Canadian Cattle Ranching Frontiers*. Toronto: University of Toronto Press, 1983.

British Columbia Forest Practices Board. *Special Investigation: The Effect of Range Practices on Grasslands: A Test Case for Upper Grasslands in the South Central Interior of British Columbia*. Victoria, 2007. http://www.bcfpb.ca.

Buhs, Joshua Blu. *The Fire Ant Wars: Nature, Science, and Public Policy in Twentieth-Century America*. Chicago: University of Chicago Press, 2004. http://dx.doi.org/10.7208/chicago/9780226079844.001.0001.

Burchell, Gary, ed. *The Foucault Effect: Studies in Governmentality*. Chicago: University of Chicago Press, 1991. http://dx.doi.org/10.7208/chicago/9780226028811.001.0001.

Cail, Robert. *Land, Man, and the Law: The Disposal of Crown Lands in British Columbia, 1871–1913*. Vancouver: UBC Press, 1974.

Cannings, Richard, and Sydney Cannings, *British Columbia: A Natural History*. Vancouver: Greystone Books, 2000.

Carlson, Roy. "The Later Prehistory of British Columbia." In *Early Human Occupation in British Columbia*, ed. Roy L. Carlson and Luke Dalla Bona, 215–26. Vancouver: UBC Press, 1996.

Carlson, Roy, and Luke Dalla Bona, eds. *Early Human Occupation in British Columbia*. Vancouver: UBC Press, 1996.

Carson, Rachel. *Silent Spring*. Greenwich, CT: Fawcett Publications, 1962.

Castonguay, Stéphane. "Naturalizing Federalism: Insect Outbreaks and the Centralization of Entomological Research in Canada, 1884–1914." *Canadian Historical Review* 85, 1 (2004): 1–34. http://dx.doi.org/10.3138/CHR.85.1.1.

Cawker, K.B. "Fire History and Grassland Vegetation Change: Three Pollen Diagrams from Southern British Columbia." *Canadian Journal of Botany* 61, 4 (1983): 1126–39.

Clayton, Daniel. *Islands of Truth: The Imperial Fashioning of Vancouver Island*. Vancouver: UBC Press, 2000.

Cohen, Bill, ed. *Stories and Images about What the Horse Has Done for Us: Mayx twixmntm tl q̓sapi lats k̓ulmstm I snklc̓askaxa*. Penticton, BC: Theytus, 1998.

Cosgrove, Denis. "Prospect, Perspective and the Evolution of the Landscape Idea." *Transactions of the Institute of British Geographers* 10, 1 (1985): 45–62. http://dx.doi.org/10.2307/622249.

Cronon, William. *Changes in the Land: Indians, Colonists and the Ecology of New England*. New York: Hill and Wang, 1983.

–. *Nature's Metropolis: Chicago and the Great West*. New York: W.W. Norton, 1991.

–. "A Place for Stories: Nature, History, and Narrative." *Journal of American History* 78, 4 (1992): 1347–76. http://dx.doi.org/10.2307/2079346.

–. "The Trouble with Wilderness, or Getting Back to the Wrong Nature." In *Uncommon Ground: Rethinking the Human Place in Nature*, ed. William Cronon, 69–90. New York: W.W. Norton, 1995.

Crosby, Alfred. *Ecological Imperialism: The Biological Expansion of Europe, 900–1900*. New York: Cambridge University Press, 1986. http://dx.doi.org/10.1017/CBO9780511805554.

Cunfer, Geoff. *On the Great Plains: Agriculture and Environment*. College Station: Texas A&M University Press, 2005.

Demeritt, David. "Ecology, Objectivity and Critique in Writings on Nature and Human Societies." *Journal of Historical Geography* 20, 1 (1994): 22–37. http://dx.doi.org/10.1006/jhge.1994.1003.

–. "Visions of Agriculture in British Columbia." *BC Studies* 108 (Winter 1995–96): 29–59.

Deur, Douglas, and Nancy J. Turner, eds. *Keeping It Living: Traditions of Plant Use and Cultivation on the Northwest Coast of North America*. Seattle: University of Washington Press, 2005.

Drago, Harry Sinclair. *The Great Range Wars: Violence on the Grasslands*. New York: Dodd, Mead, 1970.

Dunlop, Thomas. *DDT: Scientists, Citizens and Public Policy*. Princeton, NJ: Princeton University Press, 1981.

Edwards, Elwyn Hartley. *Wild Horses: A Spirit Unbroken*. Stillwater, MN: Voyageur Press, 1995.

Egerton, Frank. "Changing Concepts of the Balance of Nature." *Quarterly Review of Biology* 48, 2 (1973): 322–50. http://dx.doi.org/10.1086/407594.

Elton, C.S. "Periodic Fluctuations in the Numbers of Animals: Their Causes and Effects." *Journal of Experimental Biology* 2 (1924): 119–63.

Evans, Clinton. *The War on Weeds in the Prairie West: An Environmental History*. Calgary: University of Calgary Press, 2002.

Evenden, Matthew. "The Laborers of Nature: Economic Ornithology and the Role of Birds as Agents of Biological Pest Control in North American Agriculture, 1880–1930." *Forest and Conservation History* 39, 4 (1995): 172–83. http://dx.doi.org/10.2307/3983958.

–. "Locating Science, Locating Salmon: Institutions, Linkages, and Spatial Practices in Early British Columbia Fisheries Science." *Environment and Planning D: Society and Space* 22, 3 (2004): 355–72. http://dx.doi.org/10.1068/d20s.

Faure, Jacobus. "The Phases of the Rocky Mountain Locust *Melanoplus mexicanus*." *Journal of Economic Entomology* 26 (1933): 706–18.

Ferguson, Barry. *Remaking Liberalism: The Intellectual Legacy of Adam Shortt, O.D. Skelton, W.C. Clark and W.A. Mackintosh, 1890–1925*. Montreal and Kingston: McGill-Queen's University Press, 1993.

Fiege, Mark. *Irrigated Eden: The Making of an Agricultural Landscape in the American West*. Seattle: University of Washington Press, 1999.

–. "The Weedy West: Mobile Nature, Boundaries, and Common Space in the Montana Landscape." *Western Historical Quarterly* 36, 1 (2005): 22–48. http://dx.doi.org/10.2307/25443100.

Fielding, Dennis, and Merlyn Brusven. "Livestock Grazing and Grasshoppers: An Interregional Perspective." *University of Idaho College of Agriculture Bulletin* 786 (1996): 1–12.

Fisher, Robin. *Contact and Conflict: Indian-European Relations in British Columbia, 1774–1890*. Vancouver: UBC Press, 1977.

Flannery, Tim. *The Eternal Frontier: An Ecological History of North America and Its People*. New York: Atlantic Monthly Press, 2001.

Flores, Dan. "Place: An Argument for Bioregional History." *Environmental History Review* 18, 4 (1994): 1–18. http://dx.doi.org/10.2307/3984870.

Foran, Max. *Trails and Trials: Markets and Land Use in the Alberta Cattle Industry*. Calgary: University of Calgary Press, 2003.

Foucault, Michel. *Discipline and Punish: The Birth of the Prison*. New York: Vintage Books, 1977.

–. *Security, Territory, Population: Lectures at the Collège de France, 1977–78*. New York: Picador, 2007. http://dx.doi.org/10.1057/9780230245075.

–. *Society Must Be Defended: Lectures at the College de France, 1975–1976*. New York: Picador, 2003.

Friedel, M.H. "Range Condition Assessment and the Concept of Thresholds." *Journal of Range Management* 44, 5 (1991): 422–26. http://dx.doi.org/10.2307/4002737.

Galois, Robert, and Arthur Ray. "The Fur Trade in the Cordillera, to 1857." In *Historical Atlas of Canada*. Vol. 2, *The Land Transformed*, ed. R. Louis Gentilcore, Plate 19. Toronto: University of Toronto Press, 1993.

Garner, Richard T., and Andrew Oldenquist. "Utilitarianism." In *Society and the Individual: Readings in Political and Social Philosophy*, ed. Richard T. Garner and Andrew Oldenquist, 194–203. Belmont, CA: Wadsworth, 1990.

Gayton, Don. *British Columbia Grasslands: Monitoring Vegetation Change.* Kamloops: Forrex – Forest Research Extension Partnership, 2003, http://www.forrex.org/sites/default/files/forrex_series/FS7_Part1.pdf.

–. *Landscapes of the Interior: Re-Explorations of Nature and the Human Spirit.* Gabriola Island, BC: New Society Publishers, 1996.

Golinski, Jan. *Making Natural Knowledge: Constructivism and the History of Science.* Cambridge: Cambridge University Press, 1999.

Gordon, Iain, and Herbert Prins, eds. *The Ecology of Grazing and Browsing.* Berlin: Springer, 2008. http://dx.doi.org/10.1007/978-3-540-72422-3.

Grant, George M. *Ocean to Ocean: Sanford Fleming's Expedition through Canada in 1872; Being a Diary Kept During a Journey from the Atlantic to the Pacific with the Expedition of the Engineer-in-Chief of the Canadian Pacific and Intercolonial Railways.* Toronto: J. Campbell and Son, 1873, http://eco.canadiana.ca/view/oocihm.30275/3?r=0&s=1.

Griffiths, Tom, and Libby Robin, eds. *Ecology and Empire: Environmental History of Settler Societies.* Edinburgh: Keele University Press, 1997.

Gutting, Gary, ed. *The Cambridge Companion to Foucault.* Cambridge: Cambridge University Press, 1994. http://dx.doi.org/10.1017/CCOL9780521403320.

Hacking, Ian. *The Social Construction of What?* Cambridge, MA: Harvard University Press, 1999.

Haines, Francis. "The Northward Spread of Horses among the Plains Indians." *American Anthropologist* 40, 3 (1938): 429–37. http://dx.doi.org/10.1525/aa.1938.40.3.02a00060.

Hämäläinen, Pekka. "The Rise and Fall of Plains Indian Horse Cultures." *Journal of American History* 90, 3 (2003): 833–62. http://dx.doi.org/10.2307/3660878.

Harris, Cole. "Archival Fieldwork." *Geographical Review* 91, 1–2 (2001): 328–34. http://dx.doi.org/10.2307/3250834.

–. "How Did Colonialism Dispossess? Comments from an Edge of Empire." *Annals of the Association of American Geographers* 94, 1 (2004): 165–82. http://dx.doi.org/10.1111/j.1467-8306.2004.09401009.x.

–. "Industry and the Good Life around Idaho Peak." *Canadian Historical Review* 66, 3 (1985): 315–43. http://dx.doi.org/10.3138/CHR-066-03-01.

–. *Making Native Space: Colonialism, Resistance, and Reserves in British Columbia.* Vancouver: UBC Press, 2002.

–. *The Resettlement of British Columbia: Essays on Colonialism and Geographical Change.* Vancouver: UBC Press, 1997.

Harris, Cole, and John Warkentin. "British Columbia." In *Canada before Confederation: A Study in Historical Geography,* 288–311. Ottawa: Carleton University Press, 1991.

Harris, Douglas. *Landing Native Fisheries: Indian Reserves and Fishing Rights in British Columbia.* Vancouver: UBC Press, 2008.

–. "The Nlha7kapmx Meeting at Lytton, 1879, and the Rule of Law." *BC Studies* 108 (Winter 1995/96): 5–25.

Harvey, David. *The Condition of Postmodernity: An Enquiry into the Origins of Cultural Change.* Cambridge, MA: Blackwell, 1990.

–. *Justice, Nature and the Geography of Difference.* Cambridge, MA: Blackwell, 1996.

Hayden Brian, ed. *A Complex Culture of the British Columbia Plateau: Traditional Stl'atl'imx Resource Use.* Vancouver: UBC Press, 1992.

Hays, Samuel P. *Conservation and the Gospel of Efficiency: The Progressive Conservation Movement.* Pittsburgh: University of Pittsburgh Press, 1999.

Hayter, Roger. *Flexible Crossroads: The Restructuring of British Columbia's Forest Economy.* Vancouver: UBC Press, 2000.

Hearle, Eric. "Notes on a Serious Outbreak of Tick Paralysis in Cattle." *Proceedings of the BC Entomological Society, March 1933* (Victoria, 1933): 11–16.

Hebda, Richard. "British Columbia Vegetation and Climate History with Focus on 6 KA BP." *Géographie physique et Quaternaire* 49, 1 (1995): 55–79. http://dx.doi.org/10.7202/033030ar.

–. "Postglacial History of the Grasslands of Southern British Columbia and Adjacent Regions." In *Grassland Ecology and Classification Symposium Proceedings*, ed. A.C. Nicholson, A. McLean, and T.E. Baker, 157–92. Victoria: Ministry of Forests, 1982.

Heyboer, Maarten. "Grass Counters, Stock Feeders, and the Dual Orientation of Applied Science: The History of Range Science, 1895–1960." PhD diss., Virginia Polytechnic Institute, 1992.

Hoodicoff, C. *Badger Prey Ecology: The Ecology of Six Small Mammals Found in British Columbia.* Victoria: Ministry of Environment, 2006. http://www.env.gov.bc.ca/wld/documents/techpub/wr109.pdf.

Hulme, Peter. "The Spontaneous Hand of Nature: Nature, Savagery, Colonialism and the Enlightenment." In *The Enlightenment and Its Shadows*, ed. Peter Hulme and L.J. Jordanova, 16–34. London: Routledge, 1990.

Igler, David. *Industrial Cowboys: Miller and Lux and the Transformation of the Far West, 1850–1920.* Berkeley: University of California Press, 2001. http://dx.doi.org/10.1525/california/9780520226586.003.0008.

Isenberg, Andrew. *The Destruction of the Bison: An Environmental History, 1750–1920.* New York: Cambridge University Press, 2000. http://dx.doi.org/10.1017/CBO9780511549861.

Jacoby, Karl. *Crimes against Nature: Squatters, Poachers, Thieves, and the Hidden History of American Conservation.* Berkeley: University of California Press, 2001.

Jenkins, Stephen, and Michael Ashley. "Wild Horse." In *The Smithsonian Book of North American Mammals*, ed. Don Wilson and Sue Ruff, 1148–63. Washington, DC: Smithsonian Institution Scholarly Press, 1999.

Jordan, Terry. *North American Cattle Ranching Frontiers: Origins, Diffusion, and Differentiation.* Albuquerque: University of New Mexico Press, 1993.

Keegan, John. *A History of Warfare.* New York: Vintage Books, 1994.

Kelm, Mary Ellen. *Colonizing Bodies: Aboriginal Health and Healing in British Columbia, 1900–1950.* Vancouver: UBC Press, 1998.

–. "Diagnosing the Discursive Indian: Medicine, Gender and the 'Dying Race.'" *Ethnohistory* (Columbus, OH) 52, 2 (Spring 2005): 371–406.

Kennedy, Michael. "Fraser River Placer Mining Landscapes." *BC Studies* 160 (2008/09): 35–66.

Kingsland, Sharon. *Modeling Nature: Episodes in the History of Population Ecology.* Chicago: University of Chicago Press, 1995.

Kirkpatrick, Jay, and Patricia Fazio. "Ecce Equus." *Natural History* 117, 4 (2008): 30–31.

Kohler, Robert. "Place and Practice in Field Biology." *History of Science* 11 (2002): 189–210.

Krech, Sheppard. *The Ecological Indian: Myth and History.* New York: W.W. Norton, 1999.

Kuhn, Thomas. *The Structure of Scientific Revolutions.* Chicago: University of Chicago Press, 1970.

Langston, Nancy. *Forest Dreams, Forest Nightmares: The Paradox of Old Growth in the Inland West*. Seattle: University of Washington Press, 1996.

–. *Where Land and Water Meet: A Western Landscape Transformed*. Seattle: University of Washington Press, 2003.

Latour, Bruno. *Science in Action: How to Follow Scientists and Engineers through Society*. Cambridge, MA: Harvard University Press, 1987.

Laycock, W.A. "Stable States and Thresholds of Range Condition on North American Rangelands: A Viewpoint." *Journal of Range Management* 44, 5 (1991): 427–33. http://dx.doi.org/10.2307/4002738.

Livingstone, David. *Putting Science in Its Place: Geographies of Scientific Knowledge*. Chicago: University of Chicago Press, 2003. http://dx.doi.org/10.7208/chicago/9780226487243.001.0001.

Locke, John. "The Second Treatise of Government; An Essay Concerning the True Original, Extent, and End of Government." In *Society and the Individual: Readings in Political and Social Philosophy*, ed. Richard T. Garner and Andrew Oldenquist, 126–40. Belmont, CA: Wadsworth, 1989.

Lockwood, Jeffrey. *Locust: The Devastating Rise and Mysterious Disappearance of an Insect That Shaped the American Frontier*. New York: Basic Books, 2004.

–. "Taxonomic Status of the Rocky Mountain Locust: Morphometric Comparisons of *Melanoplus spretus* (Walsh) with Solitary and Migratory *Melanoplus sanguinipes* (F.)." *Canadian Entomologist* 121, 12 (1989): 1103–9. http://dx.doi.org/10.4039/Ent1211103-12.

Loo, Tina. "Of Moose and Men: Hunting for Masculinities in British Columbia, 1880–1939." *Western Historical Quarterly* 32, 3 (2001): 296–319. http://dx.doi.org/10.2307/3650737.

–. *States of Nature: Conserving Canada's Wildlife in the Twentieth Century*. Vancouver: UBC Press, 2006.

Mack, Richard. "Alien Plant Invasion into the Intermountain West: A Case History." In *Ecology of Biological Invasions in North America and Hawaii*, ed. Harold Mooney and James Drake, 191–213. New York: Springer, 1984.

–. "Invaders at Home on the Range." *Natural History* 2 (1984): 40–46.

–. "Invasion of *Bromus tectorum* L. into Western North America: An Ecological Chronicle." *Agro-ecosystems* 7, 2 (1981): 145–65. http://dx.doi.org/10.1016/0304-3746(81)90027-5.

Mack, Richard, and John N. Thompson. "Evolution in Steppe with Few Large, Hooved Animals." *American Naturalist* 119, 6 (1982): 757–73. http://dx.doi.org/10.1086/283953.

Mackenzie, John. *The Empire of Nature: Hunting, Conservation, and British Imperialism*. Manchester: Manchester University Press, 1988.

MacLachlan, Ian. *Kill and Chill: Restructuring Canada's Beef Commodity Chain*. Toronto: University of Toronto Press, 2001.

Madeson, David. "A Grasshopper in Every Pot." *Natural History* 98, 7 (July 1989): 22–25.

Malin, James. *The Grasslands of North America: Prolegomena to Its History*. Gloucester: P. Smith, 1967.

McEvoy, Arthur. *The Fisherman's Problem: Ecology and Law in the California Fisheries, 1850–1980*. Cambridge: Cambridge University Press, 1986. http://dx.doi.org/10.1017/CBO9780511583681.

McFadden, Bruce J. *Fossil Horses: Systematics, Paleobiology, and Evolution of the Family Equidae*. New York: Cambridge University Press, 1992.

McFadden, Louise. "Let's Stop Killing Our Wild Horses." *British Columbia Journal* (December 1965): 11–14.

McLaren, John, A.R. Buck, and Nancy E. Wright, eds. *Despotic Dominion: Property Rights in British Settler Societies*. Vancouver: UBC Press, 2005.

McNeill, J.R. "Observations on the Nature and Culture of Environmental History." *History and Theory* 42, 4 (2003): 5–43. http://dx.doi.org/10.1046/j.1468-2303.2003.00255.x.

Meinig, Donald. *The Great Columbia Plain: A Historical Geography*. Seattle: University of Washington Press, 1968.

Melville, Eleanor. *A Plague of Sheep: Environmental Consequences of the Conquest of Mexico*. New York: Cambridge University Press, 1994. http://dx.doi.org/10.1017/CBO9780511571091.

Merchant, Carolyn. *The Death of Nature: Women, Ecology and the Scientific Revolution*. San Francisco: HarperCollins, 1990.

Miller, J.R. *Reflections on Native-Newcomer Relations: Selected Essays*. Toronto: University of Toronto Press, 2004.

Morin, Jesse, Ryan Dickie, Takashi Sakaguchi, and Jamie Hoskins. "Late Prehistoric Settlement Patterns and Population Dynamics along the Mid-Fraser." *BC Studies* 160 (2008/09): 9–34.

Mosley, Stephen. "Common Ground: Integrating Social and Environmental History." *Journal of Social History* 39, 3 (2006): 915–33. http://dx.doi.org/10.1353/jsh.2006.0007.

Murton, James. *Creating a Modern Countryside: Liberalism and Land Resettlement in British Columbia*. Vancouver: UBC Press, 2007.

Nadasdy, Paul. "'Property' and Aboriginal Land Claims in the Canadian Subarctic: Some Theoretical Considerations." *American Anthropologist* 104, 1 (2002): 247–61. http://dx.doi.org/10.1525/aa.2002.104.1.247.

Netz, Reviel. *Barbed Wire: An Ecology of Modernity*. Middletown, CT: Wesleyan University Press, 2003.

Noss, Reed F., and Allen Y. Cooperrider. *Saving Nature's Legacy: Protecting and Restoring Biodiversity*. Washington, DC: Island Press, 1994.

Orin, J. "The Cattle Herds of the Oregon Country, 1860–1890." *Agricultural History* 21, 4 (1947): 217–38.

Pedynowski, Dena. "Science(s): Which, When, and Whose? Probing the Metanarrative of Scientific Knowledge in the Social Construction of Nature." *Progress in Human Geography* 27, 6 (2003): 735–52. http://dx.doi.org/10.1191/0309132503ph4590a.

Perry, Adele. *On the Edge of Empire: Gender, Race and the Making of British Columbia*. Toronto: University of Toronto Press, 2001.

Pfadt Robert, E. *Field Guide to Common Western Grasshoppers*. Laramie, WY: Agricultural Experiment Station, 2002.

Pielou, E.C. *After the Ice: The Return of Life to Glaciated North America*. Chicago: University of Chicago Press, 1991. http://dx.doi.org/10.7208/chicago/9780226668093.001.0001.

Pokotylo, David, and Donald Mitchell. "Prehistory of the Northern Plateau." In *Handbook of North American Indians*. Vol. 12, *Plateau*, ed. Deward E. Walker Jr., 81–102. Washington, DC: Smithsonian Institution Scholarly Press, 1998.

Porter, Theodore M. *Trust in Numbers: The Pursuit of Objectivity in Science and Public Life*. Princeton, NJ: Princeton University Press, 1995.

Preece, Rod. *Brute Souls, Happy Beasts, and Evolution: The Historical Status of Animals*. Vancouver: UBC Press, 2006.

Pyne, Stephen. *Awful Splendour: A Fire History of Canada*. Vancouver: UBC Press, 2007.

–. *Fire in America: A Cultural History of Wildland and Rural Fire*. Princeton, NJ: Princeton University Press, 1982.

Rabinow, Paul, ed. *The Foucault Reader*. New York: Pantheon Books, 1984.

Ray, Arthur. "The Fur Trade in North America: An Overview from a Historical Geographical Perspective." In *Wild Furbearer Management and Conservation in North America*, ed. Milan Novak, 21–30. Ontario: Ministry of Natural Resources, 1987.

Raz, Joseph. *The Authority of Law: Essays on Law and Morality*. Oxford: Clarendon Press, 1979. http://dx.doi.org/10.1093/acprof:oso/9780198253457.001.0001.

Records of the Hudson's Bay Company Relative to the Thompson's River Post (Kamloops, BC) 1821–65, http://142.36.5.21/thomp-ok/river-post/index.html.

Reid, Joanna. "The Grassland Debates: Conservationists, Ranchers, First Nations, and the Landscape of the Middle Fraser." *BC Studies* 160 (2008/09): 93–118.

Riegart, Paul. *From Arsenic to DDT: A History of Entomology in Western Canada*. Toronto: University of Toronto Press, 1980.

Ritvo, Harriet. "Animal Planet." *Environmental History* 9, 2 (2004): 204–20. http://dx.doi.org/10.2307/3986084.

Rose, Gillian. "Practicing Photography: An Archive, a Study, Some Photographs and a Researcher." *Journal of Historical Geography* 26, 4 (2000): 555–71. http://dx.doi.org/10.1006/jhge.2000.0247.

Rowley, William D. *U.S. Forest Service Grazing and Rangelands: A History*. College Station: Texas A&M University Press, 1985.

Russell, Edmund. "Science and Environmental History." *Environmental History* 10, 1 (2005): 80–82.

–. "Speaking of Annihilation: Mobilizing for War against Human and Insect Enemies, 1914–1945." *Journal of American History* 82, 4 (1996): 1505–29. http://dx.doi.org/10.2307/2945309.

–. *War and Nature: Fighting Humans and Insects with Chemicals from World War I to Silent Spring*. New York: Cambridge University Press, 2001.

Russell, Edmund, and Richard Tucker. *Natural Enemy, Natural Ally: Toward an Environmental History of Warfare*. Corvallis: Oregon State University Press, 2004.

Ryan, Simon. *The Cartographic Eye: How Explorers Saw Australia*. New York: Cambridge University Press, 1996.

Ryder, June. "Surficial Geology of the Grasslands." In *Grassland Ecology and Classification Symposium Proceedings*, ed. A.C. Nicholson, A. McLean, and T.E. Baker, 63–94. Victoria: Ministry of Forests, 1982.

Said, Edward. *Orientalism*. New York: Vintage Books, 1979.

Sampson, Arthur. "Natural Re-Vegetation of Rangelands Based upon Growth Requirements and Life History of the Vegetation." *Journal of Agricultural Research* 3, 2 (1914): 93–147.

–. *Range and Pasture Management*. New York: John Wiley and Sons, 1923.

–. "Succession as a Factor in Range Management." *Journal of Forestry* 15, 5 (1917): 593–96.

Sanders, Deidre, Naneen Stuckey, Kathleen Mooney, and Leland Donald. "What the People Said: Kwakwaka;wakw, Nuu-chah-nulth, and Tsimshian Testimonies before the Royal Commission on Indian Affairs for the Province of British Columbia." *Canadian Journal of Native Studies* 19, 2 (1999): 213–48.

Sandlos, John. *Hunters at the Margin: Native People and Wildlife Conservation in the Northwest Territories.* Vancouver: UBC Press, 2007.

Schwartz, Joan. "The Geography Lesson: Photographs and the Construction of Imaginative Geographies." *Journal of Historical Geography* 22, 1 (1996): 16–45. http://dx.doi.org/10.1006/jhge.1996.0003.

Schwartz, Joan, and James Ryan, eds. *Picturing Place: Photography and the Geographical Imagination.* New York: I.B. Tauris, 2003.

Scott, James C. *Domination and the Arts of Resistance.* New Haven, CT: Yale University Press, 1990.

–. "Everyday Forms of Peasant Resistance." *Journal of Peasant Studies* 13, 2 (1986): 5–35. http://dx.doi.org/10.1080/03066158608438289.

–. *Seeing Like a State: How Certain Schemes to Improve the Human Condition Have Failed.* New Haven, CT: Yale University Press, 1998.

–. *Weapons of the Weak: Everyday Forms of Peasant Resistance.* New Haven, CT: Yale University Press, 1985.

Seed, Patricia. *Ceremonies of Possession in Europe's Conquest of the New World, 1492–1640.* New York: Cambridge University Press, 1995.

Shapin, Steven. "Placing the View from Nowhere: Historical and Sociological Problems in the Location of Science." *Transactions of the Institute of British Geographers*, n.s., 23, 1 (1998): 5–12. http://dx.doi.org/10.1111/j.0020-2754.1998.00005.x.

Sluyter, Andrew. "The Ecological Origins and Consequences of Cattle Ranching in Sixteenth Century New Spain." *Geographical Review* 86, 2 (1996): 161–77. http://dx.doi.org/10.2307/215954.

Smith, Tim. *Scaling Fisheries: The Science of Measuring the Effects of Fishing, 1855–1955.* New York: Cambridge University Press, 1994. http://dx.doi.org/10.1017/CBO9780511470868.

Sorenson, W. Conner. *Brethren of the Net: American Entomology, 1840–1880.* Tuscaloosa: University of Alabama Press, 1995.

Spence, Mark. *Dispossessing the Wilderness: Indian Removal and the Making of the National Parks.* New York: Oxford University Press, 1999.

Strickton, Arnold. "The Euro-American Ranching Complex." In *Man, Culture and Animals*, ed. M. Harris and E.B. Ross, 229–58. Washington, DC: Smithsonian Institution Scholarly Press, 1965.

Taylor, Alan. "Unnatural Inequalities: Social and Environmental Histories." *Environmental History* 1, 4 (1996): 6–19. http://dx.doi.org/10.2307/3985275.

Taylor, Joseph. "Boundary Terminology." *Environmental History* 13, 3 (2008): 454–81. http://dx.doi.org/10.1093/envhis/13.3.454.

–. *Making Salmon: An Environmental History of the Northwest Fisheries Crisis.* Seattle: University of Washington Press, 1999.

–. "The Political Economy of Fishery Science and the Road Not Taken." *Journal of the History of Biology* 31, 1 (1998): 33–59. http://dx.doi.org/10.1023/A:1004253405353.

Teit, James. *Mythology of the Thompson Indians.* New York: AMS Press, 1975.

–. "The Salishan Tribes of the Western Plateau." In *Forty-Fifth Annual Report of the Bureau of American Ethnology to the Secretary of the Smithsonian Institution, 1927–1929*, ed. Franz Boas. Washington, DC: Government Printing Office, 1930.

Thomas, Gregory. "The British Columbia Ranching Frontier, 1858–1896." MA thesis, University of British Columbia, 1976.

Tisdale, Edwin. "The Grasslands of the Southern Interior of British Columbia." *Ecology* 28, 4 (1947): 346–82. http://dx.doi.org/10.2307/1931227.

–. "Grazing of Forest Land in Interior British Columbia." *Journal of Forestry* 48, 12 (December 1950): 856–60.

Tisdale, Edwin, A. McLean, and S.E. Clarke. "Range Resources and Their Management in British Columbia." *Journal of Range Management* 7, 1 (1954): 3–9. http://dx.doi .org/10.2307/3894618.

Thomson, Duane, and Marianne Ignace. "They Made Themselves Our Guests: Power Relationships in the Interior Plateau Region of the Cordillera in the Fur Trade Era." *BC Studies* 146 (2005): 3–35.

Thomson, Lt. Col. H. "Our Military Horses." Lecture to the Aldershot Military Society, London, 10 December 1895.

Tough, Frank. *As Their Natural Resources Fail: Native Peoples and the Economic History of Northern Manitoba.* Vancouver: UBC Press, 1996.

Turkel, William. *The Archive of Place: Unearthing the Pasts of the Chilcotin Plateau.* Vancouver: UBC Press, 2007.

Turner, Nancy J. "Burning Mountainsides for Better Crops: Aboriginal Burning Practices in British Columbia." *Archaeology in Montana* 32, 2 (1991): 57–73.

Turton, Andrew. "Patrolling the Middle Ground: Methodological Perspectives on Everyday Peasant Resistance." *Journal of Peasant Studies* 13, 2 (1986): 36–71. http://dx.doi. org/10.1080/03066158608438290.

Tyrell, Ian. *True Gardens of the Gods: California-Australian Environmental Reform, 1860–1930.* Berkeley: University of California Press, 1999.

Tyrell, J.B., ed. *David Thompson's Narrative of His Explorations in Western North America 1784–1812.* Toronto: Champlain Society, 1916.

Uvarov, Boris. *Locusts and Grasshoppers: A Handbook for Their Study and Control.* London: Imperial Bureau of Entomology, 1928.

Vale, Thomas R., ed. *Fire, Native Peoples and the Natural Landscape.* Washington, DC: Island Press, 2002.

Venables, E.P. "Fifty Years of Entomology in the Interior of British Columbia." In *Proceedings of the Entomological Society of British Columbia* 48 (1953): 19–22.

Vibert, Elizabeth. *Traders' Tales: Narratives of Cultural Encounters in the Columbia Plateau, 1807–1846.* Norman and London: University of Oklahoma Press, 1997.

Walker, Deward, and Roderick Sprague. "History until 1846." In *Handbook of North American Indians.* Vol. 12, *Plateau,* ed. Deward E. Walker Jr., 138–48. Washington, DC: Smithsonian Institution Scholarly Press, 1998.

Warren, Louis. *The Hunter's Game: Poachers and Conservationists in Twentieth Century America.* New Haven, CT: Yale University Press, 1997.

Weaver, John. *The Great Land Rush and the Making of the Modern World, 1650–1900.* Montreal and Kingston: McGill-Queen's University Press, 2003.

Weir, Thomas. *Ranching in the Southern Interior Plateau of British Columbia.* Ottawa: Queen's University Press, 1955.

Westoby, Mark, Brian Walker, and Imanuel Noy-Meir. "Opportunistic Management for Rangelands Not at Equilibrium." *Journal of Range Management* 42, 4 (1989): 266–74. http://dx.doi.org/10.2307/3899492.

White, Richard. "American Environmental History: The Development of a New Historical Field." *Pacific Historical Review* 54, 3 (1985): 297–335. http://dx.doi.org/ 10.2307/3639634.

–. "Animals and Enterprise." In *The Oxford History of the American West,* ed. Clyde Milner, 237–73. New York: Oxford University Press, 1994.

–. *Land Use, Environment, and Social Change: The Shaping of Island County, Washington.* Seattle: University of Washington Press, 1980.

–. "The Nationalization of Nature." *Journal of American History* 86, 3 (1999): 976–86. http://dx.doi.org/10.2307/2568602.

–. *The Organic Machine: The Remaking of the Columbia River.* New York: Hill and Wang, 1995.

Whorton, James. *Before Silent Spring: Pesticides and Public Health in Pre-DDT America.* Princeton, NJ: Princeton University Press, 1974.

Williams, Michael. "The Relations of Environmental History and Historical Geography." *Journal of Historical Geography* 20, 1 (1994): 3–21. http://dx.doi.org/10.1006/jhge.1994.1002.

Williams, Raymond. *The Country and the City.* London: Chatto and Windus, 1973.

Winston, Mark, L. *Nature Wars: People vs. Pests.* Cambridge, MA: Harvard University Press, 1999.

Wister, Owen. *The Virginian.* New York: Macmillan, 1955.

Wood, Ellen Meikens. *The Origins of Capitalism: A Longer View.* New York: Verso, 2002.

Wood, Paul, and Laurie Flahr. "Taking Endangered Species Seriously? British Columbia's Species at Risk Policies." *Canadian Public Policy – Analyse de Politiques* 30, 4 (2004): 381–99. http://dx.doi.org/10.2307/3552521.

Wooliams, Nina. *Cattle Ranch: The Story of the Douglas Lake Cattle Company.* Vancouver: Douglas and McIntyre, 1979.

Worster, Donald. *Dustbowl: The Southern Plains in the 1930s.* New York: Oxford, 1979.

–. *Nature's Economy: A History of Ecological Ideas.* Cambridge: Cambridge University Press, 1985.

–. *Rivers of Empire: Water, Aridity, and the Growth of the American West.* New York: Oxford University Press, 1985.

–. *Under Western Skies: Nature and History in the American West.* New York: Oxford University Press, 1992.

–. *The Wealth of Nature: Environmental History and the Ecological Imagination.* New York: Oxford University Press, 1993.

–. "World without Borders: The Internationalizing of Environmental History." *Environmental History Review* 6, 2 (1982): 8–13. http://dx.doi.org/10.2307/3984152.

Worster, Donald. "Transformations of the Earth: Toward an Agroecological Perspective in History." *Journal of American History* 76, 4 (1990): 1087–147. http://dx.doi.org/10.2307/2936586.

Wyatt, David. "Nicola." In *Handbook of North American Indians.* Vol. 12, *Plateau,* ed. Deward E. Walker Jr., 220–22. Washington, DC: Smithsonian Institution Scholarly Press, 1998.

Wynn, Graeme. "A Fine Balance? Geography at the Millennium." *Canadian Geographer* 43, 1 (1999): 220–43.

–. "The Rise of Vancouver." In *Vancouver and Its Region,* ed. Graeme Wynn and Timothy Oke, 69–148. Vancouver: UBC Press, 1992.

–. "Shall We Linger along Ambitionless? Environmental Perspectives on British Columbia." *BC Studies* 142/143 (2004): 5–68.

Young, Christian C. "Defining the Range: The Development of Carrying Capacity in Management Practice." *Journal of the History of Biology* 31, 1 (1998): 61–83. http://dx.doi.org/10.1023/A:1004205522191.

Young, James. "Cheatgrass." In *Noxious Range Weeds*, ed. Lynn James, 408–18. Boulder, CO: Westview Press, 1991.

–. "Hay Making: The Mechanical Revolution on the Western Range." *Western Historical Quarterly* 14, 3 (1983): 311–26. http://dx.doi.org/10.2307/969623.

Young, James, and B. Abbott Sparkes. *Cattle in the Cold Desert*. Logan: Utah State University Press, 1985.

Zeller, Suzanne. *Inventing Canada: Early Victorian Science and the Idea of a Transcontinental Nation*. Toronto: University of Toronto Press, 1987.

Index

Note: "f" following a page reference denotes a figure.

Aboriginal peoples: approach to nature and animals, 160; archaeological evidence on grasslands, 33; creation of Indian reserves, 6; gold rush, impact of, 35–36; horses' importance in culture, 33–34, 65, 77; strategic burning of grasslands, 20, 21; treaties not signed with government, 6, 40. *See also* Indian reserves

Aboriginal peoples, dispossession of: centrepiece of *Resettling*, xvii; chiefs' testimony to Commission re lack of resources on reserves, 50–54; commonages, abuse and disallowance, 43–45, 48–49, 122, 125, 157; diseases' (flu, measles, smallpox) impact, 34–35; exclusion from meadow commons, 47; fur trade's impact, 34–35; gold rush (after 1858), impact of, 35; grazing permits required for Crown land (1919), 56, 57–58; lowland (winter) ranges taken over by settlers, 36–37; Native rights or needs re land not considered, 122, 125, 157; Oregon Treaty (1846), 35; pastoral leases and, 36, 39, 45; reserves unsuitable for cattle (lacking range and water), 28, 31, 50–54, 56, 67; "seasonal curfew" for horses on Crown range, 59–61; settlers' indifference about Native land problems, 43–44, 48–49, 122, 125, 126; settlers' lands blocking access to fisheries, 40–41; treaties not signed with government, 6, 40. *See also* Indian reserves

Aboriginal rights and title to land: Allied Tribes of British Columbia formation (1916), 65; appeal to Queen re rights, 13–14; assertion of by Nlaka'pamux, 13–14, 70, 73

Act for the Extermination of Wild Horses (1896), 28

Act to Protect Winter Stock Ranges (1879), 22, 132–33

Act to Provide for the Better Protection of Cattle Ranges (1876), 22

Administration of British Columbia Ranges (McLean), 155

agriculture: Aboriginal peoples not agricultural and therefore not civilized, 111; concept linked with colonialism and civilization, 111; idealized view of, vs reality, 110–13, 116

Alexis Creek range, 74

Alkali Lake Band: cattle herd, 15; land holdings, 116; Royal Commission on keeping horses, not cattle, 54; testimony at Royal Commission re lack of grazing land, 52

Alkali Lake Ranch, 37, 50, 116, 121

Allied Tribes of British Columbia, 64–65

American Society for Range Management, 78

Anaham people, 47–49, 74

Anderson, James, 27, 28

Anderson, Virginia, 97

Animals Act (1908, 1923), 30–31, 62

Annals of the Former World (McPhee), xx

Arctic Dreams (Lopez), xx

Ashcroft Indian Reserve, 55

Ashley, Michael, 25

Ashnola Band, 53

Ashnola John, Chief, testimony at Royal Commission, 53

Ballard, Robert, 81

bark beetles, 143–46, 146f

BC Cattle Company, 53, 109, 115, 116

BC Stockbreeders Association, 68–69

Beak, C.M., 45

Bearcroft, Norma, 77, 79

beavers: beaver dams and hay meadows, relationship, 45–46; collateral damage to clearing range for cattle, 160; increase by mid-1950s, 46; reduction and resulting degradation of ranges, 132

Beets, Marty, 80

Begbie, Matthew, 112–13

Benedict, R.R., 116–17

Berlin, Isaiah, xii

Big Bar range, 25, 50, 98, 120–21

blackleg (disease) in Nicola Valley, 123

Bonaparte Band chief's testimony at Royal Commission, 52–53

Boston Bar, 3

British Columbia: animals deemed non-useful viewed as pests, 15–16, 24–26, 159; collateral death toll of "non-useful" animals, 159–60; colony established (1858), 36; forest policy on fire suppression, 142–43; land policy and range monopoly, 116–17; "new liberalism" approach to intervention, 57; scientific resource conservation (early 1900s on) to promote resource exploitation, 56–57; transition pre- to post-contact, 158–59

Brown, W.H.: on Aboriginal land title claims, 70; commonage mock-up, 125; instruction to shoot wild horses, 72; on Native aversion to poison on reserve lands, 106; on preparation for poisoning grasshoppers, 105–6

Buckell, E.R.: conference presentation on grasshopper control, 148; description of grasshoppers swarms, 104–5; explanation of grasshopper plague in 1944, 151–52; on grasshopper plagues in 1940s, 149; on human impact on grasshopper population dynamics, 95, 100, 101; on overgrazing's impact on grasshopper irruptions, 100; on ranchers' lack of cooperation re poison for grasshoppers, 106–7, 126; war imagery in battle against grasshoppers, 94; work on grasshopper populations in BC, 97, 98–99, 100

Buckskin, Felix George, 13

bunchgrass: adaptation to dry conditions, 4; in different grassland zones, xv, 4, 18, 18f; grasshoppers and, 90–91, 98; "hard grass" suitable for winter grazing, 37; in Intermountain West area, 18, 18f; recovery in exclosure on Nicola Range, 136, 136f, 137, 137f; tree/shrub encroachment, 19–20, 41, 61, 140–43; vulnerability to overgrazing and trampling, 16–17

Cameron Bar, 3

Camille, Chief of Canoe Creek, 55

Camille, Chief of Canoe Creek, testimony, 50–51, 53, 55

Canada Wild Horse Society, 77

Canadian Entomologist, 149

Canadian Pacific Railway (CPR), 114

Canoe Creek Band, 50–51

Cariboo-Chilcotin region: book on

(*Spirit in the Grass*), xi; carrying
capacity degraded over time, 131;
description of region, xiii–xiv;
ecological history in *Resettling*, 4;
Okanagan River valley, xiv, xvii, 15, 16,
45, 106, 116; Similkameen River valley,
xiv, 37, 45; Thompson River valley, xiv,
36, 37. *See also* Fraser River valley;
Nicola River valley

Castonguay, Stéphane, 96

cattle: breeds, 114; cattle numbers (1951 to
1960), 156; cattle size and quality (in
1940s), 147; cattle size and quality (in
1950s and '60s), 156; as "creatures of
empire," 97; largest herds, 4, 15, 36, 114,
121; shift to grain-fed yearlings and
calves (1950s), 155–56

Caverhill, Peter, 72, 155

cheatgrass: colonization of bunchgrass
ranges, 139–40, 139f, 140f; on grasslands
(1895–1914), 19, 55

Chilco Ranch, 31, 37, 50, 157

Chilcotin River valley: BC land policy
and range monopoly, 116–17; best
winter lowlands, 37; carrying capacity
degraded over time, 131; cattle herds
along, 4; grasshopper irruptions, 88, 90,
93; ranches in, 49–50, 49f, 97, 116–17,
121; wild horses in, 62, 66, 68, 75, 80

Chilliheetza, John (chief of Nlaka'pamux),
62–64, 66, 70

Coldwater Indian reserve, 73

colonialism: idealized view of agriculture,
vs reality of ranches, 110–13; link
(unacknowledged) with killing of wild
horses, 77–79; linked with agriculture,
111; parkland imagery by early settlers,
111–13

commonages: amendment to law needed,
120–21, 125; availability to all ranchers,
108, 120–21, 123; disallowed later by
province, 44–45; Douglas Lake and
Okanagan Lake commonages, 23, 43,
44; ecological condition bad in Nicola
Valley, 125; effort to protect cattle
ranges, 23, 43; grasshopper infestation
(1920s), 125; Hamilton Commonage,
108, 109, 125; Lundbom Commonage,

108, 125, 136, 136f; Meadow Marsh
Commonage, 108, 109; Native rights/
needs not considered or disregarded,
43–45, 48–49, 122, 125, 157; principle
doubted by Grazing Commissioner,
124–25; smallholders' disputes with
large landholders about, 123–24;
smallholders' protests against large
ranchers' extensive use of, 108, 122–23;
smallholders' requests to government
for, 50, 108. *See also* range degradation;
ranges

Cooperrider, Allen, 60–61

Copley, George, 137–38, 138f, 156–57

Cornwall, Clement, 23

Cornwall ranch, 36

corporate and large ranches: Alkali Lake
Ranch, 37, 50, 116, 121; antimonopoly
and anticorporate sentiment (early
1900s), 116; BC Cattle Company, 53,
109, 115, 116; BC land policy in part
responsible for range monopoly, 116–17;
Chilco Ranch, 31, 37, 50, 157; concern
of smallholders/government about size
of large ranches, 110; corporatization
and industrialization after railway, 115,
116; expansion/consolidation of cattle
economy (late 1800s), 114–16; Guichon
Ranch, 50, 51f, 110, 116–17, 157, 164;
horizontal consolidation of land and
water, 103; irrigation and reorganization
of environment, 115–16, 161; lack of
proper regulation led to abuses, 132–33;
land accumulation, methods, xvii–xviii,
37, 45, 50, 108–10, 124; land holdings,
36, 37, 103, 109, 110, 116; lax land laws
and accumulation of huge tracts,
113–14, 116; location of large,
intermediate, small ranches, xv–xvi,
xviii; poison for grasshoppers, attitude
toward, 127–28; shift to grain-fed
yearlings and calves (1950s), 155–56; size
in late 1960s, 157; system of range rights
and control, 121–22; Western Canadian
Ranching Company, 53–54. *See also*
Douglas Lake Cattle Company; Gang
Ranch; range monopoly and conflict

Coutlee, Joe, 149

Cox, William, 37–38
Craig, R.D., 140
Criddle, Norman, 151
Cronon, William, 4, 98
Crosby, Alfred, 158

Dawson, George, 21
Debeck, H.K., 78, 79
Demeritt, David, 86, III
Ditchburn, William: on effort to enlist Native people in poison control of grasshoppers, 128; frustration with Native resistance, 72; on lack of value of Aboriginal horses, 64–65; letter from Mackenzie re range damage by horses, 61; preference for Aboriginals raising cattle rather than horses, 64, 69; on shooting of Aboriginal horses, 64, 68; view that more Native rangeland not needed, 67
Dog Creek Reserve, 54
Dominion Geographical Branch, 5
Dominy, Michèle, xiii
Douglas, James, 37–38, III
Douglas Lake Band, 50, 51f, 106
Douglas Lake Cattle Company: acquisition of land, xvii–xviii, 45, 50, 108–10; concern of smallholders/government re size, 110; corporate and extensive operation, 103, 115, 117; as example of "injurious" effects of large landholdings, 117; financial difficulties in 1920s, 103–4; grazing fees (ca. 1920), 165; holdings of land, 37, 103, 109, 157; "horizontal consolidation" of land and water resources, 103; profiting from grasshopper irruptions, 93; winter ranges and grasslands at Douglas Lake, 50, 51f
drylands of interior British Columbia. See grasslands
Dunwoody Pond (Janovy), xxi

East Kootenay Valley and wild horses, 74
Ellis, Thomas, 116
Elton, Charles, 99
Empire Valley Ranch, 116

enclosures: of common grazing grounds to prevent degradation, 23; grazing permit system a form of enclosure, 57–58; as improvement to range, 161; ranchers' promotion of, 23
Engstrom, Victor, 16
Esk'etemc Band. See Alkali Lake Band
exclosures, 135–37, 136f, 137f

Faure, Jacobus, 149–50
Ferguson, Barry, 57
Fifty Years of Entomology in the Interior of British Columbia (Venables), 154
fire patterns on grasslands: Aboriginal burning, 19–21; changes to and tree/shrub encroachment, 19–20, 41, 61, 140–41; disrupted by Europeans, 21; fire suppression, consequences, 142, 143; fire suppression to benefit timber industry, 142–43; fire's ecological functions, 20–21, 141–42
Fisherman's Problem (McEvoy), 4
Fletcher, James, 48, 87, 89, 96
Flores, Dan, xx
Ford, Lillian, 26
Fountain Indian reserve, 73–74
fox hunting, 30
Fraser, Simon, 33
Fraser River valley: best winter lowlands, 37; Big Bar range, 25, 50, 98, 120–21; changing landscape going north, 4; grasslands and undulating plateau areas, xiv; horse laws contested into the 1940s, 73; rain shadow environment, 4; ranches along middle Fraser, 45, 49–50, 49f; sequence of human occupation, 3–4; wild horse situation, 14, 31, 68, 73–74. See also Gang Ranch
fur trade and Aboriginal culture, 34–35

Gang Ranch: assembly (1870 to 1883), 50; BC land policy and range monopoly, 116–17; incorporated, 115; industrial ranch in Riske Creek, 98; land holdings, 37, 109, 157; location, 49f; photographs of, 118f–119f; protein pellets used (after 1940), 155; vertical integration, 115; on wild horses as "evil," 15

Gayton, Don, xi–xii, xx, 19–20
gold rush, 35–36
Grandidier, C.J., xvii, 39–40
Grant, George, 111
Grasshopper Control Act (1930), 128–29
grasshopper irruptions: assumptions re
    scale and frequency of irruptions, 89,
    100–101; assumptions re specific
    weather conditions, 90, 101; beneficial
    for bunchgrass and grasslands (pre-
    ranching), 91; in commonages (in
    1920s), 125; damage to crops and range,
    88, 89–90; detailed records only after
    1890, 86, 100; identity of "problem"
    grasshoppers, 86, 90, 99; Indian
    reserves' severely affected, 91–92;
    irruptions in Nicola Valley (1898,
    1943-46), 88, 148–49; locust
    transformation theory, 149–51;
    Melanoplanus mexicanus (new genus) in
    1944 outbreak, 150–52; plagues
    (1943-46), 148–49; population
    dynamics, 101; research hampered by
    assumptions and lack of funding,
    101–2; small-scale ranchers, impact on,
    92–93; swarm sizes, 89–90, 104–5;
    unpredictability of, xix
grasshopper irruptions, causes:
    overgrazing and creation of habitat, 9,
    90, 95–96, 99, 101; part of grassland
    ecology, 86, 89; poor land-use practices,
    85, 94–96
grasshopper irruptions, control efforts:
    campaign against revealed economic
    inequalities among ranchers, 10, 128,
    129; chemical pesticides to control
    (mid-1940s), 152–54; collateral death toll
    among wildlife, 154, 160; ecological
    approaches, 153; government
    demonstration of poisoning's efficacy,
    127–28; Grasshopper Control Act (1930),
    128–29; grasshopper control zones, 128,
    148; injuries to workers, 127; insect
    problems on Prairies drained federal
    funding, 101–2; military terms used in
    "war" against, 89, 90–91, 94, 148; natural
    controls and "hopperdozers," 87; in

Nicola Valley, 128, 130, 148–49; poison
    gas proposed, 93–94; poisoning, 9, 86,
    87–88, 93, 103, 105–7; poisoning,
    government management of, 126–27;
    poisoning's failure, 86, 93; range
    conservation deemed too slow, 96,
    102–3, 104, 130, 161
grasslands: in Cariboo-Chilcotin region of
    BC, xiii–xiv; efforts to protect cattle
    ranges, 22–24; environmental history in
    Resettling, xiii; environmental history
    of, 32–33; fire, changing patterns and
    results, 19–21, 41, 61, 140–43; grades of
    range, 41–42; grazing pressure low
    pre-contact, 18–19; initial trip by
    author, 3–4; microbiotic or
    "cryptogrammic" surface crust, xiv;
    park-like pre-contact, 111–13, 141;
    photography by Chris Harris, xi–xii;
    plant communities, east vs west
    Rockies, 18; plant succession, 60–61;
    rain shadow environment, 4, 17–18;
    susceptibility to grazing and trampling,
    19; transition to accommodating just
    "favoured" animals, 158–59; as viewed
    by early settlers, 111–13. *See also*
    bunchgrass; ranching; range
    degradation; ranges
Grasslands Conservation Council, xvii
grazing: Grazing Act (1919), 9, 56, 62,
    133; grazing capacity, attempts to
    establish, 41–43; grazing pressure low
    pre-contact, 18–19; grazing zones/
    grades, xiv–xv, 41–42; problems for
    ranchers (1940s), 147; spring turnout
    times and range degradation, 121,
    130–31; stocking ratios, xv, 21–22, 36,
    47, 60, 121, 123; transhumance
    (moving cattle from range to range),
    xv–xvi, 22; on unfenced upland
    (Crown range), xv, xvi, 4; upland
    meadows and altercations with
    Anaham peoples, 45–47, 47–49;
    weather and markets interactions, 22.
    See also overgrazing
Grazing Act (1919): amendment (1923) for
    seasonal curfew for wild horses, 62;

inability to overcome "social order" of large ranchers, 133; new land-use practices, 9; range management a government responsibility, 56
Great Plains, 18–19
Greaves, J.B., 45, 109
Grimmett, M.L., 13
Guichon, Joseph, 40–41
Guichon, Lawrence: concern over range degradation, 137; efforts to eradicate wild horses, 66; on grasshopper control, 127–28; purchase of formerly leased land, 45; smallholders' protests against large ranchers' extensive use of commonages, 122–23
Guichon Ranch: BC land policy and range monopoly, 116–17; grazing fees (ca. 1920), 164; land holdings, 110, 116, 157; winter ranges and grasslands at Douglas Lake, 50, 51f
Guildford, Richard, 110, 126

Hall, J.A., 94
Harper, Thaddeus, 45
Harris, Chris, xi–xii
Harris, Cole: colonial attitude toward Aboriginal peoples, 27; concept of agriculture linked with colonialism, 111; on explosive Native-settler situation (by mid-1870s), 40; percentage of land in Indian reserves, 6; on quality of early Indian reserves, 38; on ranching history in BC, 85–86
Harris, Douglas, 63
Hayne, J.B., 29–30
Haynes, J.C., 38, 45
Heat-Moon, William Least, xx
Hjort, Johan, 99
hopperdozers (grasshopper traps), 87
Hopping, Ralph, 144–45, 146
horses. See wild horses
Hughes, Tom, 77
Hutchinson, Andrew, 125

Igler, David, 103
Indian reserves: Aboriginal complaints re reserves' size, 38–40; Aboriginals'

deep dissatisfaction with, 28, 31, 38–40; along middle Fraser and Chilcotin rivers, 49–50, 49f; creation, 6, 37–38; at Douglas Lake in Nicola Valley, 50, 51f; grasshoppers, impact of, 91–92; Joint Indian Reserve Commission (JIRC), 40; Kamloops reserves, 38, 92; Okanagan Lake reserves, 37–38; overgrazed reserve, 74, 75f; Royal Commission's decision to change nothing, 56; settlers' intrusion onto Native winter ranges, 43–44, 48–49; testimony re reserve shortcomings at Royal Commission, 50–54; unsuitability for cattle, 28, 31, 50–54, 56, 67, 92; unsuitability for cattle ignored by authorities, 31, 54–55, 56, 67, 69, 73; weed infestation blamed on Natives, 55. See also Aboriginal peoples; Aboriginal peoples, dispossession of indigenous peoples
Industrial Cowboys (Igler), 103
irrigation works: damage by pocket gophers, 152; by large ranches, xvii, 53–54, 115–16, 161; need for better irrigation (late 1800s), 23–24; productivity increase and costs, 147, 155; reorganization of environment, 115–16

Janovy, John Jr., xxi
Jenkins, Stephen, 25
Joint Indian Reserve Commission (JIRC), 40
Jordan, Terry, 114

Kingsland, Sharon, 99
Kirkpatrick, T.G., 16
Kler.klick.ten (Louis), 38

Land Use, Environment, and Social Change (White), 4
Lapp, Tenas, Chief of Bonaparte Band, testimony to Royal Commission, 52–53
Lemare, Percy, 121–22, 142
Leopold, Aldo, xx

Locke, John, 111
Lockwood, Jeffrey, 150
locusts: confusion with grasshoppers, 86;
    destruction on Prairies, 86; locust/
    grasshopper transformation theory,
    149–51; Rocky Mountain locust extinct,
    150–51
Lopez, Barry, xx
Louis, Chief of Stone Band, testimony at
    Royal Commission, 51, 55
Lounsbury, Charles, 93
Lower Nicola Indian reserve, 73

Mackenzie, John, 30
Mackenzie, Thomas: Aboriginal horses a
    Dominion problem, not provincial, 31,
    63–64; advocate of segregation of settler
    and Native livestock, 59, 63;
    commonage principle doubted, 125;
    delayed implementation of restrictive
    grazing law in Southern Interior, 66,
    68; determination to remove wild
    horses, 59, 61; dispute between large
    ranchers and smallholders, 124–26;
    frustration with Native resistance,
    70–71, 72; government range
    management, 125–26; on grasshopper
    control methods, 93–94; on
    grasshopper irruptions, causes, 95;
    insect problems on Prairies more
    urgent economically, 102; meeting with
    Nlaka'pamux re shooting horses, 13–14,
    72–73; Nlaka'pamux horses shot in
    Nicola Valley, 67–68; on poor land use
    by ranchers, 102; on ranchers' lack of
    cooperation re poison for grasshoppers,
    126; reaction to Native letter re their
    property (horses), 63; scientific range
    management promoted, 59–60; on
    shooting of Aboriginal (not wild)
    horses, 68; on unregulated grazing, 102,
    154–55; view that more Native
    rangeland not needed, 67. See also wild
    horses, eradication
MacLachlan, Ian, 114
Maher, Susan Naramore, xx–xxi
Marshall, Paul, 152–53
McEvoy, Arthur, 4

McFadden, Louise, 78–79
McIntyre Creek ranch, 79
McKay, John, 16
McKee, R.G., 76
McKenna-McBride Commission. See
    Royal Commission on Indian Affairs
    (McKenna-McBride Commission)
McLean, Alastair, 155
McPhee, John, xx
Melrose, George, 130–31, 139–40
Michel, Myers, 13
Miller & Lux cattle company, 103
Mitchell, Sam (chief of Fountain
    people), 74
Moore, John, 24–25
Murton, James, 57

Native peoples. See Aboriginal peoples;
    Aboriginal peoples, dispossession of
Netz, Reviel, 7–8
"new liberalism" in British Columbia, 57
Nicola River valley: Aboriginal wild horse
    situation, 15–16, 29, 66–68, 70–71, 73;
    BC land policy and range monopoly,
    116–17; best winter lowlands, 37;
    blackleg (disease) in, 123; carrying
    capacity degraded over time, 131; cattle
    herds, 4, 114; commonage use by large
    ranchers, protests against, 122–23;
    commonages, 23, 108–9, 125; elk
    extirpation, 34; exclosures on
    Lundbom Commonage, 136, 136f;
    grasshopper control zone with
    poisoning, 128, 130, 148–49;
    grasshopper irruptions, 88, 90, 148–49,
    151, 153; grasshopper poisoning,
    resistance to, 106–7; grassland/dry
    forest, xiv; grazing fees (ca. 1920), list,
    164–66; Indian reserves in, 44, 50, 51f;
    land holdings by large ranchers, 45;
    Native people with large number of
    livestock, 55, 65; overgrazing, 15, 131;
    range law cause of settler discontent,
    66; restrictive grazing law,
    implementation delayed, 66, 68;
    smallholders' protest against large
    ranches, 108. See also Douglas Lake
    Cattle Company; Guichon Ranch

Nlaka'pamux First Nation: assertion of
Aboriginal rights and title to land,
13–14, 70, 72–73; aversion to poison
(for grasshoppers) on reserve, 106;
horses shot by settlers, 67–68;
importance of horses in culture, 34;
legal argument to protect their horses
(1924), 62–64; protest against
disallowance of commonages, 44–45;
protest against shooting wild horses
(1930), 13–14, 72–73; on ranchers'
attempt to control all grazing land, 66
Noss, Reed, 60–61

Okanagan First Nation, 37–38, 40
Okanagan River valley: grasshopper
irruptions, 106; grasslands, xiv, xvii;
ranches in, 45, 116; wild horses in, 15, 16
Okanagan Valley ranches, 45, 116
Oregon Treaty (1846), 35
O'Reilly, Peter, xix, 15, 44, 47–48
overgrazing: on fenced vs unfenced
ranges, 131–32; on Indian reserves, 74,
75f; link with grasshopper outbreaks, 9,
90, 95–96, 99, 101; little done to correct
pre-1960, 154–55; overgrazing and
trampling of ranges, 16–17, 25, 41–42

Parham, Henry, 79
Parminter, John, 143
pests on cattle ranges: animals not valued
by humans, 15–16, 24–26, 159; arsenic
and DDT to control grasshoppers, 9;
beavers' damage to upland meadows,
46; collateral death toll of various
animals, 159–60; costs of
extermination, 163–64; elimination an
"improvement," 161; entomologists'
preference for range restoration, 9;
extermination as tool of range
improvement, 159; pocket gophers, 152.
See also grasshoppers; wild horses
Place, J.S., 26
Plan for the Reclamation of British
Columbia's Wild Horses, 76
Plotnikov, V.I., 150
pocket gophers, 152
Porter, Theodore, xix–xx, 9

Powell, Isaiah, 38–39
Pragnell, George, 65–66, 67, 69
PrairyErth (A Deep Map) (Heat-Moon),
xx
Prentice, J.D., 15–16
Pyne, Stephen, 142–43

ranchers and settlers: approach to nature,
using and improving, 160; BC land
policy partly responsible for range monopoly, 116–17; changes in range management difficult to implement, 9, 161–62;
large ranches (see corporate and large
ranches); lax land laws and accumulation of huge tracts, 113–14; system of
range rights and control, 121–22. See
also Guichon, Lawrence; range monopoly and conflict; smallholders; Ward,
Frank
ranching: BC land policy and range
monopoly, 116–17; dominant land use
(late 1800s, early 1900s), 4–5, 5f;
ecological history of, 4, 5–7, 7–10;
expansion/consolidation of cattle
economy, 114–16; factory feedlot system
(by late 1960s), 156; financial difficulties
in 1920s, 103–4; grazing problems for
ranchers (1940s), 147; idealized view of
agriculture vs reality, 110–13, 116;
modern capitalist institution, xviii, 161;
productivity increase (1950s and 1960s),
155; railway's impact (1890s), 114;
requirement for land, 35–37; shift to
grain-fed yearlings and calves (1950s),
155–56; system of range rights and
control, 121–22; weather and markets
interactions, 22. See also Aboriginal
peoples, dispossession of; range
degradation; ranges
Ranching on the Southern Interior Plateau
(Weir): on environmental factors
shaping regional economic landscape,
6; geographical analysis of impersonal
forces, 7; "standard" study of cattle
ranching since 1950s, 5–6
range degradation: beavers hunted and
water less available, 132; carrying
capacity degraded over time, 131–32;

cheatgrass and sagebrush problem, 19,
55, 139–40, 139f, 140f; enclosure efforts,
23, 57–58, 161; example in Riske Creek,
133–37, 134f–137f; exclosures, 135–37,
136f, 137f; on fenced vs unfenced
ranges, 131–32; grazing problems for
ranchers, 147; overgrazing and
grasshopper outbreaks, 9, 90, 95–96,
99, 101; overgrazing and trampling,
16–17, 25, 41–42; photographs of,
134f–137f; regulation lacking or poor, 7,
102, 132–33, 154–55; reseeding with
introduced grasses, 137–38, 138f; spring
turnout times and, 121, 130–31; tree/
shrub encroachment, 19–20, 41, 61,
140–43; upland problems with trees
killed by bark beetles, 143–44
range monopoly and conflict: commonage
usage by large ranchers, 108–10, 121–24;
concern of smallholders/government
about size of large ranches, xviii, 110,
116–17, 119–21; concern re large ranches'
monopolizing resources, xvii–xviii,
108–10, 121–24; continuing tension
between small and large ranchers,
156–57; efforts to reform grazing rights,
119–25; grasshopper control through
poisoning, 107, 126–28; re underhanded
methods of land accumulation by large
ranchers, 108–10; system of range rights
and control, 121–22. See also
commonages; corporate and large
ranches; smallholders
ranges: carrying capacity, 61, 119–20, 131;
cattle herds, location of largest ones, 4,
15, 36, 114, 121; "deferred-rotation"
grazing, 59–61; enclosure efforts, 23,
57–58, 161; government management
(1920), 125–26; grades of range in
grasslands, 41–42; lowland (winter)
ranges taken over by settlers, 36–37;
management a government
responsibility, 56, 125–29; pastoral
leases, 36, 39, 45; plant succession in
grasslands, 60–61; scientific range
management, flaws of, 60–61; stocking
ratios, xv, 21–22, 36, 47, 60, 121, 123;
transhumance (moving cattle from

range to range), xv–xvi, 22;
unregulated/poorly regulated grazing,
7, 102, 132–33, 154–55; upland meadows
and altercations with Anaham peoples,
45–47, 47–49. See also commonages;
enclosures; grazing; range degradation;
range monopoly and conflict
Raz, Joseph, 63
Redstone Indian Reserve, 55
Resettling the Range (Thistle): dispossession
and marginalization of Aboriginal
peoples the centrepiece, xvii; ecological
history of ranching, 4, 7–10;
environmental problems not separated
from social and ecological contexts, 10;
focus on wild horses and grasshoppers,
7; regional environmental history of the
grasslands, xiii
Resh, Lyle, 80
Ricou, Laurie, xx
Riske Creek range: damage caused by
grasshoppers, 90; grasshopper feeding
and breeding habits evolving, 99;
grasshopper irruptions, 88, 90;
indigenous settlement pre-contact, 97;
location, 5f; propertied range and
overgrazed by 1920s, 98–99; ranching
on a large scale, 97–98; range
degradation, 133–37, 134f–137f
Roberts, Art, 110
Ross, William, 119–20, 142
Royal Commission on Indian Affairs
(McKenna-McBride Commission):
Aboriginal testimony re shortcomings of
reserves and dispossession, 50–54;
assumption that Native peoples not good
at land-use management, 54–55; belief
that cattle preferable to horses (despite
Native concerns), 54; decision that no
need for changes in Indian reserves, 56
Royal Commission on the Timber
Industry, 143
Russell, Edmund, 94
Ryan, Simon, 112

Sampson, Arthur, 60, 61
Samson, Chief of Alkali Lake Band,
testimony at Royal Commission, 52

Sand Country (Leopold), xx

Sanger, Owen, 55, 120–21, 141

Saul, John, 15

science: belief and skepticism in "science wars of 1990s," xix; overridden by economic and political considerations, 9; relevance in environmental history, 9–10; science-based range management and "new liberalism," 56–57; scientific range management and its flaws, 60–61; secondary influence on range policy, 9

Seager, Alan, 114

Secwepemc First Nation, 34, 97

Similkameen River valley, xiv, 37, 45

Sloan, Gordon, 155

smallholders: commonages, petition to government to create, 50; community fields to exclude large ranchers' cattle, 157; community pasture request rejected, 123, 126; concern re large ranches' monopolizing resources, xvii–xviii, 108–10, 121–24; continuing tension between small and large ranchers, 156–57; denunciation of "drift toward oligopoly," xviii; description of typical ranch, 110, 115; disputes with large landholders re commonages, 122–24; grasshoppers' impact on, 92–93; large, intermediate, and small ranches, location of, xv–xvi, xviii; poison control campaign, resistance and reaction, 126; range law cause of settler discontent, 66; resistance to large ranches' monopoly of resources, xvii–xviii, 108–10, 121–24; sheep, permission to hold, 123; war on grasshoppers, 107, 126–28. *See also* ranchers and settlers; range monopoly and conflict

Smith, John, 55

Society for the Prevention of Cruelty to Animals (SPCA), 76

South African War Land Grant Act, 109

Spencer, George, 152–53

Spirit in the Grass (Harris), xi–xii

Sproat, Malcolm: colonial attitude toward Aboriginal peoples, 27; grades of range in grasslands, 41–42; grazing capacity, attempts to establish, 41–42; inability to stop settler abuse of Native land use, 43–44; on injustices against First Nations, xvii, 40; on settlers' lands blocking Native access to fisheries, 40–41

St. Mary's Reserve, 75f

Stegner, Wallace, xx

Stl'atl'imx First Nation, 21

Stock Ranges Act (1876), 50, 108, 132–33

Stone Band, chief's testimony at Royal Commission, 51

Swaine, J.W., 144

Swakum, Jack, 13

Sys-sy-as-cut, complaints to authorities re size of reserves, 38

Talbot, W.L., 148

Teit, James, 34

Thistle, John, xvi–xvii, xx–xxi. *See also Resettling the Range*

Thompson, David, 14–15, 33

Thompson River valley, xiv, 36, 37

Thomson, H., 29

Thomson, L.B., 131–33

Thoreau, H.D., xx

Tisdale, Edwin, xv, 27, 133

Tod, John, 20

Tranquille Range, 139, 139f

Treherne, R.C., 94, 95–96, 101–2

Trespass Act (1923), 62

Tsilhqot'in First Nation, 97

Turkel, William, 79

Union of South Africa, 127–28

upland meadows: beavers' impact on, 46; exclusion of Native people, 47–49; origins, 45–46; protests by Anaham people at exclusion, 47–49; types of, 46–47

Uvarov, Boris, 148, 150

Vancouver Daily Province (newspaper), 29

Vancouver Sun (newspaper), 13–14, 77, 80

Venables, E.P., 89, 154

Vernon, Forbes, 44, 45

Victoria Colonist (newspaper), 13

Victoria Daily Times (newspaper), 106

Walden (Thoreau), xx

Ward, Frank: allegation re introduction of blackleg (disease), 123; on choice of poison over range conservation to control grasshoppers, 104; concern over range degradation, 137; critic of Aboriginal horses, 71; Douglas Lake Ranch's financial difficulties (1920s), 103–4; efforts to eradicate wild horses, 66; grasshopper plagues in mid-1940s, 149; manager of Douglas Lake Cattle Company, 66; on re-introduction of long-term pastoral leases, 124; serious problems for ranchers (1940s), 147; smallholders' protests against large ranchers' extensive use of commonages, 122–23

Weaver, John, 161

Weir, Dan, 75

Weir, Thomas: approach to ranching and the grasslands, xvi–xvii, 7; grassland zones, xv; on overgrazing, xvi, 7; *Ranching on the Southern Interior Plateau*, 5–7; ranching patterns in different grassland zones, xv–xvi; on shift to grain-fed yearlings and calves (1950s), 156; on three kinds of grazing practice, xiv–xv

Western Canadian Ranching Company, 53–54, 116

Wheatgrass Mechanism (Gayton), xi–xii, xxi

White, Richard, 4, 128, 158–59, 160

Whitford, H.N., 140

wild horses: Aboriginal horses viewed as "wild" by settlers, 15; definition problems, 14, 71–72; despised by most ranchers and range officials, 15–16, 24–26, 159; difficulty in determining if wild or owned, xix, 14, 26–27; disease and interbreeding, arguments vs the horses, 15–16, 28; horse pastures on federal land refused by Native people, 67; necessary for Aboriginal travel and hunting, 65; numbers, 14–15, 17, 26; origins (simplified and otherwise), 14, 77, 78. *See also* wild horses, eradication

wild horses, eradication: Aboriginal (not wild) horses shot, 67–68; Act for the Extermination of Wild Horses (1896), 28; alleged to be a Dominion problem, not provincial, 31, 63–64; alternative solutions rather than killing, 76, 77; Animals Act (amendments, 1908, 1932), 30–31, 62; arguments for eradication, 15–16, 80; arguments for segregation of Native horses, 59, 63, 71; avoiding conflict with Aboriginal peoples, xix, 14, 26–27, 31; bias in laws against Native people, 62; colonial attitudes toward Aboriginal peoples, 27–28; concerns (ethical and other) about, 75–79; costs of extermination, numbers killed, and their fate, 68, 80–81, 163–64; difficulty in determining if wild or owned, xix, 14, 26–27; fencing desired by government but payment disputed, 64; grazing non-equivalent to cattle grazing, 16–17, 25; Indian reserves unsuitable for stock raising, 28, 31, 50–54, 56, 67; legality of discriminatory range law, 65–66; link (unacknowledged) with colonialism, 77–79; mixed acceptance of horse roundup and reduction, 73–74; Native legal argument protecting their property, 62–64; Nlaka'pamux horses shot, 67–68; overgrazing and trampling of range, accusations of, 16–17, 25; roundups after 1930, 79–80; season curfew for Crown range (January to May), 62; solutions proposed, 27–31; "special shooters" with bounty paid, 62; "war" against horses dispossessed Aboriginal peoples, 10

Williams Lake District, 92

Wilson, John, 36

Wilson, Tom, 89–90

Wolf Willow (Stegner), xx

Wood, Ellen Meikens, 161

Wooliams, Nina, 109

Worster, Donald, 161

Wynn, Graeme, xi–xxi

NATURE|HISTORY|SOCIETY

Claire Elizabeth Campbell, *Shaped by the West Wind: Nature and History in Georgian Bay*

Tina Loo, *States of Nature: Conserving Canada's Wildlife in the Twentieth Century*

Jamie Benidickson, *The Culture of Flushing: A Social and Legal History of Sewage*

William J. Turkel, *The Archive of Place: Unearthing the Pasts of the Chilcotin Plateau*

John Sandlos, *Hunters at the Margin: Native People and Wildlife Conservation in the Northwest Territories*

James Murton, *Creating a Modern Countryside: Liberalism and Land Resettlement in British Columbia*

Greg Gillespie, *Hunting for Empire: Narratives of Sport in Rupert's Land, 1840–70*

Stephen J. Pyne, *Awful Splendour: A Fire History of Canada*

Hans M. Carlson, *Home Is the Hunter: The James Bay Cree and Their Land*

Liza Piper, The *Industrial Transformation of Subarctic Canada*

Sharon Wall, *The Nurture of Nature: Childhood, Antimodernism, and Ontario Summer Camps, 1920–55*

Joy Parr, *Sensing Changes: Technologies, Environments, and the Everyday, 1953–2003*

Jamie Linton, *What Is Water? The History of a Modern Abstraction*

Dean Bavington, *Managed Annihilation: An Unnatural History of the Newfoundland Cod Collapse*

Shannon Stunden Bower, *Wet Prairie: People, Land, and Water in Agricultural Manitoba*

J. Keri Cronin, *Manufacturing National Park Nature: Photography, Ecology, and the Wilderness Industry of Jasper*

Jocelyn Thorpe, *Temagami's Tangled Wild: Race, Gender, and the Making of Canadian Nature*

Darcy Ingram, *Wildlife, Conservation, and Conflict in Quebec, 1840–1914*

Caroline Desbiens, *Power from the North: Territory, Identity, and the Culture of Hydroelectricity in Quebec*

Sean Kheraj, *Inventing Stanley Park: An Environmental History*

Justin Page, *Tracking the Great Bear: How Environmentalists Recreated British Columbia's Coastal Rainforest*

Daniel Macfarlane, *Negotiating a River: Canada, the US, and the Creation of the St. Lawrence Seaway*

Ryan O'Connor, *The First Green Wave: Pollution Probe and the Origins of Environmental Activism in Ontario*